Donated in loving memory of
my dear friend, the author,
Jack L. Levin.

Muriel Weiss
Sept 15, 2003

Fighting the Good Fight

The Writings of Jack L. Levin

edited by

Dr. Robert O. Freedman

A PROJECT OF THE AMERICAN JEWISH CONGRESS, MARYLAND CHAPTER
WITH THE ASSITANCE OF THE AMERICAN CIVIL LIBERTIES UNION OF MARYLAND

American Literary Press, Inc.
Baltimore, Maryland

Fighting the Good Fight
The Writings of Jack L. Levin

Copyright © 2003 American Jewish Congress,
Maryland Chapter

All rights reserved under International and Pan-American copyright conventions. No part of this book may be reproduced, stored in a retrieval system, or transmitted in any form, electronic, mechanical, or other means, now known or hereafter invented, without written permission of the author. Address all inquiries to the author.

Library of Congress
Cataloging-in-Publication Data
ISBN 1-56167-822-8

Published by

American Literary Press, Inc.
8019 Belair Road, Suite 10
Baltimore, Maryland 21236

Manufactured in the United States of America

Preface

Preparing this book has been a process that has given me a great deal of personal satisfaction because Jack Levin was such an exceptional human being.

Going through his writings reinforced Jack in my memory, as I hope it will in the memories of all who knew him. For those who never had the pleasure of meeting Jack, I hope this book will be an introduction to a man who was the model of a Jewish social activist of the second half of the 20th century.

There are many people who helped me with the book. First and foremost I would like to thank Bill Engelman who headed the special American Jewish Congress Committee that had responsibility for raising the funds and organizing the material that went into the book. Bill also helped edit one of the sections of the book. I would also like to thank the other section editors, Alan Shecter, Elaine Fedder, Jonathan Finkelstein Ph.D., Sidney Hollander, Jr. and Aaron and Dorothy Margolis.

Special thanks go to Mal Sherman, for his advice, counsel and generosity, and to Alan Shecter for his generosity and advice throughout the entire project. I would also like to thank Roz Wills for helping to assemble the documents utilized in the book and Sandy Levy, the librarian of the Sun Papers for her help in locating the Op-Ed articles which Jack had submitted to the Sun. Among the donors I would like to thank are the Benjamin and Esther Rosenbloom Foundation, Dr. Robert Feinberg, and the Sidney Hollander Family Fund and The Associated: Jewish Community Federation of Baltimore.

I would also like to thank all the members of the American Jewish Congress and American Civil Liberties Union whose support for this project is deeply appreciated.

Robert O. Freedman
February 2003

Editors note and acknowledgement:

The writings of Jack Levin found in this book are composed almost entirely of Op-Ed articles originally published in the *Baltimore Sun* and *Baltimore Evening Sun* as well as published and unpublished Letters to the Editor in those newspapers.

Since much of the material was taken from Jack's files, not every document was dated. However, the recurring themes that permeate this book make this only a minor problem. Finally, in the presentation of the documents in this book every effort has been made to give as comprehensive as possible a portrait of Jack's thinking.

Table of Contents

	Page
Preface	
Dr. Robert O. Freedman	i
Introduction	
Alan Shecter	1

Part I: Baltimore, Maryland and America

The Holocaust and Discrimination Against Blacks and Jews
    Dr. Jonathan Finkelstein 9

Civil Rights, Civil Liberties, the ACLU, and the Problems of Poverty
    Sidney Hollander, Jr. 40

Judaism and Church/State Controversies
    Aaron Margolis 137

Of Cabbages and Kings: Jack Levin on Key Figures in American Life
    Elayne Fedder 150

The Jewish Museum of Maryland
    Elayne Fedder 179

Part II: International Affairs

Israel and the Arab-Israeli Conflict
    Dr. Robert O. Freedman 205

The Struggle for Soviet Jewry
    Dr. Robert O. Freedman 244

On Peace and War
> Dr. Robert O. Freedman 253

Part III: At the Close of Life
Nostalgia, Aging, and Death
> William H. Engelman 269

Photographs follow page 136

FIGHTING THE GOOD FIGHT
Introduction
by
Alan Shecter

In his last years, when his blindness had become total, my uncle Jack wore a large button on his lapel that read, "I HAVE NO VISION".

His intent was to anticipate and quickly inform, without the awkwardness of spoken words, as to why he did not recognize or respond to people who approached him as he moved around at work and at the meetings and social events that filled his later years. He would then put people at ease by explaining that the message on the button should not be interpreted as a declaration of his candidacy for President of the United States!

The glaring irony concerning the anecdotal lapel button is that no one who knew him ever doubted that Jack L. Levin had remarkably perceptive and far-reaching vision. As these essays will readily reveal, his formidable ability to communicate persuasively what he "saw" established him as a serious source and force in the social and political arenas in his time. To be sure, his comprehensive vision was framed not only by historical perspective, but by what, he felt certain, *could* and *should* be.

Perhaps that view derived from his having been beaten and abused, frequently, in childhood.

There are many remarkable instances where the tragedy of an abusive youthful experience is overcome and where the victim sublimates his rage and emerges, almost miraculously, with stunning creative energies and nearly incessant productivity.

What can we understand about this "sublimator," who in the midst of personal achievement and business success, became inspired to channel still further his resources and talents toward attacking – with insight, effectiveness and anger – some of the miseries that co-exist with the pervasive good, both internationally and in American society? Miseries like equal opportunity denied ... justice ignored ... hunger overlooked ... intolerance unchallenged

... civil and human rights trampled upon ... enlightenment and understanding not even attempted.

It is not widely known that Jack was awakened and beaten – for years – night after night by his compulsively intoxicated father. Though rarely mentioned, it's a fact with too much consequence to omit, an experience the pre-teen Jack bore and which he was innately driven to make relevant and constructive.

On the few occasions when he told me about his childhood, he would grin bitterly and shake his head slowly, reflecting still unresolved bewilderment and a hint of his deep-seated rage at the memories. But oddly, paradoxically, his overriding recollections of his childhood, as he related them to me, focused on his friends, the daily antics of school and after school fun. He seemed almost amused, almost nostalgic at how poor his family was, and how the Levin family survived. The term "child abuse" was not part of the lexicon when Jack was a boy and, if it had been, it would not have occurred to Jack that he was the victim of it. A quick sense of humor and high grades at school were his primary defenses.

Self-pity was never an issue; but fear was inevitable, and Jack's accompanying terror and anxieties gave way to anger. It was the anger that endured, finally and steadily relieved by an enormous, spontaneous wit and an insatiable craving for literature, history and sociological insight. He understood, early on, the immense power of the pen, and developed a deep, very stubborn, empathetic sense of caring – qualities so very visible in and between the lines of his writings.

For sure, Jack's unenviable childhood experience sharpened his instincts, strengthened his resolve, and made a fighter of him. While he won more than his share of fistfights, he understood that such victories were ultimately meaningless. And as he matured, he contemplated more worthwhile fights. What began to make sense to him were battles where meaningful change was possible and feasible. He wanted his "wins" to matter.

When Jack wrote motivating articles and speeches, organized seminars and public rallies, coordinated the efforts of countless organizations and activists across religious, political, racial and governmental boundaries, or mediated between mutually hostile groups, how cognizant and connected was he to the contemptible, brutal beatings by his intoxicated father?

When I asked him this question, he told me, "It's not personal. The issues I care about simply relate to what's fair." But in a 1993 interview in *The Baltimore Jewish Times*, he stated, "I inherited some of my father's combativeness, his easy outrage at things that shouldn't be a certain way. Instead of using my fists, I pound a typewriter." Pounding and fighting for what he believed was fair – in society, politics, judicial and Constitutional questions – because the cruelties of poverty, discrimination and lack of equal opportunity in our prosperous society were "seen" by Jack as reversible, even as his childhood thrashings were not.

****

Jacob Leon Levin was born in East Baltimore in 1912 and died on January 25, 2001. Sixteen and a graduate of Baltimore City College High School, he had already demonstrated superior writing skills. At the peak of the Depression, he was able to obtain employment in the Advertising Department of the Hecht Company in downtown Baltimore. He attended The Johns Hopkins University at night, earning his degree and marrying Ester Shecter in 1934. He then joined his brother-in-law, Louis E. Shecter, (my father), in the advertising agency business and ultimately became managing partner in Shecter & Levin Advertising Agency. The partnership prospered for more than sixty years, attracting prominent local and several national advertisers in an era when it was rare for a Baltimore firm to have national clients.

Employing his literary skills commercially, Jack's advertising and public relations work "paid the bills" while enabling him to work with and ultimately lead as president such local organizations as American Jewish Congress, American Civil Liberties Union, and Jewish Historical Society. He also became one of only two Life Members of the Baltimore Jewish Council and wrote speeches for mayors, governors and U.S. senators. Senators Mathias, Mikulski, and Sarbanes considered him an important resource on Jewish and Israeli issues.

On occasion, Jack bitterly recalled how, in 1940, when he was 28, Nobel Laureate Sinclair Lewis produced Jack's play, *The Good Neighbor*. Jack always insisted that the play, about injustice and insensitivity in America, was so altered and "doctored" by script editors, that it was no longer "his" play when it opened. It closed quickly, following wretched reviews. Lewis dropped a bundle of cash and Jack never forgave those editors. Nevertheless, his versatility and the financial backing by such a respected and renowned writer enhanced Jack's self-confidence, particularly in his word skills and ideas.

Jack was quick to understand the Nazi threat. He condemned and railed against fascism as early as 1932. In 1936, a German battleship, The Emden, flying the swastika and carrying some 600 Nazi naval trainees, docked at Baltimore's Fells Point for a courtesy visit in Baltimore. A swastika-emblazoned flag flew at Baltimore's City Hall for the occasion. Plans were announced for a welcoming agenda that included hospitality in upscale Roland Park homes. Baltimore was flattered! When the ship arrived, Jack was there to rain on the city's parade, leading a furious protest against the visit and against Nazi-German ambitions.

In the early 1940s, there were rumors about atrocities against Jews, and then there were confirmations of it. Jack helped organize rallies, letter-writing, and lobbying campaigns for immediate action by Congress and the President. But, as we know too well, the annihilation went on. The critical need for a Jewish homeland in Palestine became an understandable obsession and was the inspiration for a rally at the Fifth Regiment Armory, organized with strategic promotional help from Jack Levin and his partner, Lou Shecter. An estimated throng of 15,000 raised enough cash in connection with the event to purchase three fighter aircraft for the fledgling Jewish military, which later played a critical role in Israel's War of Independence.

The Holocaust nightmare caused many liberals and intellectuals to attend meetings and join organizations that looked to Russia as a resource to stop the unimaginably massive Nazi gassing and burning of Jews and others. History later taught that this naivety about the Russian government was to have doubly negative consequences. In the early 1950s, when U.S. Senator Joseph McCarthy was at the peak of his anti-communist, blacklisting witch-hunt, Jack, although not an attorney, became chairman of Baltimore's ACLU chapter. He helped lead the fight against branding idealistically misdirected innocents, including many artists, writers and people from virtually all areas of society, as traitors. Treason by association! To Jack, the ACLU was a key resource for exposing and stopping "patriotic demagoguery." He often stated and wrote that ACLU represented what America and patriotism are REALLY all about – the Bill of Rights.

The war in Vietnam appalled and frustrated Jack, particularly because proponents in Washington were so able to discredit protesters by simply stereotyping them as irresponsible, unpatriotic hippies. To counter this, Jack, together with successful businessmen and friends that included Henry Niles, president of a prominent life insurance company; James Rouse, creator of the city of Columbia, Maryland; and Malcolm Sherman, a respected real estate executive, conceived the idea of organizing an activist group in Baltimore known as Business Executives Move for Vietnam Peace. The organization quickly grew into a national one; it wasn't long before a growing cadre of successful, credible business leaders from all around the U.S. began lobbying their senators and representatives to stop the war. The group made a significant impact because its impressive "establishment" membership – the extreme antithesis of the hippie stereotype – made protesting the war "respectable," just as Jack intended and knew it would.

****

In the 1950s and early 1960s, the power of united minorities – Jews and Blacks in particular, "battling" together – helped to win victories in Congress, in Selma, Alabama, in Mississippi, and in the courts of both north and south. Unity works. But the highly effective alliance of Blacks and Jews, which facilitated revolutionary changes in American society in those years, subsequently began to split apart, reaching a peak of alienation and feelings of rejection among and between these groups in the wake of the Martin Luther King assassination on April 4, 1968.

Quotas in medical school enrollment at University of California at Davis (the Allan Baake Supreme Court case) and the recall of United Nations Ambassador Andrew Young after unauthorized contacts with the Palestine Liberation Organization were other issues that drove a deep and bitter wedge in what had been a highly effective Black-Jewish alliance.

Wanting to re-establish understanding and at least *some* unified political leverage to deal with issues like affirmative action, civil rights legislation, poverty, hunger and improved urban schooling, Jack was in the forefront of a group that, in 1978, created the Black-Jewish Forum of Baltimore, which came to be known as "The BLEWS (Blacks/Jews). The loss of unity and common effort between these two groups, each of which had known – first hand – about prejudice and discrimination, caused Jack much distress and disappointment. Constructive dialogue between these minorities and a foundation for joint efforts and communication were established, although at the time of his death, the meaningful effectiveness of the BLEWS still remained to be achieved. Fighting "the good fight" is not synonymous with winning, but in Jack's mind, victories begin with carefully conceived strategies and with people talking and listening to each other.

Anti-Semitic experiences were also a part of Jack's youth, including most of the fistfights to which I have already alluded. He became sensitive to the concepts of religious tolerance and understood the urgency of maintaining constitutional separation of religion from government. In Jack's mind, issues such as mandatory prayer in public schools and state-sponsored vouchers for religious schools were perils to the integrity of the First Amendment's "establishment clause," potentially treacherous threats to minorities. He also saw the issue of a woman's right to choose abortion as a largely religious issue with First Amendment ramifications. Jack's essays quickly demonstrate, with scholarly articulation and consuming passion, how his angry reaction to these threats was directed into positive, thoughtful action.

Ultimately, Jack defined his own Jewishness primarily in terms of social justice, occasionally citing the biblical tenet, "Justice, justice shalt thou pursue." The goals of eliminating hunger, homelessness, poverty and substandard educational employment opportunities were like ancient psalms that drove him almost relentlessly.

Prejudice, injustice, inferior education, slum housing, and the lack of equal opportunity for blacks and other minorities in America regenerated some of Jack's childhood indignation and, sadly, too many opportunities for a "good fight." He fought with fervor, but always civilly, with words and ideas. His weapons included seemingly endless energy, clear focus, enormous intellectual gifts, and an unfailing sense of his convictions.

Somehow, Jack consistently made time for Ester ("my bride ... always beside and behind me") and son David. Later, there was joyful time with his devoted daughter-in-law, Randi, and his adoring grandchildren, Joey and Lauren. He found time for reading – fiction, non-fiction, intellectual treatises – and time each week for the gym. He always kept himself fit, trim and muscular.

He enjoyed playing his harmonica and told uproarious jokes and anecdotes with perfect timing and inflection. His ability to stand on his head for long minutes always dazzled the children of his friends, if not his wife. Beyond his countless honors, awards, achievements and successful campaigns, Jack is also easily remembered as a "barrel of fun!"

A "good" fight? There are always, unfortunately, too many from which to choose   Prolific, inexhaustible, and committed, Jack attacked on many fronts. Some of the battles in which he joined were won in his lifetime, at least incrementally, such as fair housing and employment legislation.

In these pages, some of Jack's admirers, and some of the current leaders of the organizations he once led, have joined together – using Jack's own words – to record just some of his inspiring "fights" and to preserve his vision and his voice.

In the more enduring sense, Jack never did lose his vision. Perhaps a young reader somewhere will be stimulated by Jack's expressions to fight a few more "good fights."

Part I

Jack Levin on Life in Baltimore and America

Chapter 1

Jack Levin's Views of the Holocaust and Condemnation of Discrimination against Blacks and Jews
by
Jonathan C. Finkelstein, Ph.D.

From the vantage point of 2002, the technological, scientific and medical advances of the 20th century capture one's attention because they are incredible. The development of powered flight and travel in outer space, of conceptions of the relations among time, space and gravity, and of drugs and vaccines to effectively fight diseases are but a tiny few examples of these advances. Perhaps some persons in the late 19th century, with keen appreciation of the human imagination, foresaw some of these inventions.

What was not foreseen at that time was the extent to which human hate and aggression would scar much of the new century. The "longest hate," anti-Semitism, had powered local pogroms in Russia and Poland, but it became the core philosophy of German Naziism. The resulting Holocaust consumed six million European Jews and millions of other people in the first half of the 20th century. Other totalitarian movements and regimes in the Soviet Union, Africa and Asia would multiply the intentional devastation of peoples (genocide) before the century's end.

The conquest of the Nazi Germany and its allies, in 1945, did not eradicate anti-Semitism. However the United Nations, chartered in the same year and dedicated to promoting the fundamental human rights and dignity of all persons and peoples, did take part in the birth of the State of Israel in 1948. Israel became a member of the U.N. in 1949. Israel's first 50 years have been momentous with a ten-fold growth in population from the in-gatherings of Jewish refugees from post-World War II Europe, most middle eastern Arab lands, the Soviet Union and Ethiopia.

The welfare of the nation and even its existence, however, were not assured. Over that period, Israel fought four wars, endured an Intifada, starting in 1987, by Palestinians and suffered Iraqi SCUD missile attacks during Operation Desert Storm in 1991. The prospects for peace with the Palestinians, based on the Oslo Accords (1993), after peace agreements with Egypt (1979) and Jordan (1994), were yet to be realized as the 20th century drew to a close.

The United States took part in two World Wars and numerous overt and covert military endeavors during the 20th century. The expression of anti-Semitism in America, which was never as virulent as in Europe, faded across the century and Jews of various denominations and ethnicities participated to an ever greater extent in American life. By the end of the century, a modern Orthodox Jew was selected as the Vice Presidential nominee of the Democratic party in the Y2K (2000) election. The Republicans won, however.

There was virulent racism in the United States during the 20th century and it was directed against African Americans, a designation used in the 1990s that replaced the term "Blacks" (late 1970s) and "Negroes" or "Colored People" (before 1960). Horrific murders by lynching witnessed by crowds of adults and children marked the early part of the century. De juro segregation of African Americans from Whites in virtually every sphere of life prevailed through mid-century in many parts of the country and their opportunities for education and training, entry into many vocations and professions and to residence in certain neighborhoods remained severely restricted almost through the second half. The National Association for the Advancement of Colored People (NAACP) and the American Civil Liberties Union (ACLU) were instrumental in striking down laws supporting segregation with landmark cases in the post WWII period of the 1940s. The momentum of the Civil Rights movement increased through the second half of the century and brought about meaningful changes in American society. The Reverend Dr. Martin Luther King, Jr. championed a non-violent approach to confronting segregation and racism and led marches and sit-ins in both southern and northern cities. More aggressive and even violent elements of the African American community rose to leadership with Dr. King's assassination in 1968 and the close and compatible involvement of American Jews with the Civil Rights movement weakened as "Black Power" replaced civil rights as the apparent goal. Nevertheless, the affinity that Jews have felt for African Americans – perhaps based on a common history of slavery – continues to motivate efforts at inter-racial understanding and betterment.

Jack L. Levin participated actively in some of the major events and issues of the 20th century. We now call the 20th century history. Having entered the 21st century without him, he nevertheless serves as a model for participating in the continuing struggles for human rights, social equality and the welfare of the State of Israel and the Jewish people.

When the Nazis visited, Baltimore put out the welcome mat

Over half a century ago, I felt for the first time a frustration I have often experienced since as an incorrigible do-gooder: being attacked, ignored or ridiculed by those I ventured to warn about what I perceived as an immediate and growing threat to us all.

On that day, April 22, 1936, the frustration was caused by community resistance or indifference to our protest rally against the symbolic "good will" visit to Baltimore of the Nazi training ship *Emden*. Its well-scrubbed, white-clad cadets, putting a happy face on Nazism, smiled at Baltimore and Baltimore smiled back, with hugs and kisses.

Today the feeling returns as some of us try ineffectually to yank off the grinning don't-worry-be-happy mask that hides the ugliness of spreading poverty in the midst of plenty. Few seem bothered by increasing disparity between obscene extremes of wealth and misery, health and sickness, feast and famine that mock our Judaic-Christian values.

I make no claim to prophesy of prescience – only to readiness to acknowledge a monstrous reality that is staring us in the face. I also admit to an incurable optimism compelling a belief that something can and must be done or attempted. The frustration comes not from others' failure to oppose evil but from their insistence on denying that it exists, on giving it a pretty name and turning away. It comes from those who excuse every outrageous injustice with "it's only human nature."

Fifty-four years ago, we "premature anti-fascists" could not penetrate the willful blindness of those who refused to see Hitler, Mussolini, Hirohito and company as anything but "bulwarks against communism."

Today, we premature anti-fantasists cannot pierce the blindness of those who will not see danger in the growing chasm between rich and poor that is making the U.S. into another banana republic.

We point to the recent Census Bureau analysis on budget and policy priorities showing that the gap between the fat cats and the hungry in 1988 was wider than in any year since the Census began collecting this data in 1944. But few of us seem to want to read the handwriting.

Likewise, few were upset or the least discomfitted by the Emden's campaign to win the hearts and minds of pre-war Baltimoreans. In fact, official and influential Baltimore gave Hitler's emissaries a royal welcome.

Mayor Howard W. Jackson, as host to the Emden's Capt. Hans Bachman, made him at home by displaying the Nazi swastika flag in the mayor's office in City Hall.

Maryland Gov. Harry W. Nice boarded the ship to extend complimentary greetings. Debutantes had their hands kissed by dashing Nazi officers and joined them in sipping champagne and Rhine wine.

Hitler was toasted by many Baltimore officials and dignitaries on his birthday April 20. There were rousing chouses of "Happy Birthday, Dear Fuehrer." When the ship's band finished playing "Deutschland uber alles" the arms and voices of 450 were raised in heiling Hitler.

He also received roaring ovations at the Emerson Hotel, where the pastor of Baltimore's Zion Lutheran Church led prayers, toasts, a lavish buffet for 225 guests and much heiling.

The *Sun* news story on our April 22 protest demonstration at the foot of Broadway recreation pier reflected the popular mood. Its headline: "One Arrested as Nazis' Foes Jeer Crew of Emden." The subcaption: "2,000 at Protest Rally – Police Take Prisoner as they Drive Demonstrators Back."

The story went on to focus on the "one arrest," a drunk who, when 300 policemen began pushing people to move on, pushed back and was hauled off in the paddy wagon. The "arrest" and the "jeering" suggested a disorderly mob of churls being inhospitable and rude to invited guests. There was no mention of such respected speakers as James Waterman Wise, son of Rabbi

Stephen Wise, and others who came down from New York to discuss the meaning of the ship's visit. Meanwhile, the news story went on, the German sailors just smiled and "strolled about on the outskirts of the crowd. Many persons stopped to talk to [them] and obtain their autographs."

How can we be so concentrated on Willie Horton, flag factories and no-new-taxes, and so distracted from the wealthiest fifth of all families receiving 44 percent of the national income while the poorest fifth receive less than 5 percent? How can we pretend that the rising tide lifts all boats?

How can we be so preoccupied with Star Wars, unstealthy bombers and the good life that we ignore the growing gray underclasses of hungry, homeless and ailing fellow Americans who can't afford medical treatment? How can we load our crushing debts onto our children?

How can we stand on one shore of the shrunken Atlantic, knowing that on the other shore, in sub-Saharan Africa, 413 million fellow humans have a per-capita income of $330 a year, knowing that the life expectancy of the average Ethiopian is 42 years, knowing that we co-occupy a small global planet in the black emptiness of space, -- how can we know all of this today as we knew what was brewing in 1936, and not give a damn?

There is a ray of hope now, just as there was in 1936, that we can stop spreading the disease of delusion, the rejection of fact in a fantasy world.

Recent polls indicate that most American taxpayers express willingness to accept a modest tax increase if it is clearly stipulated to relieve the hungry, homeless and certifiably poverty-stricken.

If the band keeps playing that tune as the procession starts moving and growing, perhaps some fearless politician will come off the sidelines and rush to lead the parade.

April 20, 1990

The Other Roland Park

Roland Park today is a pleasant community where people of diverse religions, races and creeds live in peace and contentment. 'Twas not always.

Many senior Baltimoreans have less rosy memories of the old Roland Park than does Anne Stinson in her beautifully written elegy, "Easy As An Old Sweater," (*Opinion - Commentary*, Feb. 6). To them, Roland Park was not "the first planned suburban development in America." It was one of the most religiously and racially restricted developments in America before restrictive covenants were declared unenforceable by the U.S. Supreme Court.

To them, Roland Park was not a neighborhood with a "kind of wonderful, unself-conscious serenity about it," but a consciously, legally restricted area from which Jews, blacks and other minorities were cruelly excluded.

To them, Wyndhurst Road was not just the northern boundary of a segregated bit of heaven, it was the location – at Wyndhust and Charles – of a sign promoting development of Homeland and touting the Roland Park Company as "Pioneers in Restricted Development."

To them, Roland Park was not where big trees were honored but where little people were dishonored; not where streets were kept deliberately narrow but where minds were; not a place of gentility but uncivility.

My first Roland Park recollection is of 1935, when I helped to organize a protest demonstration at its Pratt Street dock against the "goodwill" visit of the Nazi warship Emden. Many of the young, smiling, pink-cheeked Nazi sailors were welcomed as house guests or "exchange students" in Roland Park homes. I have never been comfortable there since.

The official discriminatory policy was highly popular. In a *Sun* article (July 2, 1973), Mrs. Lee McCardell, widow of the *Sunpapers* writer, remembered that, in 1943, when a family that had a half-Jewish father bought a house near hers, neighbors circulated a petition asking the family not to move in – or, at least, to change their name.

In the same article, Mrs. Thomas Waxter Sr., a longtime resident, was quoted: "Roland Parkers were awful to the Jewish people." She and her husband were among the few residents who fought the surrounding ugliness, which she now says was "very fashionable at the time."

It was even worse for blacks. As late as 1973, when some Jewish families were already living in Roland Park, the *Sun* article was still headlined: "Why No Blacks in Roland Park?"

In 1948, Baltimorean Philip S. Perlman, as U.S. solicitor general, had successfully argued the *Shelley v. Kraemer* case before the Supreme Court. That historic decision had finally eliminated state-court enforcement of restrictive housing covenants. But covenants interpreted as contracts remained legal. So it took a while before the law broke down the Roland Park resistance.

Nostalgia tends to cloak the past in undeserved charm. Speaking well of the dead should not apply to dead bigots. Roland Park is much more beautiful today than it was. It practices what is preached in the preamble to the charter of the United Nations: "to practice tolerance and live together in peace with one another as good neighbors."

February 27, 1988

Holocaust

Editor: The letter writer who charged that American Jews "nagged, lectured," etc. (presumably over the Pope's bestowing respectability upon unrepentant Nazi official Waldheim) and who is repelled "when the Holocaust is repeatedly shoved in my face," etc., has unintentionally rendered a service to those of us, Jewish and Christian, who try to keep alive remembrance of what happened so that it can never happen again.

The letter shows that we err in taking for granted that the uniqueness of the Holocaust, over four decades later, has finally been recognized and accepted.

After all, the encyclopedias Americana, World Book and Britannica conceded its uniqueness, stating that the slaughter of the six million Jews was "exceptionally barbaric," that the systematic genocide of one particular people by legal sanction, the well-planned, methodical and nearly successful application of modern technology to annihilate one ancient group of humans for the crime of birth was indeed unparalleled.

Then along came the letter writer who denies the uniqueness of the Holocaust and resents being reminded of it, and others who deny it ever happened at all, and we know there is still much nagging work to be done.

August 7, 1987

Nobody Cared

Baltimore's time for remembering the Holocaust will start Sunday morning with a community observance at the downtown Holocaust Memorial, and continue Sunday evening and all day Monday with a conference at the Baltimore Hebrew College commemorating the 40th anniversary of the Warsaw Ghetto Uprising.

While remembering the six million murdered innocents, we should also remember that many of them could have been saved.

As an unfashionably premature anti-fascist in the 1930s, I remember the antagonism of friends toward one perceived as a trouble-making fellow-traveler and worse for opposing the bulwarks against communist – Hitler, Mussolini and Hirohito. Those of us who arranged a pre-war protest rally on Pratt Street in front of the visiting Nazi destroyer *Emden* pink-cheeked sailors, house guests of welcoming Baltimoreans, were reviled as inhospitable churls.

I remember the frustration of Baltimore's great humanitarian, the late Sidney Hollander, when he returned from futile pleading with the joint Senate-House Committee on Immigration in April 1939. He begged them to admit some of the terrified, homeless German Jewish children torn away from parents bound for concentration camps. His harrowing eye-witness reports of sadistic cruelties did not change the expression of what Sidney called the "stony-faced inquisitors." He got nowhere with his reminders that "America has always been kind to children" and that England, France, Holland and Switzerland had given homes to thousands of the Jewish children. Patriotic American organizations prevailed against the German Refugee Bill.

I remember that Gerhart Riegner, Swiss representative of the World Jewish Congress, tried to awaken the Western conscience in 1942, offering proof from a leading German industrialist that Hitler had ordered the extermination of all European Jews. Months of red tape later, he handed the American minister in Berne a report that began: "Millions of Jews are on the verge of complete annihilation by a deliberate policy of starvation, deportation under inhuman conditions and organized mass murder ..." The World Jewish Congress published a compendium of Nazi massacres of Jews in Riga, the desperation of a million and a half in Hungary, Italy, Romania, Bulgaria and France, the establishment of the Nazis' "vast slaughterhouse for Jews" in Eastern Europe. But millions of Jews stayed locked as the killing escalated.

On December 2, 1942, before completion of the crematoria at Auschwitz and Buchenwald, before the "final solution," Rabbi Stephen Wise appealed to his friend Roosevelt, who replied that the United States and its allies would "take every step to end the crimes." As a result, two weeks later, the U.S., Britain, the USSR and the governments in exile issued their first joint statement condemning the Nazi atrocities. Until then, not even words had been used as weapons.

But the doors stayed shut, and by this time 2 million Jews had already been killed. The refugee ships were turned back. When the British and Americans did organize the Bermuda Conference on Refugees, they put in charge of its visa division U.S. Assistant Secretary of State Breckenridge Long, an admirer of fascism, who had for years been turning a deaf ear to the cries for rescue, while enforcing idiotic visa procedures. (For example, a Jew who escaped the Gestapo had to produce an official police record from his hometown Nazi officials, attesting to his good character!)

Many could haven been saved – by aiding escapes to neutral nations, by concealment in certain areas, by temporary suspension of immigration quotas, by insisting that the Red Cross provide the same safeguards for imprisoned Jews as for prisoners of war or interned civilians, by demanding that the British stop turning the fugitives away from Palestine, the one place that would take them. With American cooperation, money and visas, Sweden, the French Underground, Romania and other countries could have saved thousands more Jewish lives.

In the spring of 1943, while the Allies conferred in

Bermuda, and the Jews fought back in the Warsaw Ghetto, Sweden, which had already admitted 35,000 Jews, offered to ask Germany to release 20,000 Jewish children, and to care for them in Sweden. The Swedes proposed that the U.S. and Great Britain agree to share the cost of food and medicine and relocate the children after the war in Palestine or some other haven. The British Foreign Office approved.

Then on June 5, 1943, Breckenridge Long and our skillful State Department began producing their specialty: endless red tape, months of delays in replying to letters. Pressed by the British, they concluded that the proposal "might antagonize the Germans," because it was limited to Jewish children – and it should be channeled through the Intergovernmental Committee anyway. So the British revised the plan to include some non-Jewish Norwegian children, and resubmitted the plan to the new U.S. committee. In January 1944, after 8 months of stalling by the U.S. – months in which many more than 20,000 children died in the Nazi ovens – the Swedes finally gave up.

The French Underground had rescued thousands of Jews – and could have saved nearly all of the 60,000 Jewish victims in France, if they had been given only two things – more money and American visas, neither available.

Romania had notified neutrals it was ready to transfer 70,000 Romanian Jews in Romanian ships to any refuge selected by the Allies. The slow murder of that proposal ended with an amazing cable from our State Department that saving the Romanian Jews "might incense the British" by granting relief to a "special group" of aliens.

Thus, "good" people did nothing while millions were being murdered for the crime of brith. There was always an excuse – preoccupation with Depression or war – but never in history have so many cared or done so little about such monstrous evil.

We need to remember that expulsion of the Jews proved to be a loss and failure to their enemies, and a gain and success to their friends, whom they rewarded with massive contributions to industry, commerce, science, art and culture.

We need to remember that the near-successful attempt to wipe out a whole race of fellow humans and the world's indifference to it are not a morbid obsession. It is necessary if we are ever to master the beast that lurks under the skin of a supposedly civilized society – and to understand the determination of survivors in Israel and elsewhere, that it must never burst loose again.

April 8, 1983

With the times again troubled, could another such leader arise?

Could anything like Hitler's coming to power 60 years ago ever happen here in the land of the free?

History never repeats exactly, and the differences between the Germany of January 1933 and the United States of 1983 are enormous. Yet, one disturbing similarity in the sullen loss of faith in republican government's ability to solve society's big problems.

After making customary patriotic obeisances to our system as the world's best, some citizens grumble that they are getting sick and tired of it. Election follows election, the ins and outs swap hats, but such questions as crushing unemployment, inequality of sacrifice and opportunity, drugs, crime and survival in a nuclear age remain shrouded in rhetoric, unaddressed and unanswered. Both parties claim competence, but neither assumes discipline or responsibility. The President and Congress blame each other. Nobody is accountable. Nobody is in charge.

Some propose escape from irresponsibility and stalemate through drastic revision of our Constitution to create a parliamentary system. Its advocates are not eccentrics, but solid citizens like Floyd Cutler, former counsel to President Carter; Robert McNamara, former secretary of defense, and C. Douglas Dillon, former secretary of the treasury, who calls for sharp reduction or elimination of the division of authority between the legislative and executive branches. Even incumbent congressmen are saying that the situation is becoming intolerable.

'But if – as seems likely – this major revision of the Constitution is rejected – what then? Will the frustrated ones start clamoring for radical change? Will they begin looking for a charismatic take-charge guy – not a dictator, to be sure, but an all-American someone who offers quick fixes and simple answers to questions of stupefying complexity, who will lead them through the wilderness to the promised land?

Are these desperate ones approaching the point at which, 50 years ago on January 30, 1933, President Paul von

Hindenburg, once considered by German industrialists their protector against the Nazis, appointed Adolf Hitler chancellor?

One month after the problem-solver was put in charge, the Reichstag fire ignited the conflagration that raged across Europe for the next 12 years at a cost of millions of lives.

The day following that fire, all constitutional liberties were suspended, the death sentence was imposed for "disturbing the peace" and the Jew madness began.

It is interesting to note now, when anti-Semitism holds its classic appeal for many troubled seekers of scapegoats, that it was Hitler's first and favorite instrument for eliminating opposition, consolidating support and distracting attention from his inability to work expected miracles. The brawling attacks on Jews in his beer hall days were followed as soon as he took power, by the inauguration of the great Jewish boycott.

Targets were chosen by race, not religion – not only stores, shops, restaurants and cinemas owned or partly owned by Jews, but Jewish doctors, dentists, educators, lawyers, judges and other professionals. Shut-down Jewish businesses were ordered nevertheless to keep paying their non-Jewish employees. Mass meetings exhorted the public to back the boycott.

Huge posters denounced the Jews, as did inflammatory radio broadcasts and placards on Jewish business places, so designated by informers. Every Jewish employer had to discharge at once every Jewish employee and pay an extra month's wages to each Aryan employee, or be arrested for the slightest hesitation.

Not far different from these events of 50 years ago in Germany are the anti-Semitic measures practiced today in the USSR, especially against Jews who have shown a desire to emigrate; the discrimination against Jews in education and employment harassment and imprisonment of Jewish leaders; vilification that is condoned, sanctioned and propagated by the government, and exported to Arab, African and Third World countries.

Reminiscent also are the double standards, tortured condemnations and hypocritical sanctions applied against Israel in order to isolate and delegitimize it in the United Nations. The U.N. has become a major forum for classic, crude anti-Semitism. At a meeting of the U.N. Commission on Human Rights in Geneva, Dr. Michael Novak, United States representative, declared: "Imagine my shock when I heard so much hatred, so many lies, such squalid racism, such despicable anti-Semitism – all in the name of human rights. I have heard in this chamber attacks upon Zionism in accents of a murderous hatred not heard since the days of the Nazis. It is as though this chamber has retrogressed by 40 years – as though this is not 1981 but 1941, and not in Geneva, but along the Hitler-Stalin axis."

The infamous General Assembly vote of 1975, that branded Zionism as a form of racism, was only the culmination of many attacks on the world's oldest national liberation movement.

In Europe there is a resurgence of anti-Semitic terrorism.

Less raucous yet alarming echoes are heard in the whisperings and innuendos of a few mindless Americans. They should take note of what the good, conservative Germans learned early on from the Jewish boycott a half century ago.

It opened the eyes of many nationalists to the true nature of the regime whose path to power they had smoothed. It was not that they suddenly stopped disliking or patronizing Jews. Nor were they shocked by the outrages. But these first anti-Semitic excesses made them realize what they had unleashed; a campaign of hatred and violence unlike anything they had experienced or expected.

The hope that Hitler would return them to power faded fast for the Prussians, Junkers, and Hohenzollerns. They began to perceive that the terror they had spawned against Jews, pacificists, Catholics and Marxists could be turned against themselves, which it soon was too late to stop.

It is true that the American Nazi party and Ku Klux Klan are at present only small, ludicrous bumps on the American body politic. Yet Klan and Nazi candidates have recently been able to win two or three primary election contests. Meantime, some anti-Semites disguise their intent by pretending great concern and even affection for Jews, by denouncing Nazism, fascism, racial and religious persecution, while aiding and abetting those, who are sworn to annihilate Israel.

It is true that there has been a precipitous drop in anti-Semitism, as a factor in American elections. Jews hold public office in numbers disproportionate to their percentage of the population and are not subjected to the old discrimination in employment and the professions. No significant elements of public or private life espouse or condone anti-Semitism in the U.S.

Yet the warning signs are evident in a depressed economy with over 10 percent unemployment, declining social opportunity and increasing frustration.

Millions are asking: "Who is to blame for the mess we're in? Not ourselves, we deny it. Not our government officials, they deny it. Who, then?"

The search for the cause of our social sickness haunts all who remember the long nightmare that began 50 years ago.

January 20, 1983

[Post election betrayal of Israel predicted]
... as a Baltimorean cites world-wide anti-Semitism

Three recent unrelated events suggested that the reports of the death of anti-Semitism may have been exaggerated and its death-bed scene is one of the longest playing on record.

The happenings are: news treatment of the warfare between Iraq and Iran; the selection of an actress who is an avowed enemy of Israel and champion of the PLO to portray a victim of Nazism; and the statement by the president of the Southern Baptist Conference that God does not hear the prayer of a Jew because he is a "man who says Jesus Christ is not the true Messiah. It's blasphemous ..."

Until Iraqis and Iranians began killing each other systematically and bombing each other's oil installations, thus compelling attention from the media, an avid consumer of news might have thought that the only Moslem concern was Jews and Israel.

After all, what has been the really big news all over the world?

Not the slaughter of Moslems by Russians and other Moslems in Afghanistan, Iran, Syria, Lebanon, Iraq, Libya, etc.

Not the denial of human rights to Arabs by Arabs.

Not the suppression and even enslavement of some Arab women by some Arab men; not the torture of some Arab prisoners by some Arab jailers; not the abuse and exploitation of incredibly poor Arabs by fantastically rich Arabs. Certainly not the genocidal intentions and homicidal acts of the PLO against Israelis; not the cynical sellouts of the United Nations to the oil cartel; not the spectacular sabotage of the Camp David peace efforts by the co-called moderate states of Jordan and Saudi Arabia as well as the "rejectionist" states.

No, the burning issue is that Jews want Jerusalem, whose Jewish citizens have constituted the majority of its population for over a century and whose centrality to Judaism has prevailed for millennia, to be the capital of Israel; or that Israel is proposing to buy Bedouin land on terms which some outsiders consider unfavorable to the sellers, or that an Israeli task force cleans out a nest of assassins before they can attack defenseless civilians; or, of course, those West Bank settlements which horrify all the nations that routinely attack Israel as an illegitimate occupying power.

Among these U.N. stalwarts there is hardly one that is not now abusing or has not in the past unfairly treated some of its vulnerable citizens, often Jewish. These models of propriety include Arab states whose idea of secular democracy is to ride roughshod over minority civilians, especially Jews; and that most pious, greatest occupier in all history, the USSR. In many countries of Eastern Europe, its police forces stand constantly ready to crush any movement toward unsanctioned change.

But the fact that Russia maintains some 30 divisions in four European states 35 years after the end of World War II, and continues to ravage Afghanistan, is not news; nor is the distinction between the USSR's unprovoked aggressions and Israel's self-defense against forces that tried several times to destroy it. No voice is ever raised in the U.N. questioning the legitimacy of the USSR or its right to exist. Why is embattled Israel monotonously excoriated as the Great Occupying Power for refusing to return to its enemies the launching sites for their previous attacks, while they are still refusing to make peace and are committed to exterminate the State of Israel?

Why are intransigence and belligerence associated so often with the Jewish people who worship reason and peace, who have made greater sacrifices and taken greater risks for peace than any in history; and so seldom associated with their violent enemies who are committed to destroy the Jewish state? Why the double standard?

Why does any suspicion that Jewish behavior is flawed, like that of others in the somewhat less than perfect human species rate featured news treatment and universal condemnation?

A part of the answer, of course, is oil and the foolish notion that if only Jews were nice to their enemies, then the OPEC nations would be nice to an oil-hungry world.

The basic explanation, however, is based on impossible expectations. More is expected and demanded of Jews than of any other mortals: more tolerance, patience, sacrifice and suffering; more superhuman goodness than has ever been found in evil mankind; more eagerness to invite their own annihilation by their sworn enemies.

The word for this irrational attitude, this refusal to recognize the defensiveness of Israeli actions, this deafness and blindness of the glaring fact that Jews will never again fill their assigned role of the martyr race – the word is the same now as before it fell into disrepute. It is anti-Semitism.

In Europe, where anti-Semitism was often state policy, it was used by monarchies to divert attention from social problems and by Hitler to stir the passions of racial purity. Today, in the Soviet Union it is used to promote proletarian unity against the individualist outsider.

In America, where it has never achieved legal status, it has surfaced in occasional virulent spasms of hate like those of the prewar Father Coughlin and postwar George Lincoln Rockwell, the American Nazi. The more common expressions of hostility here used to be social and economic discrimination, rejection in colleges, employment, housing and accommodations, and accusations of aggressiveness and pushiness against Jews who protested such injustices, now illegal. Unfortunately it is easier to eradicate discrimination than prejudice.

What else can you call it but anti-Semitism when nations which are piling up armaments to defend themselves against possible enemies thousands of miles away, brand as militaristic the Jewish nation whose actual enemies are pressing against its very doors and windows, threatening to break in for the fifth time in three decades?

What else can you call it when the intolerant evangelical leader denies access to God for the Jews who first worshiped Him and who wrote the book the fundamentalists profess to revere?

What else, when great moral principles contributed by

Jews to our Judeao-Christian culture are repudiated by a self-styled Moral Majority?

What else, when much of the world persistently vilifies the Jewish reactor as actor; the Jewish defender as aggressor; the Jewish victim as malefactor; the Jewish champion of liberty and life as the scourge of tyranny and death?

Today, as throughout history, anti-Semitism remains a sickness of mind and spirit, a symptom of deeper ills that had better be confronted, than blamed on the Jews – again.

The Anti-Semites Live

Sir: This is to express thanks and appreciation to *The Evening Sun* for publishing Dr. Harry Bard's excellent, informative article on the isolation of Israel by the U.N.

Dr. Bard stated well what needs to be said: that the anti-West alliance of Communist and Arab members has taken over the sub-structures as well as the General Assembly of the U.N. and effectively expelled Israel from any representation on the Economic and Social Council and the committees and commissions that work devotedly for all humankind – except the Israelis.

This exclusion is ironic, since there are no individuals better equipped than the Israelis to make significant educational, cultural, scientific and intellectual contributions to the work of these U.N. bodies.

Obviously, the guilt of generations of statesmen who participated in or tolerated centuries of anti-Semitic excesses culminating in the Holocaust has sputtered and died. It flared briefly in the U.N.'s creation of the State of Israel, but it has fizzled out. The nations are back to business as usual: exploiting Jews as scapegoats. The new U.N. twist, as Dr. Bard's article reveals, is to make Israel the demon state that must be exorcized as the simple answer to all the world's woes.

The exorcists should note that the Jewish people lives, while the nations that persecuted Jews instead of confronting problems are ruins littering the pages of history. What happened to the individual nations could happen to the United Nations, too.

March 25, 1975

General Powell

Editor: Congratulations to President Bush for his excellent appointment of Gen. Colin Powell to be chairman of his Joint Chiefs of Staff. In passing over many white generals of greater seniority and experience to move General Powell to the top job, the president was practicing – intentionally or not – the affirmative action his administration and courts oppose on grounds of "reverse discrimination." Perhaps more corporate CEOs and chairmen will be moved to emulate the chief executive by naming qualified blacks to leadership positions in their board rooms. In 1980, only 4 percent of our "color-blind" nation's managers and administrators were black.

August 17, 1989

Question and Answer

An interesting question came up at a recent meeting of the executive committee of the Black/Jewish Forum of Baltimore, known as the BL-EWS, which seeks to strengthen the relationship between Baltimore's black and Jewish communities to the city's benefit.

This was the question, raised by a black leader: "Much is known and taught about the Holocaust, and the education is necessary: but what do we know, teach or care about The Middle Passage? In fact, how many of you have ever heard of it?"

None of the Jewish members had. I found later that white Christian friends were equally ignorant. So I looked it up

The phrase refers to one of the worst crimes of modern Western imperialism, the shipment of slaves from Africa to the West Indies and East Coast America ports, including some in the Chesapeake Bay. About 10 million men, women and children, but mostly young males preferred as field hands, were corraled and herded onto the slave ships.

The European settlers of America needed labor for their expanding plantation agriculture and turned to the slave trade. It powered their export economy of sugar, cotton, indigo, tobacco and rice.

The Middle Passage from the African West Coast took an average of 30 to 32 days of indescribable horror. Packed in the stinking holds, up to a fourth of the slaves died of communicable diseases – dysentery, smallpox, measles – or in shipwrecks, sinking, pirate attacks, slave revolts, or – after landing in a strange and hostile environment – of susceptibility to unaccustomed infections. (The mortality rate was higher, of course, for slaves shipped from Africa's East Coast on a passage twice as long as from the West Coast.)

My friend's question, however, seemed to imply a mistaken equivalence of the Holocaust and the Middle Passage. Both were outrageous examples of man's inhumanity to man. Both involved the torture and sacrifice of defenseless people.

But they were different in important ways. The uniqueness of the Holocaust was that Jews, and a few other minorities, were chosen for extermination. In the Middle Passage, the blacks were chosen for inhuman exploitation. The cattle cars carried Jews to the ovens and gas chambers to die. The slave ships transported surviving blacks to the plantations to live, toil and produce profit for others. A killer/victim relationship is not the same as master/slave.

Nevertheless, a world that tolerated the Holocaust and the Middle Passage owes a debt to survivors of both and their kin. It is true that today's Germans and white Americans should not be held responsible for the crimes of their ancestors. Yet those killers were the parents and grandparents of the present generation; and those exploiters, the owners, providers, customers and crews of the slave ships, were the not-so-distant relatives of many of the living. The past is not remote.

Modern Germany acknowledged that reparations were in order for survivors and families of the victims. The United states – or most of its citizens – are inclined to accept an obligation to descendants of the only Americans who did not come here as immigrants seeking a better life, but were dragged here in chains and abused for over a century. We recognize and support successful black efforts to overcome hardship and handicaps and to realize at long last our constitutional promise of equal opportunity.

That is why affirmative action is legally and morally justified, even at the cost of some "reverse discrimination," a side effect like that produced by other useful remedies against inherited disease.

At the very least, for most fair-minded citizens, affirmative action is a rite of passage from the lingering stench of the Middle Passage. They know it is perilous to ignore history.

Tom Dulack, the author of "Incommunicado," the play about the poetic genius and bigot Ezra Pound whose pro-fascist anti-Semitic ravings made him a World War II traitor and certified madman, says in a program note: "Pound was not an aberration...

He was a representative product of ... his culture and civilization and it is sheer hypocrisy for the rest of us to pretend otherwise... The history of anti-Semitism in the West is long and lamentable. No country, no people, including the United States of America, can plead innocent. Anti-Semitism is woven into the very fabric of our culture."

A similar point was made by Philipp Jenninger, former president of the West German parliament, who was hounded from office for an unforgivable sin. He stated the truth that the German people shared responsibility for creating the monster they unleashed on humanity, and that they denied that "in 1938 a majority of Germans stood behind Hitler (and) identified themselves with him and his politics."

Likewise, racism in America is an ugly historic fact that cannot be denied and a tendency that must constantly be defied – regardless of support or opposition from the administration and Supreme Court.

No amount of reparations or affirmative action by the living can bring back the dead or repair the terrible damage done. But these compensations are civilizing influences on our brutal nature. They are also an important first step toward curing our addiction to violence; admitting that we have a problem.

That is an attempt to answer my colleague's question.

September 16, 1989

A World That Committed the Crime of Silence

Secretary of State James A. Baker III visited Israel for the first time last month. It must have been a revelation to him – especially the searing experience of Yad Vashem (literally "a monument and a name"), the Holocaust Martyrs and Heroes' Remembrance Authority in Jerusalem. It is a national shrine visited by more than a million people each year.

It must not have been easy for an American who has led a comparatively sheltered life, whose home, church and office have never been smashed and burned, who has never had to watch his children grabbed and murdered by brown-shirted savages, whose family members have died peacefully in beds instead of in ovens, to grasp the enormity of the horror inflicted on European Jewry by the Nazi bestiality which preceded birth of the State of Israel.

Secretary Baker is a busy man with a crowded schedule. Surely at Yad Vashem he had no time to pore over archives containing millions of pages of documents, testimonies and memoirs in many languages – the awesome collection relating to the Holocaust period. Nor could he have browsed among the 80,000 books in the library dealing not only with the Holocaust but also with the growth of modern anti-Semitism, fascism and Nazism, the background of World War II racial hatred so alien to this Midwest American. The agony of starving refugees and survivors of death camps pleading in vain for a haven and being returned to their Nazi executioners must have been difficult or impossible for Mr. Baker to comprehend.

While the Holocaust was happening to the millions memorialized at Yad Vashem, James Baker had been the teen-age son of a well-to-do Houston lawyer, living quietly in a comfortable home, playing youthful games, preparing to attend the fashionable Hill prep school and later the ivied halls of Princeton.

There at Yad Vashem he was confronting for the first time, however briefly, the strange, haunting, other-worldly facts about a people, a period, a country he never really knew – a people that had been running for millennia, now hunkered down at last in a small fortress state of their own that has known not a moment's peace from determined enemies in its 43-year history.

What did the healthy, normal visitor at Yad Vashem feel, starting down into unimaginably grotesque depths of evil?

At Yad Vashem, a man untouched by violence met a bloodied people with vivid collective memories of ancetors slaughtered by every exquisite variety of torture – crucified, lynched, burned, boiled, brained, strangled, smothered, beheaded, bayoneted, torn by pulling horses – not for what they had done but for what they were, and frequently for no other purpose than the sport of it all.

An innocent abroad, Secretary Baker caught a fleeting glimpse at Yad Vashem of a world he never knew, an indifferent world that stood by and watched as 6 million fellow humans were systematically massacred, a callused world that turned away children whose wretched parents pleaded for the lives of their youngsters if not their own, a world that committed the crime of silence.

Mr. Baker may have preferred to linger in the tree-lined paths of the Garden of the Righteous Gentiles, who risked their lives to save Jews. But he surely knew that for every rescuer there were thousands of killers.

Did the experience of Yad Vashem help Secretary Baker to understand the Israeli preoccupation with security, the meaning of "Never again?"

Did it help him comprehend Israel's distrust of an international conference and reluctance to assign its fate to nations which had supported the obscene U.N. resolution branding Zionism as racism – many of them still at war against Israel?

Did Yad Vashem remind him that Jews in Israel who, in this century alone, have survived extermination efforts by Nazi Germany, by Arab nations in five wars to drive them into the sea, by terrorists and recently by Iraqi Scud attacks on civilians, will not easily be convinced or coerced into accepting words of peace and good will concealing murderous hatred?

Has Yad Vashem helped Secretary Baker – and, through

him, President Bush – to understand the ferocity of determination that *Am Yisrael Chai,* (the People of Israel Live). Mere right of existence is hard to understand or appreciate for Americans protected by vast oceans and friendly neighbors. To us, it is a given. It is not, for the people Mr. Baker briefly visited. They have never been allowed, and especially for the last 43 years since founding their state, to take existence for granted. They are constantly conscious of what others experience unconsciously, like breathing and a heart-beat. Their history, ancient and recent, has given them little cause for trust.

And yet, despite their fixations on defense and survival, the embattled Israelis have shown that existence is not enough. They have struggled to achieve miracles and have in many ways succeeded. With enemy guns pressed against their heads and knives at their throats since 1948, they have nevertheless made the desert bloom. In their tiny bit of wasteland they have built a green refuge for the persecuted, a haven for the homeless, a full life for the half-dead and an oasis of democracy – still the only one in the vast Middle East. All that eludes them is peace, because the Arabs refuse to end hatred, boycott and belligerency against Israel.

If Mr. Baker did not feel any of that at Yad Vashem, he probably never can or will understand why issues perceived in Washington and New York as cold, common-sense, diplomatic and geopolitical considerations are seen in Tel Aviv and Jerusalem as matters of life or death.

April 13, 1991

Opinion & Commentary
Leaving Skeletons in the Closet
by Jack L. Levin

A funny thing happened recently. A grandson, my connection to the future, surprisingly reconnected me with my past.

It happened when our daughter-in-law brought our two grandchildren to visit. They played several games – tic-tac-toe and checkers – which the 9-year-old grandson handily won from his 6-year-old sister, who retired for consolation to the cookie jar.

Then came the surprise, Joey, who have never before shown the slightest interest in plaques, certificates and trophies awarded by social-action organizations I had led, suddenly began reading the stilted prose. His interest was to show off his newly acquired reading ability. His recitation recalled my exciting years with Americans for Democratic Action, American Civil Liberties Union, American Jewish Congress, Black/Jewish Forum of Baltimore, Conference of Christians and Jews, the city of Baltimore, the angry letters to the editor, the sit-ins, protest demonstrations, meetings and speeches.

"What does all this mean?" Joey asked.

"It means," my wife interposed, "that your zaydie worked very hard to change the ways that white people had been mistreating black people. But you wouldn't know about that. It all happened before you and Lauren were born."

"What happened?" Asked Joey.

"Oh, a lot of incredibly rotten things," I began, but then paused. Was this an opportunity to educate them about what my generation had lived through?

Should I tell them about the black family out shopping, turned away when the kids had to go to the bathroom? Should I get them ot imagine what it was like for a thirsty family to be turned away from a water fountain marked "Whites Only," or a hungry family from a lunch counter?

Back of the Bus

Should Joey and Lauren be required to lean about the humiliation of the black family forced to stand in the back of the bus, while seats were open up front. Or about how they felt when passing signs on the small back roads leading to shore places that proclaimed "Whites Only"? Must they be introduced to racial epithets they never heard: wops, kikes, chinks, spics, jungle bunnies, etc.

My doubts increased because I remembered Joey's mother telling me of an incident in a restaurant. Next to their table was a couple with a little blond girl. And next to their table was a black couple with two very young little boys. The little girl asked permission of her parents to go and talk to the little boys. The girl's mother indignantly and furiously forbade such contact.

Joey could not understand why, and when his parents explained that they were black, Joey wanted to know what that had to do with it. He and Lauren thought the woman was just mean or maybe crazy.

Another incident came to mind. Joey had told me how much he admired the quarterback on his neighborhood football team. He declared Matthew's achievements in glowing terms, but never mentioned that Matthew was black. To Joey, he was a teammate.

These recollections changed my mind. Why burden Joey and Lauren with the baggage of my earlier years? Why saddle them with identification with, or responsibility for past injustices? I suddenly realized that Joey and Lauren had achieved, as a result of attitudes imparted by his parents which I had cultivated in his father, a state of mind which most Americans claim to have, but don't. These kinds are really, truly color-blind. Why should their eyes be opened to the skeletons in the closet?

I felt a greater sense of reward for my past efforts than I had ever felt – plaques notwithstanding. With Joey and Lauren, it is beyond argument that the color of the skin means no more in people than in apples and that there are good and bad apples in all colors.

Chapter 2

Civil Rights and Civil Liberties
Sidney Hollander, Jr.

As W.E.B. DuBois famously pronounced, "The problem of the twentieth century is the problem of the color line." Jack Levin's life was encompassed by the century, and much of his lifelong activism was directed to issues of civil rights and the drive toward racial equality. While no advocate is satisfied with the present status of our black minority, the change during the century has surpassed what could have been expected by any but the most optimistic. Jack had barely reached (the then) voting age of 21 when the last Maryland lynching took place on the Eastern Shore; he lived to see a black mayor of Baltimore, a black Baltimorean appointed to the U.S. Supreme Court and another as chief judge of the Maryland Court of Appeals. Jack was engaged as speech writer for Baltimore's black state's attorney, was represented by black members of Congress and had black neighbors in the Cheswolde neighborhood where he and Ester had been perhaps the first Jewish home owners in the late 1940's.

For the first half of the century white advocates of racial equality continued to be on the political fringe. Even during World War II, uniformed blacks stationed in the South were ordered to the Jim Crow car when their southbound train crossed the Potomac River and, at their destination, to the rear of the town trolley or bus.

Baltimore was not as rigidly segregated as cities to the south; for example, its street cars observed no color line (although the inter-urban line to Annapolis required Negroes to sit in the rear). But schools, drinking fountains, places of public accommodation and housing were assigned according to race.

Challenges to discrimination appeared sporadically during and after World War II in Baltimore as elsewhere in the nation. Some were by court order, some by administrative decision, some through advocacy pressure, some voluntarily by reason of conscience and justice. By mid-century the University of Maryland under court order desegregated its graduate and professional schools, Governor McKeldin appointed black magistrates, and Baltimore City police officers were promoted to positions hitherto denied them. During these early postwar years faculty and staff activities were desegregated in the Baltimore school system, but racial barriers remained for all schools until 1952, when the School Board, under challenge, acknowledged its inability to provide a "separate but equal" equivalent to the advanced "A" course offered at Baltimore Polytechnic Institute. The board's decision thus anticipated by two years the Supreme Court ruling that abolished legally imposed public school segregation throughout the United States.

Perhaps more than any other single event, the 1954 "Brown vs. Board of Education of Topeka" decision reversed the political trend, and for the latter half of the century the presumption of equal rights (if not always the reality) became widespread. Step-by-step, federal, state and local, through agitation, litigation and legislation, resistance began to subside.

Furthermore, the accelerated progress toward civil rights for blacks became a pattern for other claimants: other ethnic groups, women's liberation, religious denominations, the physically and mentally handicapped, gays and lesbians – leading to such diverse mandates as wheelchair ramps, aids for blind voters, religion-conforming diets and other religious accommodations for prison inmates, equality of athletic budgets for girls in publicly funded educational institutions, and numerous other such requirements that would have left a citizen of 1900 wide-eyed in disbelief.

The first ten amendments to the United States Constitution, the Bill of Rights, inform this chapter of Jack Levin's opus. The subject is often seen from two aspects: Civil Rights and Civil Liberties. This distinction is subtle and not always helpful, but Jack sometimes used an aphorism to delineate them: Civil Rights, he said, permit the citizen to be like everyone else, while Civil Liberties allow the citizen to be different from everyone else.

Racial and Social Equality

I appreciate and welcome this opportunity to speak on behalf of the Baltimore Jewish Council, an agency of The Jewish Charities and Welfare Fund, and the Council's six affiliated organizations, the American Jewish Committee, American Jewish Congress, B'nai B'rith, Jewish Labor Committee, Jewish War Veterans, Federation of Jewish Women's Organizations, and Council of Jewish Women.

On some issues, there may be a bit of justifiable skepticism as to whether the spokesman truly reflects the majority opinion of those he represents.

In this case, ladies and gentlemen, I am confident that I express the overwhelming majority opinion of Jewish citizens in all areas of the city and in all walks of life in endorsing Baltimore City Ordinance 1083 for open occupancy housing. We Jews know something of inequality. We are experts.

From our long history, as a result of persecution and discrimination, the Jewish people has developed a special interest in social justice and in protecting and preserving hard-won democratic institutions and liberties.

More than 2000 years before the concept in the American Declaration of Independence that "all men are created equal," a Jewish prophet, Malachi, asked: "Have we not all one father? Hath not one God created us?"

And more than 3000 years before the inscription was put on our Liberty Bell, the Jewish Bible declared, in Leviticus 25:10, "Proclaim liberty throughout the land and to the inhabitants thereof."

We are proud to endorse this open occupancy ordinance, as we have all previous civil rights ordinances before this body.

In the early 40's, we supported the ordinance creating the Human Relations Commission, which you passed unanimously, and, later, the Fair Employment Ordinance.

Shortly afterwards we stood for broadening the Commission's authority to include public accommodations as well as employment – and, last spring, to include health and welfare services and educational institutions.

We recall that, each time a law was proposed, there were cries of impeding doom and disaster if the law should pass.

Nine years ago, when you enacted your first Fair Employment Practices legislation, it was said that the law was not needed, that it would not work, that it would bring all sorts of violent repercussions. Nothing has happened, except that justice has been done. Persons who had wanted to do right, but had feared reprisals from competitors and rivals, were released to deal decently and honorably, as they had desired all along. Since everyone was in the same boat, very few were inclined to rock it.

This acceptance of civil rights legislation has been the rule not only in Baltimore but in every city that has passed such laws, including housing laws. There has been no mass flight from affected areas. And very soon there will be no sanctuary anywhere to which the prejudiced will be able to flee.

As citizens, therefore, we know that this ordinance is not only just, but also practical – because it will actually increase property values by eliminating segregated slums.

As Jews, we know that this ordinance is right – because equality is basic in our teachings, traditions and history, and, along with justice, freedom and peace, is a pillar of prophetic Judaism.

As rational human beings, we cannot understand what force has to do with the issue:

Schooling is forced – and some people are unhappy about it.

Traffic rules are forced – and a few find them intolerable.

Zoning laws are forced – and some people resent them.

Are we to draw the line at legislating common, ordinary, human decency toward fellow citizens because it makes some people unhappy to grant it?

Most of the citizens of our city and state do not equate an open housing law with compulsion to do justly and love mercy. Most of us do not consider a law to treat a fellow-citizen as an individual any different from the laws handed down to us on Mt. Sinai. This open housing law requires us only to practice seven days a week what we preach in synagogue on Saturday and in church on Sunday.

This law demands of us only that we do with our hearts and minds what we have been doing with our lips.

This law stipulates only that we try to do better in the future than in the past, try to remove some of the burdens that have been loaded on the backs of our Negro neighbors and humiliations they have been forced to suffer through generations of injustices.

This is a good law that asks only good sense and good will of good citizens.

The choice that faces us is not whether or not we will have open occupancy. We will have it. U.S. Senator Dirksen, who is no flaming liberal, has said in endorsing civil rights legislation that there is no force on earth like the power of an idea whose time has come. The time for open occupancy housing has come – about 100 years late – but it has come. There is no longer the slightest doubt that equal opportunity will apply in housing as in all other areas where it has, at long last, become law.

Statement to City Council hearing
May 18, 1965

What did August 28th demonstrate?

Questions are being asked: Did the March for Jobs and Freedom do any good? Was it more than a picnic-revival meeting? Did it justify all the effort, expense and excitement? Did anything really result from the outpouring of nearly a quarter of a million Americans, the river of buses that rolled in from tributaries all over the nation and merged into a flood that swept through the Capital?

The answer is yes, over 200,000 times yes!!

It demonstrated for all the world watching that the United States has upgraded equality to the status of a great moral issue, regards the denial of human dignity – in the words of Rabbi Joachim Prinz, President of the American Jewish Congress, "the most urgent, the most disgraceful, the most tragic problem" of our times, and that this competitive society can be compassionate too.

It demonstrated to the lawmakers watching that there are hundreds of thousands of voters willing and eager to face inconvenience, discomfort, loss of time from jobs and studies, and the possibility of physical danger to assert that this issue concerns them personally, individually. These are voters who vote; who are sure to have nothing more important to do on election day, regardless of the weather, than vote their conviction and commitment; who can be counted upon to reward their friends and punish their enemies at the polls.

It demonstrated to cynics that American democracy is more than a tired platitude, that it lives as surely here and now as when the Bill of Rights first heralded *"the right of the people peaceably to assemble and petition the Government for a redress of grievances."*

It demonstrated to the onlookers at injustice the absurd cruelty and criminality of the Wallaces and Barnetts who, persecuting the victim and defending his assailant, charge that the demonstrators against inequality are the violent ones. On August 28th, the greatest demonstration in the history of the United States was not marred by a single shot, blow or even a single ugly word, although emotions mounted to a religious fervor.

It demonstrated to us who long ago committed ourselves to this struggle and who participated in the March that we have played a small but significant role in a mighty drama, collaborated in writing a large page in the history of our times, fought well in mankind's longest battle against the forces of darkness to free the human spirit, and experienced some of the exultation that earlier Israelites must have felt on their march out of Egypt. The hands that waved at us from other bus windows were brown, white, yellow and black. Many of the smiling eyes were red from lack of sleep and night-long riding, but all sparkled. When we looked at their signs denoting affiliation with churches, unions, social and fraternal organizations of almost every religion and nationality, and recalled the pitifully small bands of mavericks who used to fight alone in this struggle, we felt more than ever before *like members in good standing of the human race*. And when we saw them looking at our bus sign, we were proud to be identified as American Jews on this great mission.

But, above all, it demonstrated the attainability of dignity to those who have always believed the simple decencies of life to be out of reach for them and their children. It demonstrated the enormous possibilities of adding 20 million first-class citizens to the population of our country.

When our tide swept into Washington, the city that has become almost entirely black following the white flight to the suburbs, it was a holiday. Almost all those sitting on their front steps in the slum streets were Negroes – not, like our fellow demonstrators, fired with purpose and determination to improve their lot, but Negroes who had not even bothered to attend this greatest demonstration in America's history though so nearby, who had concluded long ago that the cards were stacked against them and nothing mattered and had given up. Something happened to these indifferent and defeated ones. As they watched bus after bus roaring by, new-found friends flooding past in never-ending waves, mounting evidence that perhaps, by God, somebody – an amazing lot of somebodies – *did care* about them, then even some of them were caught up in this moment of truth. More and more of them came out of their houses to sniff the strange and heady fragrance of friendship. They got up on their feet, grinned and waved, tentatively at first, then more and more enthusiastically as they, the voiceless and voteless, the forgotten ones, the flotsam and jetsam, found themselves suddenly swept into a torrent of sympathy with those who remembered them as fellow humans. There is no sight in the world like the first glimmer of hope on the blank faces of the hopeless and half-alive. Any of us who witnessed this miracle must rededicate ourselves to the struggle to keep it from flickering out, to fan into a flame of full life this glowing ember of dignity, not only for their sake and ours, but for the survival of our nation and all its cherished values.

August 28th demonstrated that a Civil Rights Bill can, will and must be passed – and soon, very soon – if this Revolution is to remain peaceful.

October 11, 1963

Distortion of Logic

Sir:

Worse than the violation of the basic rights of Negro citizens in Mississippi, worse than the denial of the ballot and the deprivation of common decencies, is the failure of those who know better to brand as wrong-doers the whites who commit crimes against fellow humans.

Why do we accept as law-abiding and respectable those who methodically, and with malice aforethought, degrade and humiliate their neighbors? Why do we apologize for, deal with and cater to them? How can we, who affect discernment in friends and colleagues, who want to be judged by the company we keep, who disdain intercourse with outlaws and outcasts, continue to associate with and indorse those who deserve only disgrace and contempt?

Above all, by what distortion of logic do we justify seating in the Congress of the United States, the world's most influential legislative body, the symbol of our democracy and foundation of our liberties, men who represent only the tormentors, because the tormented had no voice in their election?

We who work to protect the democratic freedoms of all Americans, support the challenge that has been filed against the seating, in the House of Representatives, of four Mississippi men who were not elected by all the people of their districts. Systematic, official denial of voting rights corrupted and negated the entire elective machinery that sent them to Washington. Representatives of confirmed law-breakers should not be our law-makers.

It is time to invoke the neglected sanctions in the Fourteenth Amendment, Section II of the Bill of Rights, applying to the states: "When the right to vote ... is in any way abridged .... the basis of representation therein (i.e.: the House of Representatives) shall be *reduced* (italics mine) in the proportion which the number of such male citizens shall bear to the whole number of male citizens over 21 years of age in such State." (The Nineteenth Amendment later extended this injunction to include women voters.)

It is time to give meaning to the Fifteenth Amendment, guaranteeing every citizen the right to vote, and to Article IV, Section IV of our Constitution: "guaranteeing to every state in this Union a republican form of government." Yes, even Mississippi.

January 19, 1965

Racial Discrimination

Sir:

The saddest comments on racial discrimination in public places are by those anointed few who accept and see nothing wrong in racial discrimination, who believe that the racist's license to insult and injure all dark-skinned fellow-Americans is guaranteed by the Constitution and Bill of Rights and blessed by a merciful and loving God.

The immorality of loud-mouthed bigots is disturbing, but the amorality of nice, quiet-spoken ladies and gentlemen who cannot tell the difference between pusher and pushed, and who defend the former's right against the latter – this inhumanity is depressing.

Is it possible, almost 8,000 years after Moses brought down the tablets of the law from Mount Sinai, and almost 2,000 years after the birth of Jesus, for anyone in this Judeo-Christian nation to define freedom as the right of a business man, licensed for public service, to refuse a glass of water to a thirsty child because the child's skin is not white?

Can any person in the Twentieth Century believe that the humiliation of man by man is ordained by Scripture and nature on the insane basis of skin-pigmentation?

Is there no glimmer of understanding of what civil liberties are all about – protecting the individual citizen against the abusive power of governmental authority or mob madness – defending the dignity of each human being and his right to equal treatment under law? ....

This is a time to be a participant not spectator, to move forward not backward in the constant fight against the beast lurking just under our skins; to be ashamed and angry about injustice and not to rationalize and apologize for it; to aid, not obstruct, the swift changing of conditions that have become intolerable to most of the human race.

October 13, 1961

McKeldin the Pioneer

Matthew A. Crenson's excellent examination of what makes Baltimore different in racial politics on this page September 20th was perceptive, scholarly and as thorough as space allowed. Yet, it left one large stone unturned.

Absent from the exploration was – as any veteran Marylander and Baltimorean will affirm – that rock of rectitude in our political landscape, twice-governor and twice-mayor Theodore R. McKeldin.

If, in a Baltimore election today, black and white politicians can discuss race without screaming at each other; if there is inter-racial restraint in this Southern city; if we have come a long way from the days of legally sanctioned segregation and discrimination – certainly some of the credit must go to the inspired and passionate leadership of Theodore R. McKeldin.

Books have been and will be written about his lifelong Manichean struggle against the massive racial bigotry and hatred he found in Maryland, how he – a Republican in a Democratic state – won elections while fighting popular prejudice, how he opened narrow minds and softened hard hearts with his unique personality and gifts of persuasion.

In her Forword to "Toward Equality," the chronology of Baltimore's progress toward the achievement of equal rights and opportunities for Maryland blacks, published by the Sidney Hollander Foundation and covering the decade from 1946 to 1956, Eleanor Roosevelt said: "This is the history of a decade of progress toward equality of rights and opportunities in an important American city. It is a very heartening history ....

"The decade is the postwar decade, when the country as a whole was making more progress toward ridding itself of discrimination based on race than in any comparable period since Reconstruction. It was the decade that saw the end of the legal doctrine of 'separate-but-equal' which had ruled for more than fifty years. It was the decade that saw the barriers of segregation – legal and extra-legal – begin to crumble. It was the decade that produced the first national civil rights law in three-quarters of a century.

"But these legal achievements, monumental as they are, are less the cause than the expression of changes that have come over the country since the war. As I read the chronicle of what has happened in Baltimore, it seems to me there are lessons for all of us, North and South.

The Hollander report gives the setting for the McKeldin regimes: "Negroes" were confronted at every turn by Jim Crow. They lived in a separate and unequal Baltimore – jampacked into substandard, segregated, dilapidated inner-city housing (none west of Fulton Avenue until 1945), facing hostility whenever a block "turned colored" and horrible health conditions typified by a tuberculosis rate that was a national disgrace.

Despite mandated integration of the workplace during World War II, black veterans were excluded from vocational courses and most apprentice and on-the-job training by employers and unions.

The many barriers to blacks did not fall of their own weight. They were pulled down by the persistent pleading and prodding of many citizens committed to social justice, led by Mr. McKeldin.

The sixth annual award of the Sidney Hollander Foundation went to Governor McKeldin. The jury specifically cited his appointment of blacks as police magistrates and parole officers and, for the first time in Maryland, of black members of the state boards of health, welfare and education. The citation also referred to the accomplishments of the Maryland Commission on Interracial Problems and Relations, appointed by the governor, and to his support of Jim Crow repeal and of the admission of blacks to the Poly "A" course.

Later, he abolished segregation in the Maryland National Guard; appointed the first black firefighters, paved the way for blacks in technical, professional, clerical and selling fields, and created many first openings for blacks. In the 1954 gubernatorial race, his opponent, Dr. H.C. Byrd, tried to exploit segregationist sentiment against him, but Mr. McKeldin won decisively – and surprisingly – and continued creating new openings for blacks.

In his second term as Baltimore's mayor, his major priority – along with development of the Inner Harbor – was insuring equal opportunity in employment, education, housing, welfare and public accommodations. He guided through the City Council what he termed – oratorically, but not inaccurately – "the most sweeping package of civil rights legislation enacted at one time by any major municipality within this nation."

At his death of cancer at age 73, on August 10, 1974, the New York *Times* paid this tribute to the youngest of seven children of an immigrant Irish policeman: "He was an outspoken, early and vigorous opponent of racial segregation and worked actively to bring integration to Maryland."

One of the reasons why race was not the explosive issue in Baltimore's 1983 election that it became in other cities was that Theodore Roosevelt McKeldin did so much to defuse it during his 25-year domination of Maryland politics.

September 30, 1983

Question and Answer

An interesting question came up at a recent meeting of the executive committee of the Black/Jewish Forum of Baltimore, known as the BL-EWS, which seeks to strengthen the relationship between Baltimore's black and Jewish communities to the city's benefit.

This was the question, raised by a black leader: "Much is known and taught about the Holocaust, and the education is necessary; but what do we know, teach or care about The Middle Passage? In fact, how many of you have ever heard of it?"

None of the Jewish members had. I found later that white Christian friends were equally ignorant. So I looked it up.

The phrase refers to one of the worst crimes of modern Western imperialism, the shipment of slaves from Africa to the West Indies and East Coast American ports, including some in the Chesapeake Bay. About 10 million men, women and children, but mostly young males preferred as field hands, were corraled and herded onto the slave ships.

The European settlers of America needed labor for their expanding plantation agriculture and turned to the slave trade. It powered their export economy of sugar, cotton, indigo, tobacco and rice.

The Middle Passage from the African West Coast took an average of 30 to 32 days of indescribable horror. Packed in the stinking holds, up to a fourth of the slaves died of communicable diseases – dysentery, smallpox, measles – or in shipwrecks, sinking, pirate attacks, slave revolts, or – after landing in a strange and hostile environment – of susceptibility to unaccustomed infections. (The mortality rate was higher, of course, for slaves shipped from Africa's East Coast on a passage twice as long as from the West Coast.)

My friend's question, however, seemed to imply a mistaken equivalence of the Holocaust and the Middle Passage. Both were outrageous examples of man's inhumanity to man. Both involved the torture and sacrifice of defenseless people.

But they were different in important ways. The

uniqueness of the Holocaust was that Jews, and a few other minorities, were chosen for extermination. In the Middle Passage, the blacks were chosen for inhuman exploitation. The cattle cars carried Jews to the ovens and gas chambers to die. The slave ships transported surviving blacks to the plantations to live, toil and produce profit for others. A killer/victim relationship is not the same as master/slave.

Nevertheless, a world that tolerated the Holocaust and the Middle Passage owes a debt to survivors of both and their kin. It is true that today's Germans and white Americans should not ge held responsible for the crimes of their ancestors. Yet those killers were the parents and grandparents of the present generation; and those exploiters, the owners, providers, customers and crews of the slave ships, were the not-so-distant relatives of many of the living. The past is not remote.

Modern Germany acknowledged that reparations were in order for survivors and families of the victims. The United States – or most of its citizens – are inclined to accept an obligation to descendants of the only Americans who did not come here as immigrants seeking a better life, but were dragged here in chains and abused for over a century. We recognize and support successful black efforts to overcome hardship and handicaps and to realize at long last our constitutional promise of equal opportunity.

That is why affirmative action is legally and morally justified, even at the cost of some "reverse discrimination," a side effect like that produced by other useful remedies against inherited disease.

At the very least, for most fair minded citizens, affirmative action is a rite of passage from the lingering stench of the Middle Passage. They know it is perilous to ignore history.

Tom Dulack, the author of "Incommunicado," the play about the poetic genius and bigot Ezra Pound whose pro-fascist anti-Semitic ravings made him a World War II traitor and certified madman, says in a program note: "Pound was not an aberration ..... He was a representative product of .... his culture and civilization and it is sheer hypocrisy for the rest of us to pretend otherwise.... The history of anti-Semitism in the West is long and lamentable. No country, no people, including the United States of America, can plead innocent. Anti-Semitism is woven into the very fabric of our culture."

A similar point was made by Philipp Jenninger, former president of the West German parliament, who was hounded from office for an unforgivable sin. He stated the truth that the German people shared responsibility for creating the monster they unleashed on humanity, and that they denied that "in 1938 a majority of Germans stood behind Hitler [and] identified themselves with him and his politics."

Likewise, racism in America is an ugly historic fact that cannot be denied and a tendency that must constantly be defied – regardless of support or opposition from the administration and Supreme Court.

No amount of reparations or affirmative action by the living can bring back the dead or repair the terrible damage done. But these compensations are civilizing influences on our brutal nature. They are also an important first step toward curing our addiction to violence: admitting that we have a problem.

That is an attempt to answer my colleague's question.

September 16, 1989

...A hateful state song

Walking past the open window of an elementary school classroom, I heard the children signing the familiar words of "Maryland, My Maryland" – familiar because I had sung them as a pupil some 70 years ago.

In this time of change, in Washington and throughout the world, it seems to me that the time has come to consider changing the Maryland anthem. The words are meaningless to most children (as they were to me three-score-and-ten years ago) and insulting to the Maryland Free State.

Those being urged not to "cower in the dust" were the owners and exploits of some 84,000 slaves still in bondage in Maryland when the song was written by a passionate Yankee hater, James Ryder Randall. He was a Maryland professor who was teaching at a Louisiana college in 1861, when he learned of the bloody battle at Baltimore's Camden Station, where the Massachusetts 6th Regiment, on its way to join Union forces in Virginia, was attacked by a mob of Baltimore Confederate sympathizers. Four of the soldiers and 11 of mob were killed and scores wounded on both sides. Randall's pen caught fire.

The defiant lyrics stirred the blood of those Marylanders who supported the Confederacy and wanted the state to secede. But the song's rhetoric was not appreciated by over half the citizenry, including especially about 89,000 freed slaves.

Since it is the state song, generations of Maryland school children have been required to mouth the hateful lyrics. Very few of the kids, of course, have any notion what they're singing – any more than they understand "Our father, Art, in heaven; Harold be thy name," or the pledge to "one nation invisible."

But some of the more observant children, who have been led to believe that the North won the Civil War and that emancipation of the slaves and saving of the Union were not evil events, may be a bit confused.

Why must innocent children be imploring their state to "gird thy beauteous limbs with steel" (against those fighting to save the Union)?

Why must the kids be taught that "the despot's heel is on our shore" (the despot being Abraham Lincoln, who they had been led to believe was the Great Emancipator)?

Are they pledging allegiance to the Stars and Stripes or to the flag of the Confederacy?

How many more generations of peaceful youngsters must be incited to "avenge the patriotic gore that flecked the streets of Baltimore?

Isn't it time for them to learn that the "beaming sword" of the slave owners has rusted, and that thousands of black professionals, business people, scientists, technicians, sheriffs, majors and government officials in the South signify that the War Between the States is over?

Maryland school children would be better served if they learned to sing – and more important, to understand – the "South Pacific" song, "Carefully Taught"

"You've got to be taught to hate and fear,
You've got to be taught from year to year,
It's got to be drummed in your dear little ear –
You've got to be carefully taught ...."

March 25, 1993

Two Baltimores

The greening of Baltimore's black middle class was evident in the recent opening in Govans of the second branch of the successful minority-controlled Harbor Bank of Maryland. The bank's main office is doing well at 21 West Fayette Street. Its first branch, the former Bank of Baltimore at 5000 Park Heights Avenue in Pimlico, has shown steady growth sine its opening two years ago.

The Harbor Bank of Maryland has assets of $32.5 million and a sound $22 million loan portfolio and has been profitable for the past five years, resisting the tide of unfavorable trends in the banking industry – a tide so high that it forced the federal government to take over the huge Bank of New England over the weekend.

The growing empowerment of Maryland's black business community was shown by Catherine Pugh in the recent black business supplement to *The Sun* and *Evening Sun.* Fifty black companies employ almost 8,000 people and have over $500 million in annual sales volume. One black investment firm manages $140 million in assets, and one black retail firm does $65 million in annual volume. A $37 million contract to build an 11-story office building in downtown Baltimore has been awarded to a black development firm. Blacks have succeeded in Baltimore business, government, science, art and the professions. They appear on television shows, commercials and interviews. Their pictures are in the papers; they're seen with white peers in all the best places.

Still more numerous, however, are the less visible blacks who have mot made it, who fall back on food stamps, work at below-minimum wages and crowd the shelters, soup kitchens, hospital emergency rooms (because they can't afford doctors), the streets, alleys and jails of the city.

Their children are the ubiquitous victims of poverty, hunger and illness – two to three times more so than the children of other Western nations.

According to the latest U.S. census, child poverty, mostly black, has increased to 12.6 million, almost 3 million more than in

1978. Forty-four percent of all black children are poor, compared to one in seven white children. Absent major government intervention, the figures will rise.

These poor children are likely to be born underweight, to live in substandard housing, to have adequate nourishment and health care and attend school less well-prepared than other children. Without educational help, their future, and the community's is bleak.

Additional educational resources are desperately needed, especially for pre-school child care for the nearly 60 percent of mothers who must work out of the home. The trouble starts early. By age 8 or 9, black students are twice as likely as whites to be two grades behind and three times as likely to drop out later. About half of black 17- year-olds lack the skills in math, reading and science needed to perform moderately complex tasks. Early pregnancy and substance abuse take their toll.

What is to be done, by whom, and when?

The middle class – black and white – must agree that there cannot be two Baltimores, two Marylands and two Americas; that the problems of hunger, homelessness, disease and despair cannot be walled off; that we are all in this together, and that most of us are more immediately threatened by what is happening at the center of our city than by what may happen in the Middle East.

The success of many black fellow citizens proves the tremendous potential, and the benefits to us all, in helping minorities to escape from the underclass into the mainstream of a united, healthy, productive commonwealth.

January 9, 1991

30 years later, Fair Housing Act bridging the divide

It has been a little more than 30 years since passage of the Fair Housing Act, part of the U.S. Civil Rights Act of 1968, which was approved by Congress under pressure from President Lyndon Johnson. It prohibited discrimination in the sale or rental of housing, except owner-occupied, single-family housing with four or fewer occupants, sold or rented without the aid of a broker or an agent.

The results have been mixed. Progress has certainly been made in middle and upper class suburban homeownership and in apartment housing. The city of Columbia, established by James Rouse even before the housing law's enactment is now about 25 percent non-white.

But all the news is not good. In Maryland, Baltimore Neighborhoods, Inc., a fair housing group,, last year received 247 reports of discrimination in housing that merited investigation. Seventy-one complaints were referred to the Department of Housing and Urban Development and various local agencies. BNI resolved 112 cases through negotiation in 1997 and completed 106 tests. In each test, a minority couple, which had been rejected, was followed by a white couple, with the same income and in the same social stratum which was accepted.

Thirty-seven of the cases contained significant evidence of discrimination. The situation last year in Washington was equally discouraging. There, 35 percent of the visits to a real estate office by black and Hispanic home buyers involved some form of discrimination, the Fair Housing Council reported. In every case, white testers received more courteous and prompt service from the same office. Minority applicants were told they had to qualify for a mortgage before seeing homes, while there was no such requirement for whites.

In Baltimore, many areas remain extremely segregated, for example: Gay Street/Penn Central, 98.6 percent black; Gwynns Falls/Clifton, 98.0 percent black; Beverly Hills/Harford Road, 98.7 percent white; Cross Country/Clarks Lane, 95.2 percent white; Forest Park/Garrison Avenue, 98.5 percent black; Eastern

Avenue, 99.4 percent white; and Elwood Park/Highland/Kenwood, 96.1 percent white.

In a recent study in Washington, about one-third of the minorities interviewed said that they would prefer to live in a racially diversified neighborhood rather than their present segregated community (the reality may be an even smaller number because of the tendency of interviewees to express what they think the interviewer wants to hear).

However, most are simply following the natural desire to live with their own kind. The reason lies in the nature of all living creatures; to find comfort and security in the group identified with their mothers; to have a wider choice for procreation and rearing of off-spring and to eat rather than be eaten by other species.

Some groupings do complement each other; the long-necked ostrich with keen eyesight can spot danger; the zebra with a strong olfactory sense can sniff it coming. Thus, they warn of approaching peril, live together and protect each other. The ostrich does not lose a single feather, nor the zebra a single stripe.

Also, people huddle because in previous times, the only source of help for immigrant families was their relatives and their ethnic/religious communities.

Today, however, the main provider of last resort is federal, state and local government, which gives more humanitarian aid than private foundations and charities combined. The principal benefactor is not Uncle John, but Uncle Sam.

When my wife and I were house-hunting 50 years ago, we found a partially built home in Northwest Baltimore that had the potential to meet our requirements. The builder had intended it as a gift for his newlywed daughter and son-in-law, but their marriage dissolved. We bought it immediately. All that we checked were the neighborhood schools and the proximity to our Baltimore Hebrew Congregation. We did not investigate or care about the religious or racial composition of the neighborhood, which we later found to be all white and Christian.

While we were supervising the completion of construction, neighbors dropped in with greetings, offers of aid and suggestions and invitation to their homes for dinner. Though we had not been aware of it, we had "busted the block", nevertheless, we were welcomed.

We became close friends with one family in particular. Their children and our son played together. We watched TV in each other's homes. We took trips together. They accompanied us to events at our temple and we attended affairs at their church.

At that time, our temple had not yet organized a Cub Scout pack, so our son joined the Elderslie Methodist Church Cub Scout Pack 59, which honored me by making me its program chairman and camp-out parent.

From exchanging our boyhood recollections – my neighbor's of growing up our on a small truck farm and mine of the crowded streets and alleys of a polyglot working-class neighborhood in East Baltimore – we came to understand and empathize with the problems of poverty in this wealthy nation.

We exchanged Christmas-Hanukkah gifts. We explained our holidays to them, and they did the same for us. We became, in effect, one extended family.

Forty-two years later, after our son married, and my wife and I moved to a retirement community, we sold the home to a black family which, we are told, has been embraced by the neighbors as we were long ago.

In this age, when so many natural handicaps have been overcome, when police, fire protection, national defense and humanitarian needs are mostly the responsibility of government, it may be hoped that the day will come when the ancient walls come tumbling down and people will accept and benefit from living together in racially diversified communities, instead of huddling for protection with only their own kind.

Then, indeed, Martin Luther King, Jr.'s dream of judging people, not by the color of their skin, but by the content of their character, can be realized. Then children of all races can learn from each other that loving one's neighbor is more fun than hating and fearing those whom their ancestors hated and feared, and that all people are born equal with inalienable rights. One to these is the privilege and opportunity of living with good neighbors of every race and religion, who can enrich our brief stay on this lonely planet.

May 28, 1998

When the sky didn't fall

Dire consequences are predicted should 60 inner-city families be relocated to Baltimore County suburban neighborhoods. But the heavens didn't fall on similar occasions in the past.

The clergymen's protest against racial exclusion at Gwynn Oak Amusement Park on July 4, 1963, was supposed to bring the destruction of thousands of businesses. I remember vividly. My minister, Rabbi Morris Lieberman of Baltimore Hebrew Congregation, was a leader of the protest, and I had to defend his actions against members of the congregation who disapproved of a rabbi practicing what he preached.

The three brothers who owned Gwynn Oak Park, Arthur, David and James Price, warned of the park's demise. That happened only later, when changing times – home amusements such as television, giant theme parks such as Disneyland – killed off the neighborhood family amusement park.

Integration of public accommodations spread rapidly after the Gwynn Oak protest. Already in 1959 Walter Sondheim and Martin Kohn had employed the first black female sales clerks downtown at Hochschild Kohn & Company. Now the other larger downtown retailers gradually removed the rusting bars of discrimination.

The predicted white boycotts never developed. Armageddon did not erupt when bowling leagues, ice skating rinks and even swimming pools became racially mixed.

The pessimists may be just as wrong about mixed housing. Understandably, when lifetime investments are threatened by falling property values, the acceptance of different neighbors may take longer than the adjustment to integrated public accommodations, but it will come. It has been happening for many years.

Windsor Hills was first a white Gentile neighborhood, then Gentile-Jewish and, since 1955, white Gentile-Jewish-black. By 1959, whites were moving in with black neighbors. Windsor

Hills demonstrated that integrated living can work, first as a middle-and-upper income community and later with many low-income families.

In the Belair-Edison community of about 7,000 houses, where the ratio is 60 percent white, 40 percent black, leaders are opposing slumlord takeover and white flight. One of the neighborhood residents said, "It's more like the real world. You have the opportunity to be exposed to different types of people."

Once a slum kid in a project in Detroit nearly murdered another kid. The knife point was diverted by a large belt buckle. Otherwise, he might have spent most of his life in prison. His single-parent mother subjected him to a stronger discipline and moved with him to a better neighborhood.

If that neighborhood had been Baltimore County, howls of rage would have filled the press and the talk shows. But that boy and his mother brought a lifestyle not of crime, but of study and effort. That kid is now Dr. Benjamin Carson of Johns Hopkins, a world-renowned pediatric surgeon.

Who would be the principal beneficiaries if such a motivated mother and son were welcome by new neighbors in Baltimore County? Are we so fear-blinded that we perceive every poor black person only as a carrier of drugs, crime and falling property values?

As we celebrate the Gwynn Oak protest, it is good to know that one day white and black children can share the same neighborhood as well as the same amusement park, and that former housing project residents may one day earn enough money to be accepted by whites as qualified neighbors.

May 28, 1996

Editor:

Congratulations to President Bush for his excellent appointment of General Colin Powell to be chairman of his Joint Chiefs of Staff. In passing over many white generals of greater seniority and experience to move General Powell to the top job, the president was practicing – intentionally or not – the affirmative action his administration and courts oppose on grounds of "reverse discrimination."

Perhaps more corporate CEOs and chairmen will be moved to emulate the chief executive by naming qualified blacks to leadership positions in their board rooms. In 1980, only 4 percent of our "color blind" nation's managers and administrators were black.

August 17, 1989

B. Civil Liberties and the ACLU

Dear George:

                Why I carry an ACLU card

I would like to tell Vice President George Bush, and anyone interested, why I am a card-carrying, card-waving member of the Maryland ACLU (in fact, a board member and a past board chairperson).

I believe that defense of individual rights and liberties is the glory of America. I believe that our precious, unique Bill of Rights is what distinguishes us from most other nations and makes us special.

I believe that practicing instead of just preaching liberty for all is what the United States is all about, and that the ACLU is the one organization devoted exclusively to securing the Bill of Rights in all situations – popular and unpopular – and for all citizens – good guys and bad guys alike, because if it is not for all of us it is not for any.

I believe that, in its 68 years of service, including its defense of John Thomas Scopes for daring to teach evolution, its guarding of First Amendment rights of free speech and association in the 1930s and '50s, its fight against the interning of Japanese-American citizens in concentration camps in the '40s, its civil rights struggles of the '50s, '60s and '70s – the ACLU has never served America better than in fighting off attacks on the Constitution by extreme right radicals favored by Bush's administration.

To the ACLU's everlasting honor, it has opposed – and continues to oppose – administration efforts to ignore or distort the law in order to achieve goals of government-imposed religious values, denial of rights to women and minorities, government secrecy and censorship, appointment of judges picked by Ed Meese and Jesse Helms to obstruct and defeat the laws they are sworn to uphold, and of right-wing government officials committed to sabotage their own departments.

I agree with the U.S. presidents who have highly praised the ACLU for its single-minded dedication, and with former Chief Justice Earl Warren. It was he who said: "The ACLU has stood foursquare against the recurring tides of hysteria that from time to time threaten freedoms everywhere ...

"Indeed, it is difficult to appreciate how far our freedoms might have eroded had it not been for the union's valiant representation in the courts of the constitutional rights of all people of all persuasions, no matter how unpopular or even despised by the majority they were at the time."

I am proud, also, of ACLU's accomplishments here in Maryland as well as nationally: protesting routine drug-testing of civilians without cause at Aberdeen Proving Grounds, challenging racial discrimination in fire company membership, defending government employees who were discharged for comments made off the job, attacking 19th century conditions in county jails as cruel and unusual punishment and litigating the propriety of a denominational religious display on Baltimore County property.

I am gratified that Maryland ACLU is working in coalition with such organizations as St. Johns Council for Criminal Justice II, the Maryland Coalition Against State Execution and Marylanders for the Right to Choose.

I believe that, in our system of checks and balances, one of the most important is the limitation on government and even on the democratic majority, imposed by the Bill of Rights.

That is why we civil libertarians – 5,500 in Maryland and over a quarter million nationwide – wave our ACLU cards as we wave our flag; because both symbols stand for freedom, because we fight not for what's extreme-right but for what's right.

September 9, 1988

Our Civil-Liberties Defense Force

This year's observances of Memorial Day, Flag Day, July 4th and Labor Day should be marked by an extra dimension of patriotic fervor, because this is the year of the 200th birthday of American liberty, born September 25, 1789, when the U.S. Congress passed the Bill of Rights.

The parades, fireworks, picnics and holiday oratory this year should pay special tribute to what has become one of the most remarkable and important documents in human history, a guide and inspiration to freedom-seekers all over the world.

Of course, the American Civil Liberties Union and like-minded organizations are devising multi-faceted plans to commemorate the anniversary. An education campaign will begin this fall and conclude on Bill of Rights Day 1991, the bicentennial of the bill's final ratification by Virginia, the last of the 13 original states to sign on. (Maryland was the second to ratify, December 19, 1789, following New Jersey.)

There will be programs to educate and involve the media, elected officials, lawyers, teachers, students, labor and civic groups, to increase awareness and understanding of civil liberties.

There will be articles, columns, books, lectures, seminars and documentaries. But what is also needed, besides the celebration, is celebration of the blessings of individual freedoms that make our nation the envy and hope of mankind. Each day's headlines tell us that many people are still struggling to achieve what we take too much for granted. That is cause for jubilation.

Today, Memorial Day, as we welcome summer, we can quietly rejoice that most of us continue to prize, protect and defend the freedoms for which Americans fought and died.

On Flag Day next month, as we salute the Star Spangled Banner at Fort McHenry, we can cheer that it symbolizes American liberty as well as American strength.

This Independence Day, as we watch the rocket's red glare and fireworks bursting in air, we can exult that our system, the model for other nations struggling to be free, is based on two balancing principles: first, that the majority of us rules through democratically elected representatives; and second, but equally important, that the power of the majority – even though democratic – must be limited to insure individual rights.

We can congratulate ourselves that the marching bands glorify not the government, which in every generation is trying to expand its power over the citizen, but the individuals's right to resist that expansion.

This Labor Day, we can revel in the rights that millions of workers in other nations are still fighting to win – freedoms that have their roots in the Bill of Rights' first, 13th and 14th amendments.

This is the message to the 1989 celebrants of patriotic occasions – to the Boumis, Elks, Odd Fellows, Knights, Pioneers, Moose – to all who participate in the I-Am-An American Day Parade, and to all of us who pledge allegiance.

Let's blow the bugles for freedom of religion, speech, assembly, petition and the press, and the right to a vote that counts.

Let's beat the drums for security against unreasonable search and seizure, and against deprivation of life, liberty or property without due process.

Let's wave the flag for equal protection of all citizens under the law because the hard-won liberty we save may be our own.

We might celebrate also the constant defense of the Bill of Rights by the American Civil Liberties Union. Although President Bush boasted that he is not a member of it, previous U.S. presidents have praised it, as does the majority of Americans, according to a recent survey. Its job as umpire in today's complicated contest of social issues has become difficult, involving many tough calls.

Not all the issues are on the grand scale. For example, there are the conflicting civil-liberties questions swirling about the proposed "Caller ID" system by which a phone company customer could purchase an attachment to his phone that would display the phone number of the person calling. The receiver of a late-night call would see the caller's number and, suspecting an obscene or crank call, not answer to phone.

Good? Not quite.

What about an innocent caller who has an unlisted number – who has already paid an additional fee for privacy?

What about anonymous callers to rape hotlines or AIDS crisis lines or battered-women hotlines or similar entities? Will those victims be scared off from seeking help? What will Caller ID do to their privacy and anonymity?

What about businesses which use Caller ID to find the names and addresses of everyone who calls to register a complaint or ask a question? Would that violate privacy?

Some ACLU chapters have come out in opposition to Caller ID on privacy grounds. It has been incorrectly assumed that ACLU of Maryland already opposes it, but the question is still before the organization. The ACLU wrestles with many such apparently mundane issues that affect our daily lives. Like our military defense forces, our civil-liberties defense forces deserve our patriotic pride.

May 29, 1989

Dear Sir:

So Mr. James J. Kilpatrick, in his piece on the First Amendment rights "if any" of the editor of a student newspaper ("The Sun", Friday, February 18, 1983) believes that freedom of the press is the right not of the editor but only of the publisher. If you don't own the press, advises Mr. Kilpatrick in effect, you'd better write what the publisher tells you, or shut up, or go out and buy your own press. That's what "life in the real world is all about."

Set aside that, in the case referred to, the university president who forbade publication of the legitimate news story and expelled the editor was not the publisher at all. He did not own the university presses; they were bought with public funds.

Set aside, also, that the courts have consistently supported the exercise of free press rights guaranteed by the Constitution and that, in this case, the court ordered the writer reinstated as both student and editor.

Let's be concerned, however, about the implication of Mr. Kilpatrick's patrician position: that if you can't come up with many millions of dollars to buy the newspaper, television or radio station, then your right of expression is limited, in this age of instant mass communication, to the medium you can afford – a letter, a phone call or a cry into the wind. Is effective free speech only for the free spenders?

February 19, 1983

Defending the thought we hate

When the American Civil Liberties Union defends the civil liberties of right-wingers, it is criticized from the left as reactionary. When it stands up for the civil liberties of left-wingers, the likes of Rush Limbaugh chide it for bleeding-heart liberalism.

It must be doing something right.

In fact, most ACLU cases involve neither right nor left, but middle-class Americans dealing with complex and sometimes conflicting interpretations of rights. Sometimes the rights of society clash with those of the individual. Sometimes it's a case of the establishment of religion versus its free exercise, sometimes the public's right to know versus a person's right to privacy. These are only a few of the controversies that heat up ACLU board rooms.

The Maryland ACLU was rocked by dissension from the start. Shortly after its founding in 1931, it was confronted with a case that divided its state board from its national board.

A judge ordered radio station WFBR's microphone out of the courtroom where the station was covering a trial. The Maryland ACLU backed the defendant's privacy and right to a fair trial. The national ACLU defended the public's right to know what went on at the trial. As I recall, Maryland won that one.

During the Joseph McCarthy period, when I was state board chairman, the Maryland ACLU board was divided over the case of Bethlehem Steel workers who were fired as communists and had requested their union to represent them in seeking unemployment compensation. They claimed that, as dues-paying members in good standing, they were entitled to union representation. When we filed a brief in the fired workers' behalf, several of our board members quit. (They returned to the fold later.)

A few years ago, a woman employee of the Department of Motor Vehicles displayed on the wall of her office a religious picture depicting entry to heaven through the pearly gates. Her superior ordered her to remove it, claiming it amounted to the establishment of religion in a government building. Her defense was that she was merely asserting her right of free exercise of religion – which we defended. The heavenly portals were returned to the wall.

But such differences are exceptions, not the rule. All ACLU members agree at all times on one point: that the ACLU has really only one client, the Bill of Rights. Sometimes that client is personified by a good guy, sometimes by a bad one.

Right-wing talk show hosts see the union as a bunch of "bleeding hearts", interested only in defending the liberties of liberals and communists, not those of right-wingers, the Ku Klux Klan, Nazis and anti-communists. But they know better.

The ACLU always has adhered to the standard our principal founder, Roger Baldwin, enunciated many years ago: "The test of loyalty of the ACLU to its principles lies in the impartiality with which they are applied -- there can be no favorites in defense of rights for all. This a hard test to impose against natural sympathies and prejudices; it is even harder to defend the 'thought we hate'."

That is why the ACLU has defended the Nazis and similar groups in many over-publicized and over-politicized cases. The Ku Klux Klan's right to assemble and parade has been defended at least a dozen times. The free speech rights of Sen. Joseph McCarthy and his followers were protected by the ACLU in at least five cases, the John Birch Society in another five, the National States Rights Party, the National Renaissance Party and white supremacists' interests in a few more.

In Maryland there have been national landmarks like the Madalyn Murray O'Hare case of 1963, which outlawed teacher-led school prayer and, in the same year, the Supreme Court's unanimous decision that the accused has the right to be represented by an attorney. The victory was won by the late Fred E. Weisgal, who was head of the Maryland ACLU legal panel, at that time virtually a one-man operation.

Today, over 200 volunteer lawyers are on call; 116 of

them handled cases in 1992. The cases had one thing in common – defense of the Bill of Rights:

The rights of a cook who was fired because he refused to undergo an AIDS test ...

The rights of residents in a rehabilitation hospital who were routinely abused, neglected, injured and unnecessarily restrained ...

The rights of the disabled inmates of a Hagerstown correctional institution who were denied equal access to various programs ...

Those of Talbot County road workers who were racially segregated and given less desirable work assignments than white co-workers ...

Those of black applicants denied membership in a Western Maryland club ...

Those of an African-American school superintendent on the Eastern Shore who was dismissed for no apparent cause ...

Those of politically powerless minority communities where environmental wastes were being dumped ...

Those of women who were denied equal access to membership in organizations and employment in various capacities, including jury duty.

If the ACLU is unpopular with those who resent and resist the restraints imposed by the Bill of Rights, that is understandable. They cannot forgive us for actually practicing what they fervently believe should be preached exclusively.

April 13, 1994

Mr. Stanley Sollins, Director
The Baltimore Jewish Council
101 West Mt. Royal Avenue
Baltimore, Maryland
October 9, 1985

Dear Stanley:

    Several weeks ago I learned that a Jewish group aligned with the New Jewish Agenda had requested of the Jewish Community Center to hold a meeting there. The speaker on the controversial topic of U.S. policy in Central America would be John Ranz, founder of "The Generation After" and President of "Holocaust Survivors." He was a leader and hero of the anti-Nazi Resistance in Poland and survived 3 years in concentration camps. The quoted $300 rent was acceptable. Jerry Shavrick told them he would have to consult with the Baltimore Jewish Council for permission to rent and left them with the clear impression that a stalling process was under way.

    Since this request obviously concerned important aspects of JCC policy and the First Amendment right of a Jewish group to assemble peaceably in an agency of the tax-exempt Associated Jewish Charities to hear a respected Jew seek redress of perceived grievances affecting Jews, I visited you at your office and we discussed why I felt the meeting should be allowed to proceed routinely and that it would foolish to make a "federal case" of it.

    I expressed the view that refusal to rent under these circumstances would be:

1)   Undemocratic – the "town-hall meeting" is in the best American tradition of freedom of speech and assembly to discuss controversial issues openly;

2)   Un-Jewish – if there is a difference of opinion, argue it out, as Jews have been doing since the beginning of time and do today with great vigor in the Israeli Knesset;

3)   Unintelligent and un-productive – in fact, counter-productive, since the uproar surrounding the denial of the

forum would attract to the topic a far greater audience than would ever have attended without the hype, hoopla and fanfare.

You indicated that my views were persuasive and that you would present them to the authorities. Apparently, they were less vulnerable to reason than you, and opted for rejection, which of course was devoutly sought by some organizers of the meeting to assure its success. Before, they were not sure, but now they know: attention must be paid!

If there is any doubt about the counter-productivity of this JCC policy, consider the following:

A) Front page, local section, featured story with screaming headline: "JCC: No speech. Holocaust survivor denied hall" – and lead paragraph "The Jewish Community Center will not allow the President of a Holocaust survivors group to speak there." (Thursday, 10/3) in Baltimore News American – circulation 124,354;

B) Also in the News American (10/4) follow-up half-page-wide photo of Jews picketing the JCC, with clearly readable signs: "Freedom of Speech and Judaism Should Be Indivisible," "JCC Denies Holocaust Survivors Right to Address Baltimore Jews," "Jewish Speech Verboten," etc. – circulation 124,354;

C) Back-page "Maryland Newswatch" story and photo in the Baltimore Evening Sun (10/4) featuring the refusal to rent space at the JCC to a Holocaust survivor, and picket-sign messages as above – circulation 155,607;

D) Both major newspapers and The Jewish Times have expressed far greater interest in covering the event now than they would ever have had if the meeting had been held routinely – like so many other JCC events that they ignore or cover with yawning indifference;

E) Talk shows and news coverage on television and radio stations that would otherwise have shown enormous disinterest in the program;

F) Homewood Friends Meeting House presentation of the

program on 10/18 will attract a far greater attendance than it would have had without this publicity buildup;

G) So will the Sunday morning (10/20) address of John Ranz in Columbia, Maryland;

H) Most importantly, there will be a JCC meeting anyway – despite all the efforts to stop it – only outside on the front steps where it can attract more notice than it ever would have inside. Further, there will be less opportunity for respectable response from opposing speakers who would have expressed their dissent under the focused and controlled situation indoors.

To sum up, as a result of the decision to deny this Jewish speaker and Jewish group the right to reach an audience, at best, of a few hundred, a "corporal's guard," they will carry their message, rendered now even more distasteful than before, to an audience of several hundred thousand. They weren't shut up; they were built up.

I think it's time for a very careful examination of JCC policy to avoid further cutting our nose to spite our face.

All of the above concerns the "controversial" issue raised by the AJCWF Executive Committee – that of free speech – rather than the original "controversial" issue that would have been raised for discussion at long last in the Jewish community – U.S. policy in Central America.

Not every Jew considers discussion of this issue – in the wisdom of our local leaders – "not in the best interest of the JCC and the AJCWF."

Rabbi Alexander M. Schindler, President of UAHC, said in his address (11/83) to its 57th General Assembly:

> "There must be an end to U.S. military intervention in El Salvador and Honduras, an end to the covert war against Nicaragua. Instead, we must seek a negotiated solution .... and make a permanent commitment to democracy, economic reform and social justice."

Whether or not we agree with such views, they deserve a hearing at the JCC, which claims to be "an agency for informal

Jewish education" for Jews living in Greater Baltimore.

cc: Mr. Stephen Solender, President
    Association Jewish Charities & Welfare Fund

Human rights today: U.N. hypocrisy, U.S. reality

This week includes the anniversary of two events of vital importance to all who cherish freedom: the ratification of the American Bill of Rights by the states on December 15, 1791, and of the adoption of the Declaration of Human Rights by the United Nations.

The latter event occurred just 35 years ago – on December 10, 1948. The Universal Declaration was adopted by 48 votes for, none against, and eight abstentions – the USSR and its satellites, plus South Africa and Saudi Arabia.

Among the rights it declared were:

- All persons are born free and equal in dignity and rights – without distinction as to race, color, sex, language, religion, political or other opinion, national or social origin, property, birth or other status.
- All have the right to life, liberty and security of person.
- No one shall be enslaved or tortured.
- No one shall be subjected to arbitrary arrest, detention or exile, or interference with his privacy.
- All are entitled to equal protection of the law, right of presumption of innocence until proved guilty, of freedom of movement, of emigration and return, of seeking and enjoying asylum in other countries while retaining nationality.
- Every person has the right of voluntary marriage, protection of family, ownership of property.
- Everyone has a right to freedom of thought, conscience, religion, expression, peaceful assembly and association, participation in government, elections, social security, equal pay for equal work, trade unions, and a standard of living "adequate for health and well being of himself and of his family."
- Each person has the right to an education, to participation in cultural life and the benefits of art and science, and "free and full development of his personality."

Representatives of many nations stressed the everlasting significance of the Declaration. Typical comments were:

Chile: "No one can infringe upon the rights proclaimed in it without becoming an outcast from the community of nations."

Bolivia: "Humanity will enter upon a new phase which should lead to the establishment of a true international constitution, founded on the limitations of the sovereignty of states for the benefit of the individual."

Lebanon: "Destined to mark an important stage in the history of mankind."

Cuba: "The Declaration expressed in particularly clear and precise terms the most noble aspirations of 20th century man."

Uruguay: "Human rights will in the future be protected and defended by all peoples of the states that are members of the United Nations."

It does not come as a revelation that the U.N.'s noble expectations have not been realized.

Jonathan Bower, in his preface to "Amnesty International – The Human Rights Story," published in 1981, says: "Nearly half the 154 governments of the United Nations are believed to be holding prisoners of conscience – people imprisoned for their beliefs or origins, who have not used or advocated violence. Over the last five years there have been allegations of the practice of torture in 60 nations. In more than 50 countries, citizens can be detained without trial or charge. In 134 countries the death penalty is in force, in many for politically related offenses."

He looks at the record in the Soviet Union, Latin America, Central Africa, Asia, even countries of Western Europe with terrorist gangs – and it is not pretty. The details are enough to turn the strongest stomach.

So much for the bad news about the 35-year-old document.

The good news is that the 192-year-old U.S. Bill of Rights has come as near to fulfilling its promise as can be hoped for in the present stage of human development. The cost of its implementation has been high – in blood, sweat and tears – but the

Bill of Rights lives in the United States. It has a long way to go to reach full implementation, as demonstrated at the recent 20th anniversary observance of the March on Washington. But it has come a long way from conditions preceding the 1963 march of a quarter million.

Such massive protests can be held here peacefully without the jailing, harassment, torture, and disappearance of dissidents. The media can bring down a demagogue like Joseph McCarthy or even a president like Richard Nixon. The people can force the government to stop fighting an unpopular war and not to start an unwinnable war of mutual annihilation.

Despite continuing efforts of leaders to lead a retreat on civil liberties, the majority of Americans stands firm or advances.

We recognize that individual freedom, the main difference between us and our adversaries, must be preserved. We are determined to cherish and conserve this respect for individual that undergirded the American Revolution and distinguished it from those authoritarian and totalitarian revolutions that some right-wing radicals are cooking up.

Despite efforts to empower police to conduct illegal searches, we still enjoy the right to be secure in our persons, homes, papers and effects, against unreasonable searches and seizures.

Despite efforts to breach the wall of separation between church and state with prayer in public schools and tax credits, we make no laws respecting an establishment of religion.

Despite efforts to remove restraints in pursuit of suspected criminals, we do try not to deprive any person of life, liberty or property without due process of law, and not to deny equal protection of the laws or speedy trial by an impartial jury.

Despite efforts to tamper with the voting rights laws, government here cannot get away with denying or abridging the right to vote on account of race, sex or color.

Despite efforts to control and manipulate information – in CIA censorship, denying scholars, books and publications entry into the U.S. and intrusion into academic freedom – the right to disseminate information and freedom of press and speech are relatively secure.

We take for granted freedoms that others would fight to the death to achieve. We bask in an open society among autocracies, bureaucracies and assorted hunkered-down tyrannies. We can pour into Washington to shake fists at government, like an occupying army, and nobody is jailed or shot. We excoriate the President in the full glare of national and international media coverage and nobody disappears.

Considering the annihilation of human rights elsewhere at the anniversary of the Declaration, on the eve of Orwell's 1984, we free citizens of the United States have many blessings to count as we celebrate Bill of Rights Day.

December 16, 1983

Do Americans Want to Keep the Bill of Rights

The intent of the creators of the Bill of Rights, whose bicentennial we are celebrating, was to reinforce the claims of rights that a citizen may assert against the government – rights such as freedom of speech, press, association and assembly, religious liberty, personal privacy and due process of laws in general, the right of a citizen to limit the power of the state to restrict his personal freedom, the right for which many of our forebears fought and died.

Is that still our intent?

We celebrate the 200th anniversary of these great human freedoms which are the envy of peoples throughout the world – but do we really want them? Apparently not, if it can be assumed that recent Supreme Court decisions are giving us what we voted for in 1980, '84 and '88.

Do we agree with the court's 5-4 decision that a coerced, involuntary confession is just a "harmless error" which no longer necessarily entitles the defendant to a new trial?

Or do we believe, with Justice Byron White, that this appalling decision is out of step with decades of legal history and that the Court majority dislodged "one of the fundamental tenets of our criminal justice system"?

As we concerned that the court has agreed to "re-examine" such fundamental issues as separation of church and state, censorship and a defendant's right to file a writ of habeas corpus?

Does it bother us that the court's *Webster* decision has taken away a woman's right to choose abortion and turned it over to mostly male state legislators; and that women's basic rights will thus depend on who they are, where they live and how much they can afford to pay? Or that a federal appeals court in Philadelphia recently rejected a key part of Roe v. Wade in upholding Pennsylvania's anti-abortion laws?

Does it trouble us that individual rights, the glory of the United States and the distinguishing superiority of our system over others, are becoming casualties in the administration's "wars"?

Does it matter that the administration's many "wars" – against crime, drugs, etc. – are used as justifications to erode the fourth Amendment right of the people "to be secure in their persons, house, papers and effects against unreasonable searches and seizures?"

Do we still believe that no person – however hated – shall be compelled in any criminal case to be a witness against himself or be deprived of life, liberty or property without due process of law; and that the accused shall be entitled to a speedy and public trial by an impartial jury, without excessive bail, without cruel and unusual punishment, no matter how heinous the crime?

Or do we shrug it all off as problems for others – bad people – never for us good guys, until ourselves or persons close to us get into trouble?

Civil liberty is under constant pressure, not only from government and large private institutions such as corporations, universities, unions and special interests, but also from us the people. Long ago, Edmund Burke wrote: "Of this I am certain, that in a democracy the majority of citizens is capable of exercising the most cruel oppression upon the minority."

A more recent authority, Charles Reich, characterized civil liberty as "an unnatural state for man or society .... essentially contrary to the self-interest of the majority."

Civil liberty requires the majority to restrain itself, especially difficult under conditions of stress like the present recession. Growing unemployment provokes discrimination, ethnic rivalries and repression of dissent. The dependent and powerless poor suffer the most.

Jurist Learned Hand said: "Liberty lies in the hearts of men and women. When it dies there, no constitution, no law, no court can save it. No constitution, no law, no court, can even do much to help it."

The real question confronting us today is not whether civil liberty lives in the Reagan/Bush -appointed Supreme Court, or in the White House or in Congress and state legislatures, but whether it lives in our hearts. Of all the grave problems besetting the nation, none is more threatening than the loss of faith in civil liberty or – worse – its perception as evil liberty.

The genius of this nation's founders was to recognize that power is inevitably used wantonly and that a bill of rights is as necessary to defend an individual against the majority in a republic as against a king in a monarchy.

In fighting for addition of a bill of rights to our constitution, none of the anti-Federalists was more passionately effusive than Maryland's Luther Martin in attacking the unamended constitution (which Ronald Reagan later endorsed in attempts to weaken the Bill of Rights).

The unamended constitution, said Martin, would be "certain death to your liberty as arsenic could be to your bodies." He protested again before Maryland delegates in April 1789 voted 63 to 11 for ratification of the Bill of Rights. "We consider (the unamended constitution) very defective and that the liberty and happiness of the people will be endangered if (it) be not greatly changed and altered.

In the USSR and Eastern European countries today, those who confused Western-style consumerism with freedom, who have learned that liberty does not mean guaranteed cradle-to-grave food, health care, job and apartment, are having second thoughts. Many are not, as in the GE television commercial, waltzing around exclaiming how happy they are. There as here, a price must be paid for liberty. We must decide if we are ready to pay, or if we want liberty only when it is free of charge.

We would not be the first people in history to swap the risks of freedom for the illusion of security. But we might be the last. For it is won't work here after 200 years of testing, in the best of all worlds, it won't work anywhere.

December 12, 1991

For Free Speech

Sir: Please accept the congratulations and appreciate of Maryland civil libertarians for your excellent editorial censuring the Baltimore high school students who attacked a man selling a Socialist publication because they disliked his views.

Yesterday's odd-balls often become today's national heroes. Their unpopular ideas, then called blasphemy, now are revered by all right-thinking solid citizens as holy writ. Tom Paine, Henry Mencken, Abraham Lincoln, Eugene Debs, Franklin D. Roosevelt – our history is full of so-called crackpots who changed America for the better. The great danger today, however, is not failure to tolerate free speech, but failure to exercise it.

Domestically, many huge problems still demand attention: internationally, the issues loom even larger. A life-or-death struggle rages everywhere between us and our enemies for control over the ------ of millions of them are on the march to a better life, turbulence in which we could ourselves crush the values we are fighting to preserve. And above all this turmoil hang the bombs that threaten to achieve the quiet for which so many seem to yearn.

Who is going to meet these challenges? Not the young man who aspires only to serenity, success and a pension, who fears that he may stand out from the corporate crowd, who is the spectator and not the participant in assuming the responsibilities of freedom. The man expressing the unpopular views outside the high school may have none of the answers either, but we will never find them by shutting the mouths of heretics and the ears of the faithful.

February 26, 1960

What the flag means

Sir: The American flag merits honor not for one week, but for every day of our lives; not only by a few of us asserting obedience, servility or hate, but by all of us expressing independence, freedom and love; and not in the manner of German or Japanese Fascists and Russian or Chinese Communists hailing the power of the state, but of American affirming the dignity and liberty of the individual.

After all, dictatorships of the left and right have always excelled at producing colossal displays of flag-worship, with casts of millions waving red banners, swastikas, or the sayings of Mao Tse-tung.

But none of those symbols has ever stood for what the American flag means to the citizen who uses his head for something other than a hat rack; the right of dissent, the right of a single puny citizen to challenge and defy the giant of government when believes it to be following a wrong course that will dishonor and destroy the nation he loves – courses such as slavery, prohibition, discrimination, or the waging of immoral and unwinnable war.

Let's honor the flag for the right reasons – that there has never been another like it in all of mankind's long struggle to achieve; and deserve, liberty and justice for all.

June 18, 1970

The Sabbath

Sir: It is good to know that Congressman Carlton R. Sickles has introduced a bill to eliminate, in Federal agencies, discrimination against persons because their religious obligations forbid their working on certain days, and to allow them to work on alternate days whenever possible.

We in the American Jewish Congress especially appreciate this long-overdue correction of an injustice that affects not only the Orthodox Jews who cannot work on Friday evenings or Saturday, but also such members of other religions as Seventh Day Adventists and Baptists. As Congressman Sickles points out, the Federal government, instead of discriminating against persons who conscientiously observe their religious obligations, should lead the way "in making it possible for the devout to pursue their beliefs."

There are sound constitutional, social and historical-legal reasons for Sabbath exemption.

The very first statement in the First Amendment of our Bill of Rights is that Congress shall make no law prohibiting the free exercise of religion. If Congress shall make no such law then Federal agencies should make no such rule.

The social practice in our country is for all groups to recognize and respect this injunction. At the 1964 conference of the Protestant churches, acting through the Department of Religious Liberty of the National Council of Churches of Christ, this legislation: We recommend that wherever the principle of a common day of rest remains established in the law, thus tending to create an inequitable situation for those who keep another day of rest, such law is to be rewritten or construed as to seek to remove such inequity.

Historically, all Sunday laws go back to the Fourth Commandment. However, the Sabbath of the Bible generally was not the first but the seventh day of the week. Even in the New Testament, the Sabbath is still the seventh day of the week, and for that reason there are some Christian sects which observe the Sabbath on Saturday. The early Christian church fathers changed the Sabbath to Sunday. In ancient Rome, Sunday was the day of the Sun-god. The first known compulsory Sunday law was promulgated by Emperor Constantine as part of his program to unify the Roman Empire. One American court summarized the history of Sunday laws as follows: "All Sunday legislation is the product of pagan Rome; the Saxon laws were the product of the Holy Roman Empire. The English laws are the expansion of the Saxon, and the American are the transcript of the English." Sunday laws are thus historically the product of a union of church and state which American colonists brought here from the Old World.

     Congratulations to Congressman Sickles on his decisive step in the right direction.

July 17, 1965

Going to the Source
What the Bible says on prayer

Evangelicals calling for mandatory and preferably Christian prayer in the public schools might note the words of one of the first four Evangelists, Matthew quoted in the New Testament (Matt. 6:5):

"And when thou prayest, thou shalt not be as the hypocrites are: for they love to pray standing .... in the corners of the streets, that they may be seen of men."

Isn't this one of the reasons why prayer is being urged for school children: " that they may be seen?" It must be, because there is nothing now to stop children from praying unseen, in school or anywhere else.

Matthew also warned his fellow Evangelists (Matt. 15:7-9):

"Well did Esaias prophesy of you, saying. This people draweth nigh unto me with their mouths; and honoureth me with their lips, but their heart is far from me. But in vain they do worship me ...."

In his epistle to his disciple Titus; the Apostle Paul said (Titus 1:16):

They profess that they know God, but in works they deny Him, being abominable, and disobedient, and unto every good work reprobate."

The Old Testament teaches us and our children (Isaiah 1:15) "And when ye spread forth your hands, I will hide Mine eyes from you; yea, when ye make many prayers; I will not hear; your hands are full of blood, wash you, make you clean ... cease to do evil, learn to do well, seek justice, relieve the oppressed, judge the fatherless, plead for the widow."

And Isaiah advises further, as a substitute for displays of penitence (58:6-7): ".... deal thy bread to the hungry .... bring the poor that are cast out to thy house .... thou seest the naked .... cover him."

But perhaps most noteworthy in the current campaign for

enforced official school prayer and recitation of religiosity is the biblical comment by the Apostle James (2:14-26):

"As the body without the spirit is dead, so faith without works is dead also."

What about "works?" Adults who must perform them tomorrow are today's children.

If children are to learn about the works that need doing – without which prayers are "the body without the spirit" – the teacher might well devote to meaningful prayer the time she would have spent presiding over a mindless sectarian incantation.

A few suggestions for the children to implore, beseech and entreat:

- Pray for a verifiable bilateral nuclear freeze, that our nation renounce a nuclear first-strike and cancel weapons designed for that purpose, and that humankind of develop the capacity to comprehend present nuclear arsenals more powerful than a million Hiroshimas.
- Pray that our leaders come to understand the deep-rooted, ages-old misery and despair in our own hemisphere and throughout the world, which fuels the revolutionary fires that our leaders call communist plots.
- Pray that the parents not visit upon the children and grandchildren, the obligation to reduce America's horrendous, disastrous budgetary deficits.
- Pray that the majority not turn away from over 34 million of our fellow-Americans who live below the poverty level.
- Pray that we not continue to cut programs to aid our poor and elderly neighbors; school lunch and nutrition, food, shelter and medical assistance.

One such prayer each morning would cover a five-day week. The schedule could be repeated each week, or until the words start losing meaning, as most prayer. Then, some of the following might be substituted:

- Pray for the preservation of American unity-in-diversity, or majority, respect the equal rights and dignity of minorities.

- Pray that no effort be made, under the guise of religion, to enforce conformity by young children by making them feel like outcasts if they pray differently or not at all, or like a sub-class of dubious ----- that is suffered out of the goodness of the believers.
- Pray to broaden our minds and help us to feel concern not only for ourselves and fellow citizens and fellow nations but also our fellow humans, millions of whom are starving and enduring daily torment to us unimaginable.
- Pray to understand that "humanitarian" is not a dirty word meaning "atheist" or "subversive" or worse, gut defined as a "person devoted to prompting the welfare of humanity, especially the elimination of pain and suffering."
- Pray to live by the words of an American general-statesman-editor humanitarian, Carl Schurz, who said, "Our country, right or wrong. When it has to be kept right; when wrong to be kept right."

Such daily supplications in the ---- might lead future generations to do the "works" without which faith is dead.

Meanwhile, denominational praying continue to thrive where it has long he finished, in the churches, synagogues, tents, mosques, homes and hearts of the faithful. Nowhere in the Old or New Testament or the constitution of the United States public school children instructed to ---- some homogenized mockery of religion.

January 8, 1990

The Prayers our Schoolchildren Should Say

President Clinton was right to oppose a constitutional amendment to promote teacher-led prayer in the public schools. There is nothing in our customs or constitution to prevent anyone from praying in public now.

The amendment was defeated in the House of Representatives, even though many House members support public prayer in the schools and elsewhere.

It should be pointed out to Congress and all religious citizens that the Bible disapproves of public displays of religiosity. Evangelicals on the Christian right who call for mandatory and preferably Christian prayer in the public schools should note the words of one of the four evangelists, Matthew: "And when thou prayest, thou shalt not be as the hypocrites are: for they love to pray standing .... in the corners of the streets, that they may be seen of men."

Isn't this one of the reasons why prayer is being urged for schoolchildren – "that they may be seen?"

Matthew also warned: "Well did Isaiah prophesy of you, saying, "This people draweth nigh unto me with their mouths, and honoreth me with their lips, but their heart is far from me. But in vain they do worship me."

The Old Testament teaches: "And, when ye spread forth your hands, I will hide Mine eyes from you ; yea, when ye make many prayers, I will not hear."

Isaiah advises, as a substitute for displays of penitence, "Deal thy bread to the hungry ... bring the poor that are cast out to thy house ... thou seest the naked ... cover him."

Even more noteworthy is the Apostle James' comment: "As the body without the spirit is dead, so faith without works is dead also."

Works that need doing
What about "works?"

If children are to learn about the works that need doing – without which prayers are "the body without the spirit" – teachers might as well choose meaningful prayers instead of rote incantations.

A few suggestions:

Pray that we understand that present nuclear arsenals are more powerful than a million Hiroshimas;

Pray that our leaders come to understand the deep-rooted, ages-old misery and despair in our own hemisphere and throughout the world, which fuel revolutionary fires.

Pray that the majority not turn away from millions of our fellow Americans who struggle to live below the poverty level.

Pray that we stop cutting programs to aid our poor and elderly neighbors, child care, school lunch and nutrition, food, shelter and medical assistance.

One such prayer could be offered each morning, until the words start losing meaning, as most prayers do. Then children might be encouraged to make different entreaties.

They might pray for respect for the equal rights and dignity of minorities.

Pray that no effort be made, under the guise of religion, to enforce conformity on young children by making them feel like outcasts if they pray differently or not at all.

Pray to understand that a "humanitarian" is not a wimp or an atheist or a subversive, but someone devoted to promoting the welfare of humanity, especially through the elimination of pain and suffering.

Pray to live by the words of a great American general-statesman-editor-humanitarian, Carl Schurz, who in 1899 said: "Our country. When right, to be kept right; when wrong to be put right."

Such daily supplications in the schools might lead future generations to the "works" without which faith is dead.

Meanwhile, denominational praying can thrive where it has long flourished – in churches, synagogues, temples, mosques, homes and hearts of the faithful.

June 18, 1998

Sunday Blue Laws

Sir: An interesting point in the Legislative Council hearings on the bill to liberalize Sunday closing laws: the conservative, traditional view is that of the opponents of "blue laws," who want to keep the state and church separate.

There is no new-fangled notion, but one of our basic liberties that impelled our ancestors to leave their homelands and risk lives and fortunes in search of religious freedom. It is enshrined in the first words of our Bill of Rights to the effect that there shall be no law respecting an establishment of religion.

The advocates of a law respecting an establishment of religion should not regard themselves as righteous protectors of the status quo against the onslaught of infidels and agnostics, for they are actually defending a radical denial of one of our fundamental rights.

Blue laws are illegal because they infringe on the religious freedom provisions of the First Amendment, as applied to the states by the Fourteenth Amendment to the Federal Constitution, and discriminate unfairly among religions, penalizing thousands whose faith teaches them that the Lord's Day is not Sunday.

These persons are deprived of their right to use Sunday as they see fit, and, if they follow their own religious practices, by closing their places of business on their Sabbath, they are placed at a severe economic disadvantage. Thus, the law is punishing Jews and Seventh Day Adventists who put their religious convictions into practice.

Protection of welfare of employees could be achieved by limiting work to six days per week without specifying the special day to be reserved. To such a law there would be no objection, as it would allow each individual to choose his own holy day to be reserved.

August 4, 1960

Mayor's Prayer

Editor: Now that the holy smoke from the Mayor's Prayer Breakfast has cleared, an appraisal is in order.

About 1,000 persons attended. Hundreds of thousands of Marylanders did not come.

Some stayed away because the principal speaker was the Rev. Jerry Falwell, who holds that God does not answer the prayers of "unredeemed" Gentiles and Jews and is not their father.

Many others, like myself, who consider Mayor Schaefer not only Baltimore's but America's best mayor, stayed away because we believe that it is not the mayor's business to sanction a sectarian prayer meeting held in his name and bearing the official seal of the city of Baltimore.

We pray for the welfare of our city, state and nation and for the leaders of our government.

But we do it in our own way, in our own synagogue or church, not in the Convention Center. And we are led by our own rabbi or minister, not the mayor, budget director, state comptroller or any politician with a passion for uniformity. None of them, and certainly not Reverend Falwell, can speak for us in addressing the almighty.

June 30, 1984

Stop Meese

Editor: In all the controversy about the ugly possibility of Judge Robert Bork as Supreme Court justice, we ignore the ugly reality of Ed Meese as attorney general.

There is a 50-50 chance that Mr. Bork might impose on us his far-out, radical views against individual rights, including the right to practice birth control and buy contraceptives, the right of our children to attend public school without having the majority's religion forced on them, the right of protection of free artistic expression and even some political expression and the right of protection against sex discrimination.

But thee is a 100 percent chance that Ed Meese as incumbent attorney general can impose on us such far-out, radical views as: if you're a suspect, you must be guilty: the Bill of Rights shouldn't apply to the state; 60 years of Supreme Court decisions were all wrong; and the Miranda rule should be reversed, denying suspects rights before police interrogation.

There is a clear and future danger from Judge Bork.

There is a clear and present danger from Mr. Meese.

His comment (as America's chief law enforcement office) that 'if a person is innocent of a crime, then he is not a suspect" is as disturbing as anything Mr. Bork has said.

His fights in Congress and the courts to eliminate a woman's right of choice of abortion, to stall on the enforcement of laws, to reverse decades of progress and generations of struggle on civil rights and civil liberties and to inhibit political debate are as irrational as any of Judge Bork's positions.

Mr. Meese is trying to restrict the amount of government information available to the citizen. He is calling for sweeping restrictions on constitutionally protected speech, proposing lifetime censorship agreements on government workers, undermining the integrity and independence of the federal courts, violating the principle of separation of church and state by supporting direct government financial aid to religion and teacher-led prayer in public schools.

He wants to restrict the historic writ of *habeas corpus*. He opposes, and fails to enforce, civil rights laws supported by every president in recent years, both Republican and Democrat, the 20-year old executive order, promoting minority employment in the federal government and Justice Department support of about 50 such agreements made by local and state governments.

Mr. Bork could be one of nine Supreme Court justices. But Mr. Meese is our one and only attorney general of the United States, sworn to protect our liberties. He is an arsonist as fire chief in a government of flaming radicals.

October 7, 1987

C. Problems of Poverty
The Quiet Ones

Sir:

The recently reported malnutrition survey of poverty groups in the United States indicates problems as bad or worse than those found in underdeveloped countries: growth retardation, anemia, vitamin deficiencies, and "hidden hunger." Senators are shocked. Dr. Arnold E. Schaefer, chief of the survey, noted that it is unreasonable in an affluent society to discover such signs and that the nation should be concerned.

The record suggests that most of the nation will not be concerned at all, and will accept it as another hard fact of life – for others to face. When the others get tired of facing it, and begin to protest vehemently their famine in the midst of plenty, they will become shouters and demonstrators, whom right-thinking citizens abhor.

The latter, in the words of President Nixon, are "the great, quiet, forgotten majority – the non-shouters and the non-demonstrators, the millions who ask principally to go their own way" etc. They are proud of themselves, and the President is obviously proud of the quiet ones he claims to represent. What is their great virtue? That they not only failed to deal with problems, but also kept quiet about discrimination, injustice, inequality and indecency, through centuries of shame?

That they remained silent while millions of Jewish fellow-humans were slaughtered and while millions of Negro fellow-citizens were sickeningly mistreated and robbed of their rights and dignity? That they went about their business with magnificent detachment, sterling unconcern, and a grand red-white-and-blue indifference to the needs and frustrations of the barefooted ones who were expected to lift themselves by their own bootstraps? That they piously preached platitudes – about brotherhood, peace, love of neighbor and the golden rule, while practicing the opposite.

Of course, there are no shouters or demonstrators in the great quiet majority who see themselves stoically bearing burdens, enduring membership in the world's most overindulged and undertaxed industrial society. Why should they cry out while others suffer? When the fire is burning their own feet, perhaps then the quiet ones will be less quiet. Then at last silence will be recognized as a crime. But then it may be too late.

January 28, 1969

Figments and Facts

The conventional wisdom, distilled from post-mortems on last fall's mid-term election, is that the determining factor was the raging of the great white male.

Translation: Many of the working white poor have seen their barely adequate income actually decline in the past few years of general prosperity. They are the boats stuck on the bottom in the rising tide.

How different is today's crusader for the Newt Deal from his passionate counterpart of 62 years ago who championed the New Deal. As one of the white male Franklin D. Roosevelt revolutionaries of 1932, I do not claim that we were more virtuous than the Gingrich gang. Just vastly different.

Then, we voted mainly *for* ourselves; today's angry white males vote *against* others.

Then, the majority did not vote to deny help to needy racial minorities. Because then the majority members saw themselves, not those others, as the needy, or soon-to-be needy. Government was then perceived as possibly rescuing us, with someone else – the "economic royalists" – paying the bill. In 1994, it was a different story. Most voters were against the rescue of them by us; the hard-working taxpayers rebuffed the "freeloaders."

Then, it was taken for granted that the white male, especially the WASP male, would be first in line for government jobs and largess, and would not have to compete against women and minorities (including Jews who were still excluded from certain professions).

Then, we voted for laws to protect that part of the nation which was "ill-fed, ill-clothed and ill-housed." Many of today's white males would demolish those laws, seeing themselves as benefactors instead of putative beneficiaries. The truth is that most of what they voted against exists only in their fevered imagination.

Here are some of the figments and facts:

Figment: Most of the poor are black or assorted other minorities;

Fact: Two-thirds of those living below the poverty level, according to government statistics for 1992, are white: 24 million out of about 36 million.

Figment: Most on welfare are able-bodied adults who refused to work.

Fact: Most of the 5 million families on Aid to Families with Dependent Children consist of children, the frail elderly and the disabled who can't just be ordered to "get off your butt and go get a job."

Figment: Welfare mothers don't want to work.

Fact: Most do have some history of paid employment, which has usually required few skills, provided low wages and benefits, if any, and offered little incentive to continue.

Figment: AFDC families stay on welfare for years; it is a "way of life."

Fact: Over half of all AFDC families were on the rolls for two years or less; and only 17.66 percent have received aid without interruption for five years or more.

Figment: Welfare costs are exorbitant.

Fact: In Maryland, welfare accounts for only 2 percent of the state's General Fund. The *maximum* monthly benefit for a family of three is $366, which has to cover rent, utilities, non-food items, clothing, household furnishings, transportation, etc.

Figment: AFDC mothers are inadequate parents; orphanages would do a better job.

Fact: Much of this attitude is concealed racism.

Figment: Most teen-age mothers are nymphomaniacs.

Fact: Most teen-age pregnancies are accidental.

These facts are lost on those who want to believe otherwise. As "old stuff," they are seldom mentioned in the media, while the figments are repeated ad nauseam on endless talk shows.

Orphanages are no more of a solution to the problem of neglected children than they were in the time of Oliver Twist.

The transition of British society from rural to industrial

brought large-scale social problems: exploitation of children and women in the factories, workshops and mines. Today, society is moving from industrial high-tech with similar dislocations; poverty and destitution for the illiterate and uneducable.

It must be remembered that the conditions chronicled by Charles Dickens happened when Britain was the superpower of its time as we are of ours. It was preoccupied with its power, not its people. Could that happen here?

British writer Samuel Johnson emphasized the fact that is apparently overlooked by Newt Gingrich: "A decent provision for the poor is the true test of civilization."

So did John F. Kennedy in his 1961 inaugural address: "If a free society cannot save the many who are poor, it cannot help the few who are rich."

But the questions remain: Can we be as humane in helping their children, their elderly, sick, disabled, handicapped and unfortunate as we once were in helping our own. Does charity begin – and end – at home? Is it a valid function of government only when it helps us, never when it helps them?

With all of our unequally shared tax burdens and sacrifices, this nation still excels in the consumption of goods and services. Now if we could only raise our standard of giving as high as our standard of living.

March 23, 1995

Dear Sir:

The recently reported malnutrition survey of poverty groups in the United States, indicates problems as bad or worse than those found in underdeveloped countries: growth retardation, anemia, vitamin deficiencies, and "hidden hunger." Senators are shocked. Dr. Arnold E. Schaefer, chief of the survey, noted that it is unreasonable in an affluent society to discover such signs and that the nation should be concerned.

The record suggests that most of the nation will not be concerned at all, and will accept it as another hard fact of life – for others to face.

When the others get tired of facing it, and begin to protest vehemently their famine in the midst of plenty, they will become shouters and demonstrators, whom right-thinking citizens abhor.

The latter, in the words of President Nixon, are "the great, quiet, forgotten majority – the non-shouters and non-demonstrators, the millions who ask principally to go their own way" etc. They are proud of themselves, and the President is obviously proud of the Quiet Ones he claims to represent. What is their great virtue?

That they not only failed to deal with problems, but also kept quiet about discrimination, injustice, inequality and indecency, through centuries of shame?

That they remained silent while millions of Jewish fellow-humans were slaughtered and while millions of Negro fellow-citizens were sickeningly mistreated and robbed of their rights and dignity?

That they went about their business with magnificent detachment, sterling unconcern, and a grand red-white-and-blue indifference to the needs and frustrations of the barefooted ones who were expected to lift themselves by their own bootstraps?

That they piously preached platitudes about brotherhood, peace, love of neighbor, and the golden rule, while practicing the opposites?

- Of course there are no shouters or demonstrators in that great quiet majority who see themselves stoically bearing burdens, enduring membership in the world's most overindulged and undertaxed industrial society. Why should they cry out while others suffer? When the fire is burning their own feet, perhaps then the Quiet Ones will be less quiet. Then at last silence will be recognized as a crime. But then it may be too late.

January 24, 1969

How Clever, Mr. Block

Editor:

How clever of Agriculture Secretary John R. Block, the millionaire farmer with the $300,000 home, to undertake to prove the government's generosity in bestowing $58 a week in food stamps on the deserving poor. He says he's demonstrating that his family of four "can live within the plan and have a satisfactory diet."

What a jolly time the Block family must have had, living it up like the welfare folks for seven exciting days – a week that should have provided many delightful anecdotes to amuse the country club set.

While Mr. and Mrs. Block are acting out this merry lark for the TV cameras and loading their $58 worth of groceries into the limousine, they might consider these footnotes to their noble experiment:

In Maryland, the family of four, receiving AFDC welfare of $355 monthly, is entitled to only $195 a month in food stamps. That's not $58 but $45.30 a week.

The same family with a working breadwinner earning the minimum wage of $3.35 per hour, or $580 per month, would receive only $87 monthly in food stamps – not $58 but only $20.14 a week.

The standard of need in Maryland, according to the Governor's Commission on Welfare Grants, in 1979 was $600 a month minimum for a "decent" life for an AFDC family of four (decent for them, not for Mr. Block's family). In 1983, allowing for inflation, the monthly figure would be $775, not the present grand total of $550 including food stamps.

Unlike Mr. Block, 51 percent of food stamp families have no assets; 71 percent have no car or less than $500 equity in a car.

The average food stamp meal is a munificent 47 cents per person.

If Mr. Block and his family would live on food stamps for a month instead of a week, they might understand why 51 percent of the people who line up at emergency food centers are those who have run out of food stamps before the end of the month.

If the Block family could live on food stamps for a year or several years, as many must – with no allowance for salt, herbs, spices or any of the seasonings that make eating more than a matter of survival – they might get more of the true flavor of a grinding food stamp diet.

And if they were forced to sell or barter some of their precious food stamps to pay for urgent basic needs of health, clothing and shelter that their welfare allotment does not cover, then their feasting on food stamps might be further curtailed.

Mr. Block has carved out another monument to the insensitivity of an administration that favors haves over has-nots, because the haves also have the votes.

August 9, 1983

We need a new Civilian Conservation Corps

The 50th anniversary this year of the Civilian Conservation Corps reminds us that – no matter what our mayoral candidates may imply – neither local nor state government can make useful jobs for unskilled and uneducated youths. With most of our tax dollars going to Washington, the federal government that everyone wants off his back remains the last best hope of the hardcore unwanted unemployed, the new class of "ill-clothed, ill-housed and ill-fed." If economic recovery continues, it may provide jobs for some of them, but most cannot absorb the technological training needed to make them employable.

Just as federal agencies were created in Franklin Roosevelt's explosive 100 days – the NRA, FDIC, HOLC, AAA, PWA, TVA and CCC which saved the system by giving hope to the hopeless – so today another massive CCC is needed to employ thousands of inner-city youths missed by such efforts as Mayor Schaefer's Blue Chip-In. With all respect due to this excellent public-private partnership, it is simply inadequate.

Fifty years ago, when Maryland and its economy were much smaller and the dollar much bigger in buying power, the CCC invested almost $40 million in creating 36,000 year-round jobs in Maryland's forests and recreational parks. Thirty camps were set up. Men who had no training or aptitude were taught how to work. The CCC built 274 bridges, 3,500 erosion control dams, reforested nearly 4-1/2 million acres of land, improved another 60,000 acres of forest land, reduced 25,000 fire hazard acres and planted nearly a million trees and shrubs.

Maryland state forests and parks developed or improved by the CCC included Herrington Manor, Swallow Falls, New Germany, Gambrill, Cunningham Falls, Elk Neck, Big Run, Fort Frederick, Cedarville, Patapsco Valley and Pocomoke River state parks. CCC log cabins are still being rented to the public for recreation.

No boondoggle, this kind of useful, needed work would put money in the pockets and impart a sense of worth and pride of achievement to those who now feel wasted. It would conserve both human and natural resources.

The latter includes the approximately one-third of all the land in the United States that is owned by the federal government, with all of its debris to be removed, roads to be built or rebuilt, forests and trails to be restored, and infrastructures to be maintained.

The message that Roosevelt sent to the 73rd Congress on March 21, 1933, could be sent by President Reagan to the 98th:

"I propose to create a Civilian Conservation Corps to be used in simple work, not interfering with normal employment and confining itself to forestry, the prevention of soil erosion, flood control, and similar projects ... More important, however, than the material gains, will be the moral and spiritual value of such work ... We can take a vast army of the unemployed out into healthful surroundings ... It is not a panacea for all the unemployment, but it is an essential step in this emergency ..."

Only 10 days later, Congress gave FDR the authority to proceed. By July, 275,000 were enrolled – unemployed youths between 18 and 25 years old, unmarried, from families receiving government assistance and thousands of older men experienced in woodcraft and forestry skills, who trained and supervised the work crews.

All could enlist for six months with an option to re-enlist for six months, to a maximum of two years. They received a nominal sum per month plus room, board, clothing and tools. At army conditioning camps they exercised for days before reporting to the work camps supervised by regular army officers. In his radio address to them on July 17, 1933, Roosevelt said:

"You ... nearly 300,000 strong ... are evidence that we are seeking to get away as fast as we possibly can from soup kitchens and free rations. The government is paying you wages for actual, needed work. Through you the nation will graduate a fine group of strong young men, clean-loving, trained to self-discipline and, above all, proud to work."

This was the Roosevelt who was Ronald Reagan's hero

and role model until Reagan radically changed political colors in the 1950s. When nominee Reagan quoted to the GOP 1980 convention the wisdom of Franklin D. Roosevelt, the Republican faithful would have been less shocked if they had recalled Reagan's past worship of the original New Dealer.

He voted for FDR in '32, '36, '40 and '44. His father headed the WPA in his hometown of Dixon, Illinois. He served on the board of directors of such liberal organizations as United World Federalists. He was a founder of the California branch of Americans for Democratic Action, and later served on its national board. He campaigned vigorously for the election of Harry Truman, Hubert Humphrey, whose opponent Reagan called "the banner carrier for Wall Street," and for Helen Gahagan Douglas against Richard Nixon. Her aides kept Reagan's name off her letterhead because his reputation was too leftist. Testifying before the House Committee on Un-American Activities, in opposition to the anti-communist view of Gary Cooper and Robert Montgomery. Reagan said that the best way to combat communism was "to make democracy work."

He was right then. He would be right now to support the Mathias-Moynihan American Conservation Corps Act of 1983 which recently passed the House 301-87, and is due soon to come before the Senate. The budget resolution passed on May 19 contained $300 million for the corps. It is insufficient, but if not vetoed, it is a start.

Mathias and Moynihan should be commended, and Reagan reminded that the best way to combat communism, crime, drugs, murder, suicide, mental illness, other serious health problems, and the alienation that breeds violence is to make democracy work for the 50 percent of unemployed youth, to get them off the streets and into jobs – now. It can happen only with massive help from demon Washington.

July 14, 1983

An 'old liberal' speaks out for the 'real conservatives'

The "conservative" Heritage Foundation, the self-anointed sage and seer of mainstream America, has published a suggested agenda for the second-term Reagan administration, "Mandate for Leadership." Its recommendations include opposition of tax increases to cut the deficit, support of "privatization" and further reductions in social programs with increases for the military. It is giving conservatism a bad name. It raises the question: what is "conservative" for the United States in 1985; and what should it be?

What parts of our heritage does the Heritage Foundation want conserved? Bunker Hill or My Lai? Welcoming the tired, the poor, etc. or rejecting Jews fleeing Nazi butchers? What we've done for immigrants or what we've done to the only native Americans? Bills of attainder or the Bill of Rights? The slave ships or the underground railroad? Government of, by and for the successful only, or the unsuccessful too?

What needs and merits conserving?

The last presidential election is supposed to have shown that most voters supported the "conservative" candidate. But are they conservative? And is he?

The confusion comes when you ask people to define exactly what they mean by conservative and how they stand on issues.

Just when you think that Ronald Reagan's position is somewhere between Calvin Coolidge and Jesse Helms, you realize that he presides over the largest deficit in history, supports Red China against Formosa, and is talking more politely to the Soviets – no "evil empire" comments recently. It's enough to break the heart of a regular Reaganite.

Just when you were sure that Democrats stood for free-trade in an open society, Mondale started spouting protectionist rhetoric that sounded like classic Warren G. Harding: "We've been running up the white flag when we should be running up the American flag," said the Democratic leader, denouncing imports.

When are you being really conservative?

Let's say you're a true red-white-and-blue middle-class Reagan Republican. You dutifully despise and deride the Democrats as the party of "tax and tax; spend and spend." You don't like to be reminded that your own thrifty GOP party has loaded onto you and your middle and working class friends and your descendants, for generations to come, whatever tax burden may have been lifted off its rich friends. You'd rather not face that your fearless conservative leader is spending record-breaking sums of your and your progeny's money on super-weaponry and star-wards gadgetry for budget deficits that make the old free-spenders look like tightwads.

As a rugged individualist, you rely upon the traditional patriotic virtue of greed to get us out of our difficulties, to motivate us to do all the good things for America that it accomplished long ago when our destiny was to keep the frontier moving westward in a vast tide of migration and exploitation. So goes the theory.

But many Republicans as well as Democrats are wondering if we can still put all our faith in good old greed, now that there's no West for the young man to go to. Greed doesn't work for the entrepreneur considering a new factory when competing factories are operating at far below capacity. Greed doesn't put to work the uneducated, unskilled underclass that is useless to business.

Meanwhile, as a card-carrying conservative, do you lie awake nights figuring how to conserve the nation's basic assets – its people and infrastructures on which the free enterprise economy is built? How does greed get our roads, streets, bridges, sewers, water supply and forests preserved, repaired and rebuilt? How does it motivate us to maintain that one-third of the nation's land that is the responsibility of the federal government? How does it conserve the environment we depend on for life?

More important than conserving these natural resources is conserving human resources. If you're a real hard-bitten so-called conservative, do you really give much of a damn about conserving, repairing and rebuilding America? You made it, why can't they? Tough luck. But if the human capital programs are cut back further or eliminated – in education, job training, mother-and-child nutrition and other services designed to conserve people's health, skills and ability to cope in a competitive society – whose tough luck is it?

Don't we all become victims of such neglect – conservatives and liberals alike? When we fail to conserve our human and physical resources, we are being not conservative, but radical, because we are striking at the roots of our system. And no matter how hard-line our conservative rhetoric, no matter how aggressive our patriotism, when we shrug off millions of unemployed, hungry and homeless Americans because we're not one of them, we are as effective an enemy of our capitalist system as any communist.

It's not easy for old liberals like me to adjust to our present role of conservative – which in an important sense is what we've become. We want to conserve the social gains of the past 60 years, not smash them as the New Right radicals are trying to do. We want to conserve hard-won civil rights and civil liberties against the onslaught of the un-Americans. We want to conserve the Constitution and Bill of Rights against those who put it on a pedestal, but really as a target to be shot full of holes.

When our lawmakers endorse proposals to encourage police to conduct illegal searches, authorize judges to deny bail and imprison people without trial, bring back McCarthyism and vigilantism, remove restraints from the CIA and FBI in going after American citizens, weaken federal courts, the Voting Rights Act and Legal Services, and destroy fundamental liberties we should be striving to conserve – it's time to get government off our backs.

When the Supreme Court, bowing to the administration, dismantles legislation forbidding sex discrimination, breaches church-state separation by allowing local governments to favor religious observances, attacks First Amendment rights of expression and assembly and permits detention without trial of citizens not charged with any crime, it's time to get government off our backs.

The single most important distinction between us and our totalitarian enemies has nothing to do with weaponry, industry, national power and world influence – areas in which both sides compete and excel.

It has to do with conserving diversity, individual freedom, the right of the single citizen to petition, dissent, protest and challenge his government, and still remain secure in his home, protected by due process of law.

A national security, designed to protect the United States, which actually destroys the unique, fragile, priceless liberty that the United States stands for, is no security at all. President Reagan has the opportunity to lead the nation away from radicalism and back to the conservatism supported by a majority of Americans, including many from the minority of registered voters who twice elected him.

April 10, 1985

Passing the hat is passing the buck

Applying a Reaganism to President George Bush: There he goes again, with a thousand points of light.

Recently, in a New York Hilton speech to business, education and community leaders, Bush said: There is no problem that is not being solved somewhere in America." He exhorted his hearers to "prove that statement a thousand times over." He proposed that federal money be matched by the private sector and that banks, credit card companies and utilities include "information in their bills about how customers can serve the needy."

Partnership between government and the private sector is a fine concept. But, with all due respect to the president and his inspirational leadership of a volunteers' crusade, this call-to-arms is a cop-out and a cruel hoax on the poor and those struggling to help them.

While thousands do volunteer work and give generously of time, effort and money, and while it would be wonderful if the private sector could match government assistance, about one American in three gives a percent or less of his or her income to charity. Another one in three gives nothing at all, zilch, zero, in the face of growing numbers of homeless and hungry American families. It is hard to imagine victory in a feel-good, do-good war on poverty funded by private philanthropy and the shrinking treasuries of hard-pressed local government.

In the Depression, when a third of the nation was ill-fed, ill-clothed and ill-housed, and another third, at least, feared becoming so, there was a political majority in favor of government aid for the needy. Must we wait for another Depression to mobilize support for the government to do what only government can do? Must we wait until, once again, government is perceived as helping "us" and not "them"?

In those desperate days, the government was able, with massive public support despite ferocious opposition from the right, to institute such measures as Social Security, unemployment insurance and other kinds of aid to distressed families.

Let's face it: These were, and are, not only liberal but in fact socialist forms of "justice, not charity." For the most part, they have worked – not only in the United States but also, and to a greater degree, in other capitalist democracies.

While there are slightly fewer whites living in poverty today, there are more minorities, especially children. According to a recent Census Bureau report, 13.5 percent of Americans are poor – about one of every seven. Among blacks, the figure is 33.1 percent, one in three (one of every two black children under age 6) and 28.2 percent among Hispanics.

The report shows no change in the Reagan-era trend of the rich getting richer as the poor get poorer. The wealthiest 40 percent of the population get more than two-thirds of the income – 67.8 percent – while the poorest 40 percent of the people receive only 15.4 percent, the lowest on record.

Despite a drop in unemployment, poverty has increased, because some of the new jobs for the working poor don't pay enough to raise the family above the poverty level, now considered to be $11,600 for a family of four.

If cuts in the swollen military budget and elimination of bureaucratic waste and fraud do not suffice to cover the needs of the poor, then – heaven forbid – there may have to be a tax increased on higher incomes.

Although we complain loudly of a heavy tax burden, it is light compared to income taxes borne by citizens of other capitalist countries. Our present top federal income tax bracket is 28 percent. As of February 1987, it was 60 percent in the United Kingdom, 66 percent in Ireland (with income as small as $19,600) and up to 75 percent in Belgium, Portugal and Sweden.

The question, however, is not whether we can afford the tax (or wealth-redistribution if you will), but whether we can afford the social consequences of the widening gap between the two Americas, between those flaunting luxury and those enduring misery.

The function of federal government is to preserve the

union, to hold us together in peace with one another. Yet, our union is threatened today by an underclass of millions of Americans who have lost faith in the system and themselves, who have nothing to lose, who have given up.

Bush wants us to continue to believe the myths of decentralization, privatization and the "thousand points of light." Despite his long experience with government that works, he wants us to keep on swallowing the Reagan doctrine that government is always the problem, never the solution. He knows that although government cannot solve all problems, it can go far toward solving common problems that we all, including our leader, agree must be solved.

Instead, he should be debunking misconceptions about the federal social role: that we can't afford it, that it harms the economy, that it's a waste, that it does more harm than good, that it discourages initiative by other sectors which could do a better job and that the poor don't need or deserve more help.

Why should only some Americans be expected to relieve this intolerable poverty amid plenty, when all of us will benefit from helping to lift neighbors out of ignorance, crime, drugs, sickness, deprivation and despair?

Everybody dislikes the welfare state – taxpayers, politicians and the recipients themselves. But until there is a vast improvement in the human nature of benefactors and in the ability of the disadvantaged and working poor to help themselves in a high-tech society, it will have to do.

Passing the hat is just passing the buck.

August 18, 1989

What the Poor Need

When the children, the aged, the sick and disabled poor have to depend, not on government, but entirely on the "thousand points of light" in the private sector, they are in what our president calls deep doo-doo.

A recent study shows that, far from tithing 10 percent, most Americans given less than 1 percent (a third of us) or nothing at all (almost another third).

Maryland's private sector has many generous donors: churches, synagogues, newspapers, television and radio stations and armies of volunteers. The Maryland Food Committee, for example, through its Hunger Appeal, membership contributions, Bags of Plenty, Restaurants Sharing 10 percent (RSVVP), Auction for Action, Kids for Kids school program, Sharing is Caring lawyers' campaign and other special events, generates about $800,000 annually. About ten times that amount in market value is provided in contributions of actual food by the Maryland Food Bank and hundreds of food pantries.

But it is nowhere near enough to relieve the hunger of more than 700,000 Marylanders who require food or nutritional support at some time during the year. The reasons are many: longer periods of unemployment, lack of usable skills, growing international competition, more one-parent families due to divorce or separation, and the inadequacy of government programs.

Even if it were enough, the system is indecent. Spiritual as well as physical damage is involved. In this richest nation in world history families should not have to line up for food handouts or sleep in doorways, paying in dignity, pride and self-respect for a bowl of soup and a sandwich or a place to sleep.

The problem is not hunger or homelessness. It is poverty.

The solution is somehow to provide the poor with enough money to buy what they need in food and housing as their neighbors do. One solution worth considering is governmental action through a negative income tax.

Economist Milton Friedman explained the principle in

1962, in his book "Capitalism and Freedom":

"If an individual receives $100 taxable income, i.e. an income of $100 in excess of the exemption and deductions, he pays a tax. Under the proposal, if his taxable income is minus-$100, he would pay a negative tax, i.e. receive a subsidy. If the rate of subsidy were, say, 50 percent, he would receive $50. If he had no income at all, and, for simplicity, no deductions, and the rate were constant, he would receive $300 [when the personal exemption was $600].

".... The rates of subsidy could, of course, be graduated just as the rates of tax above the exemption are. In this way, it would be possible to set a floor below which no man's net income [defined now to include the subsidy] would fall – in the simple example $300 per person. The precise floor set would depend on what the community could afford.

"The advantages of this arrangement are clear. It is directed specifically at the problem of poverty. It gives help in the form most useful to the individual, namely, cash. It is general and could be substituted for the host of special measures now in effect. It makes explicit the cost borne by society. It operates outside the market. Like any other measures to alleviate poverty, it reduces the incentives of those helped to help themselves, but it does not eliminate that incentive entirely, as a system of supplementing incomes up to some fixed minimum would. An extra dollar earned always means more money available for expenditure ...

"The system would fit directly into our current income-tax system and could be administered along with it. The present tax system covers the bulk of income recipients and the necessity of covering all would have the by-product of improving the operation of the present income tax ...."

"A few brief calculations suggest also that this proposal could be far less costly in money than our present collection of welfare measures."

The main disadvantage, of course, is the imposition of taxes on some to pay subsidies to others and the possibility (though not probability) that, at some point in time, the "some" might be the minority and the "others" the majority. But it is unlikely that the bridge will have to be crossed in the foreseeable future. For now the poor are a politically powerless minority.

Experiments with the negative income tax in West Germany, the Netherlands, the United Kingdom, Belgium, Israel, Ireland, Luxembourg and, recently, France have not all been successful. There are problems in the concept of a minimum income, in its applications and in setting standards low enough to encourage recipients to seek work and save. But the problems are more soluble than those of the Strategic Defense initiative to which we have committed billions of dollars; and they are more threatening to the security of a nation founded on justice.

As a board member of the Maryland Food Committee, my modest efforts to help relieve hunger in Maryland make me feel good. I would gladly forgo the satisfaction and pleasure if 700,000 of my neighbors could be spared degradation and humiliation, and be enable to afford to put bread on their tables and a roof over their heads without my volunteer help, in a "kinder, gentler America."

March 15, 1989

The Civilian Economy

While the media were pre-occupied with Earth Day observances on the weekend of April 21, a Baltimore event that could have consequences to Earth's future went too unnoticed.

It was the third annual public hearing before the Baltimore City Development Commission and Mayor Kurt Schmoke, following two that have served as models for other major cities. The speak-out on demilitarization and the "peace dividend" resulted from the 68 percent cut in federal aid to Baltimore since 1980 while military spending has doubled in the same period.

Business executives, federal, state and local government officials and representatives of social action, human service and neighborhood groups testified to the urgency of converting from a military to a peacetime economy. The hearing was organized by Baltimore Jobs with Peace, directed by Sister Katherine Corr.

In the four-hour public meeting at St. Francis of Assisi Church on Harford Road, the attentive commission and large audience heard 40 voices raised in passionate protest against continuous squandering their tax dollars on military excess while human needs are neglected. Here's a sampling of the testimony:

Mayor Schmoke and former U.S. Rep. Parren Mitchell were the lead speakers. Schmoke has proposed to the Conference of Mayors a committee to investigate how hard-pressed cities can help the conversion process. He is also providing staff support to the commission.

Del. Paul G. Pinsky, D-Prince George's, discussed his bill for a state commission on conversion. It did not get out of committee this year, but will be reintroduced in the next session of the General Assembly.

Aris Melissaratos, vice president and general manager of Westinghouse Corp., discussed measures already taken by his company to facilitate conversion. "We are applying defense technology to civilian purposes," he said, pointing out application of Westinghouse capabilities to automation of the post office, commercial aviation, enhancing the nation's radar network, drug interdiction and commercial and residential security systems. "I take it as a personal challenge to keep Westinghouse workers employed," said Melissaratos. He sees tremendous opportunies for American industry opening in Eastern Europe, Africa and Central America and believes it is imperative for U.S. companies to be competitive.

Kathleen LeBlanc, a teacher in the Baltimore schools, urged the commission to address the problem of illiteracy by lowering class size and instituting a counseling program to deal with the emotional needs of children affected by drug-related violence.

Jana Meyer, of My Sister's Place, a center for homeless women and children, noted a marked increase in the numbers requiring shelter and services – many for months at time – and the desperate need for safe, affordable housing.

If we had the kind of leadership in Washington today that inspired confrontation with these problems instead of avoidance and postponement, President Bush's popularity rating might drop some, but his effectiveness rating would zoom.

Instead, we have the politics of fear, playing on the fear of crime, drugs, AIDS, each other and, worst of all, fear of peace. We are led to fear the end of the Cold War, the peace dividend, troop demobilization, the closing of obsolete military installations and factories and loss of jobs.

The fact is that military budget cuts even much bigger than any now proposed would only be a temporary setback for the economy. Short-term pain would be followed by long-term gain. Within a brief period, we could have a recovery like that following World War II, with falling interest rates, a surge in housing construction, a federal budget surplus for a change and rapid growth in capital spending and gross national product. Those are the projections not of social dreamers but of hard-nosed researchers commissioned by Business Week magazine.

Transferring tax money from Pentagon pipe dreams to investment in long-neglected infrastructure – crumbling water mains, sewers, bridges and roads – in education, nutrition, job training, drug abuse treatment and health care could produce fabulous long-term payoffs in real national security.

Converting some of the military's share of the national research-and-development dollar – now up to 67 percent – to peacetime industrial creativity could be the best way to meet and beat competition from Japan, where the best brains are not wasted on dreaming up Star Wars.

As studies show, a civilian economy generates many more jobs than military production, more money in more pockets and a better life for all, especially those mired in poverty.

When we defeat our fears, when the polls begin to show that we're not afraid to wage peace, then our poll-reading, lip-reading politicians will leave the sidelines and rush to lead the parade.

June 8, 1990

A march in behalf of beleaguered cities

The priority of Baltimore's "Save Our Cities" march on Washington October 12th is enshrined in the First Amendment to the Constitution, in the guarantee that "Congress shall make no law ... abridging ... the right of the people peaceably to assemble and to petition the government for a redress of grievances."

And Baltimore and most other cities have many grievances to be redressed. Consider some of them:

Between 1980 and 1991, essential federal capital grants to Baltimore city plummeted from $475 million to $42 million, a drop of $433 million – or 97 percent. These grants, which in 1980 covered over 70 percent of Baltimore's capital budget, in 1990 took care of only 16 percent. Federal grants for job training, so urgently needed in Baltimore, declined from $85 million in 1980, to about $9 million last year, a drop of about 90 percent.

We are an urban nation. The United States depends on cities. Most people live and work in cities. Cities are our vital centers of culture and industry. Yet our cities today stand virtually abandoned by the federal government; they are caught in a spiral of economic and spiritual decline. Our national security today is threatened not mainly by foreign enemies but by inadequate education, unemployment, homelessness, crime, despair and indifference. If our cities die, our country will soon follow.

Cities simply do not have the resources to halt their own decline. Higher local taxes drive more citizens out of the cities, leaving those who stay with an ever heavier burden. Yet the federal government has shifted the burden of taxes to the near-bankrupt cities and states.

Only at the national level are there resources great enough to reverse the downward trends of urban America.

The march on October 12th will petition the federal government to take the following emergency measures:

- Restore aid to cities for essential programs and services previously supported by federal grants which have been cut to the bone.

- Restore fairness to tax systems as proposed by Maryland's Linowes Commission.
- In keeping with the end of the Cold War, reduce military spending. End waste, fraud and abuse of funds throughout government.
- Repeal laws, such as Gramm-Rudman, which prevent funding to save our cities.

Over 65 respected organizations and a number of political, business, civic and religious leaders are supporting the march. All citizens are urged to join this call on the federal government to restore aid to Baltimore and other cities for education, food programs, housing, economic development, crime prevention, public health, environmental protection, repair and replacement of deteriorating infrastructure and fairness in a federal tax system that now inequitably burdens the middle class and poor.

These ends are patriotic, and so are the means: the petitioning of government to redress grievances. We have the hard-won constitutional right that can be the model for other cities and for people all over the world who cherish freedom. Now it is our duty to exercise the right.

September 17, 1991

Save the children ....

I don't want any privilege for myself or my family that other people do not have. It makes me uneasy in my conscience to have opportunities that are denied to other people."

So said humanitarian Sidney Hollander, Sr., Maryland's beloved warrior for social justice, who died 20 years ago. His memory was honored again recently at Har Sinai Congregation, when the Maryland Chapter of the American Jewish Congress presented its annual Sidney Hollander Award of Distinction to Ruth Wolf Rehfeld, who has served many Baltimore area community service organizations as volunteer and staff person.

If Sidney Hollander, Sr. is looking down on the society he devoted his life to improving, he might wonder if much has improved. He would see:

- Three out of four low-income Maryland families are at constant risk of running out of food, usually toward the end of each month, when food stamps have been exhausted. Over 60,000 children are hungry in the land of pleasant living.
- Hungry children suffer two to three times as many health problems as better-fed kids, and they fall behind in school or drop out.
- U.S. infant mortality statistics resemble those of impoverished Third World countries.

Seeing all this, when other Americans are splurging $50,000 on a car and hundreds of thousands of dollars on a yacht, Sidney might wonder if many today feel any twinges of conscience at having privileges and opportunities denied to the less fortunate.

He might recall his 1939 testimony, as president of the National Jewish Community Relations Advisory Committee, before the joint Senate-House Committee on Immigration, pleading to save Jewish children from the impending Holocaust. (He was advocating adoption of the German Refugee Bill, which got nowhere.)

Reporting on a fact-finding trip to Europe, he stood before

the people's representatives whom he later referred to as the "stony-faced inquisitors." They listened to the eye-witness accounts of cruelties "without change of expression."

Sidney said of the children's parents, who were facing extermination: "Such a fate they were prepared to meet, almost with resignation, for themselves; their agony was for their children. Toward these they felt as you and I would were our own left without home, without protection and at the mercy of a merciless state. The same question met me everywhere: Will America do nothing for them? Do the people there not understand?

".... Is there no chance? Will not America open its doors? I reminded her how tens of thousands have been kept alive through our help. America has always been kind to children, and America is still America."

Was it then? Is it now? Are we again abandoning our children?

Sidney Hollander died before the Reagan-Bush cultivation of self-indulgence, irresponsibility, suspicion and even hostility toward the poor.

In Sidney's time, we rejected "a flood of alien hordes." Today, we reject our own children. We have other priorities. Again we turn our backs on what we don't want to see: children in pain, denied refuge, food, shelter, nurture and life itself. We don't set them adrift on rafts; we just set them adrift on the streets and ignore them until they rob or murder us for a drug fix.

Then we pay attention and pay to support them, not in homes but in jails.

Is this the kinder, gentler America? Can we, who are so generous in responding to the plight of one child-victim publicized on TV, do little or nothing to rescue millions of kids in distress, whose stories are so common that they are not news?

In the endless debates of the current election campaign, which candidate is addressing the questions being asked by poor parents speaking for thousands and millions of poor children:

Why must we be hungry and homeless in this bountiful land?

Where do we eat and sleep tonight?

We're illiterate; how can we go to school or get job training?

We're in rags' where do we get decent clothes?

We're sick; how can we afford to see a doctor?

Will anybody take care of us while our mother is out working for minimum wages, or looking for work that does not exist?

Will any candidate talk to us who are too young to vote, or too un-middle-class?

Many Americans are listening and responding. Many are hard-working but frustrated volunteers in social service organizations whose budgets have been drastically cut or eliminated as needs multiply.

But too many of us again turn away. We say, "We've got our own troubles," without considering that one of our biggest is our forgotten children.

June 15, 1992

Misplaced priorities

The governor goes out and courts still another big-money man to buy an NFL football team. Hysterical calls flood the sports talk shows. The newspaper runs an article speculating that Baltimore will suffer a nervous breakdown if it doesn't get the ball.

Meanwhile, the Maryland Conference of Social Concern has a list that should arouse similar anxiety and attract comparable capital from patriots seeking to improve Baltimore's quality of life and boost its economy. Unfortunately, this list is greeted with yawns instead of yells.

Besides crime, drugs, children having guns and children having children, here are a few of MCSC concerns:

- Intolerable living conditions in crime-and-drug infested neighborhoods that are crying out for attention.
- A shortage of affordable housing for the poor, working poor and elderly.
- A court system flooded with cases – about 270,000 pending before only 125 judges. About three-fourths of the cases involve families. A family court system is desperately needed in Maryland.
- A health system that leaves thousands of Marylanders without coverage.
- A lack of parent involvement in the schools, to create a safe, healthy and gun-free climate.
- A lack of neighborhood cohesion. Large and small communities must come together to promote racial harmony and respect for law.
- Urban decay and the crumbling of the infrastructure, particularly in Baltimore City, which must be recognized and supported as Maryland's primary city.

The list could go on.

Can these matters get some attention while we're fixed on getting the ball? Will they be addressed if we do get the ball? Or is that we just don't get it?

Two groups of investors and now a multimillionaire from Cleveland stand ready to put up millions to buy a football franchise and millions more to operate it. Baltimore ticket buyers already have committed millions more. And lottery ticket buyers and other already have coughed up millions for a new stadium.

How much private money, time and energy are available to rid Baltimore of its potentially fatal diseases, to restore it to health and make it more livable for residents and more attractive for tourists?

Bread or circuses? A steady diet or a shot in the arm? Which will benefit Baltimore the most in the long run? What are our values?

Can we cheer only for a so-called Baltimore team actually composed of out-of-town strangers confronting another motley crew of mercenaries nine Sunday afternoons a year – or can we learn to cheer for a genuine home team tackling real challenges?

On which ball should we keep our eye?

November 17, 1993

Fighting society's silence, 35 years after march

Friday will mark the 35th anniversary of the 1963 "March for Jobs and Freedom" when a quarter-million of us gathered at the Lincoln Memorial in Washington to protest racial discrimination in America.

One address at that historic event has reverberated through the years: the Rev. Martin Luther King, Jr.'s stirring "I Have a Dream." Other rousing orations were delivered by such speakers as A. Philip Randolph, Jr., founder and president of the Brotherhood of Sleeping Car Porters; Whitney Young, Jr. of the National Urban League; John Lewis of the Student Nonviolent Coordinating Committee; the Rev. Eugene Carson Blake, United Presbyterian Church in the USA; Water P. Reuther, United Automobile Workers; and Roy Wilkins of the National Association for the Advancement of Colored People.

While all dealt with the same theme, the call for jobs and freedom so long denied to black citizens, none had the rhetorical longevity of Mr. King's "I Have a Dream" speech. None so passionately moved a quarter-million listeners then and millions more since.

However, one that made an impact on me as an American Jew was that of Rabbi Joachim Prinz. He was national president of the American Jewish Congress, of which I was then the Maryland chapter president. He was also president of the Jewish Organization of Presidents.

The theme of his speech was the crime of silence, based on his experience as chief rabbi of Berlin during the rise of Hitler.

"America," he cried, "must not become like Germany, a nation of onlookers at evil. America must not remain silent. Not merely black America, but all of America. It must speak up and act, from the President down to the humblest of us, and not for the sake of the Negro, not for the sake of the black community, but for the sake of the idea and the aspiration of America itself.

"Our children," he continued, "yours and mine in every school across the land, each morning pledge allegiance to the flag of the United States and to the republic for which it stands. They speak fervently and innocently of this land as the land of 'liberty and justice for all'.

"The time, I believe, has come to work together, for it is not enough to hope together, to pray together. We must work together to make this oath a reality in a morally renewed and united America."

Those are words to live by today also. We must not remain silent about welfare reform and quietly resign ourselves to some of its outrageous provisions.

We cannot tolerate the one-size-fits-all solution to welfare of "go find a job." Young children cannot find jobs. The elderly and disabled cannot find jobs. The mother who cannot afford child care for her several children cannot seek a job. The uneducated cannot qualify for jobs that pay enough to support a family. Such weaknesses cannot be ignored and must be revised.

We cannot accept as political correctness that millions of low-income children and pregnant women must be left without basic health insurance coverage while we squander billions of dollars on unnecessary defense and pork-barrel spending. We cannot count upon states with no program yet in place and with shabby records on social justice to give priority to the unpopular issue of needy children and the elderly. We cannot remain indifferent to growing numbers of low-income children who have far less than they need and to tens of thousands of disabled poor children who receive little or no support other than welfare.

With so much in America to be proud of, how can we live with the shame that child poverty rates in the United States are higher than in some less wealthy nations. Welfare must be reformed, not repealed.

We are too silent about politicians who claim to care about children but who don't because neither they nor their mothers are voters or contributors.

We are too silent about the shameful fact that millions Americans in this wealthy nation are hungry or malnourished.

We are too silent in the midst of plenty, millions of

children live in poverty and are not getting enough food.

We are too silent that millions of Americans are homeless.

We are too silent that millions of the elderly are forced to choose between medicine and food because they cannot afford both and that millions of Americans do not have health insurance.

It has been said that a country can be judged by how it treats its poor. By that standard, this rich and powerful nation is not doing too well. It is time to break our silence, to speak out for liberty and justice for all and review the weaknesses of the Welfare Reform Act.

We must upgrade our concern about other neighbors' children living on streets awash with drugs and bristling with guns.

Silence is a crime not only against its victims, but also against ourselves.

August 25, 1998

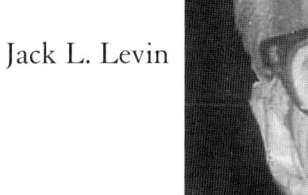

Jack L. Levin

Jack L. Levin

Mayor Theodore McKeldin and Jack L. Levin

Sidney Hollander Sr., Dr. Hyman Rubenstein, Rabbi Joachim Prinz, Jack L. Levin, Mayor Theodore McKeldin (l. to r.)

Chapter 3
Church/State Controversies
Aaron Margolis

Church and State

Following the end of World War II, the Supreme Court began to hear and decide a number of landmark cases dealing with religious freedom, in what was to become the decades long Court's involvement in church and state issues.

Many of the cases were initiated by or involved a Christian sect, Jehovah's Witnesses. They gave the impetus which secured the Court's pronouncements on religious freedom and upheld the constitutional principle of strict separation of church and state.

There were continuous efforts to whittle away that cherished principle as well as increased insensitivity of government officials to diverse religious beliefs and practices. Organizations such as the Civil Liberties Union, American Jewish Congress and Christians United for Separation of Church and State, all active in Maryland, were involved either as advocates for litigants or as "friends of the Court" in almost every case -- challenging efforts to deny or limit the separation and in ensuring its applications. These were cases involving the intrusion of religion in the public schools, local government participating in sectarian religious programs and the enforcement of Sunday "blue laws." One of the most significant cases was initiated in Baltimore challenging the practice of the recitation of prayers in opening exercises in the public schools. Most recently, the battle ground shifted to opposing the determined efforts of the Religious Right to promote Christian sectarian practices in all areas of public life.

To Jewish activists, teachings of the Torah were their guide for conduct and compassion for the oppressed, while the Bill of Rights was the bulwark of protection for the individual against the power and tyranny of the majority. Tzedakah (justice not charity) and tikkun olam (healing the world) have been the driving force in the fight for equal opportunity, effective welfare and poverty programs and in working for interfaith understanding.

      Jack Levin and other civil libertarian Jewish activists never missed an opportunity to lead that fight while acting out their Jewish heritage. To mention a few of their successes: the elimination of quotas which severely limited Jewish and other minority access to higher professional education, the enactment of fair employment practice laws and doing away with penalties for employees observing a day other than Sunday as their Sabbath. The Jack Levins of the world believe in and live the vigilance needed to preserve our religious freedom and diversity for the very orthodox believers as well as the secular humanists.

What the Bible says on prayer

Evangelicals calling for mandatory and preferably Christian prayer in the public schools might note the words of one of the first four Evangelists, Matthew, quoted in the New Testament (Matt, 6:5):

"And when thou prayest, thou shalt not be as the hypocrites are: for they love to pray standing .... in the corners of the streets, that they may be seen of men."

Isn't this one of the reasons why prayer is being urged for school children: "that they may be seen?" It must be, because there is nothing now to stop children from praying unseen, in school or anywhere else.

Matthew also warned his fellow Evangelists (Matt, 15:7-9):

"Well did Esaias prophesy of you, saying, This people draweth nigh unto me with their mouths, and honoureth me with their lips, but their heart is far from me. But in vain they do worship me ..."

In his epistle to his disciple Titus, the Apostle Paul said (Titus, 1:16):

"They profess that they know God; but in works they deny Him, being abominable, and disobedient, and unto every good work reprobate."

The Old Testament teaches us and our children (Isaiah 1:15): "And when ye spread forth your hands, I will hide Mine eyes from you; yea, when ye make many prayers, I will not hear; your hands are full of blood, wash you, make you clean ... cease to do evil, learn to do well, seek justice, relieve the oppressed, judge the fatherless, plead for the widow."

And Isaiah advises further, as a substitute for displays of penitence (58:6-7): ".... deal they bread to the hungry .... bring the poor that are cast out to they house .... thou seest the naked .... cover him."

But perhaps most noteworthy in the current campaign for enforced official school prayer and recitation of religiosity is the biblical comment by Apostle James (2:14-26):

"As the body without the spirit is dead, so faith without works is dead also."

What about "works?" Adults who must perform them tomorrow are today's children.

If children are to learn about the works that need doing – without which prayers are "the body without the spirit" – the teacher might well devote to meaningful prayer the time she would have spent presiding over a mindless sectarian incantation.

A few suggestions for the children to implore, beseech and entreat:

~ Pray for a verifiable bilateral nuclear freeze, that our nation renounce a nuclear first-strike and cancel weapons designed for this purpose, and that humankind develop the capacity to comprehend present nuclear arsenals more powerful than a million Hiroshimas.

~ Pray that our leaders come to understand the deep-rooted, ages-old misery and despair in our own hemisphere and throughout the world, which fuels the revolutionary fires that our leaders call communist plots.

~ Pray that the parents not visit upon the children and grandchildren, the obligation to reduce America's horrendous, disastrous budgetary deficits.

~ Pray that the majority not turn away from over 34 million of our fellow Americans who live below the poverty level.

~ Pray that we not continue to cut programs to aid our poor and elderly neighbors: school lunch and nutrition, food, shelter and medical assistance.

One such prayer each morning would cover a five-day week. The schedule could be repeated each week, or until the words start losing meaning, as most prayer. Then, some of the following might be substituted:

~ Pray for the preservation of American unity-in-diversity, or majority respect for the equal rights and dignity of minorities.

~ Pray that no effort be made, under the guise of religion,

to enforce conformity of young children by making them feel like outcasts if they pray differently or at all, or like a sub-class of dubious level that is suffered out of the goodness of the believers.

~ Pray to broaden our minds and help us to feel concern not only for ourselves, our fellow citizens and fellow nationals, but also our fellow humans, millions of whom are starving and enduring daily torments to us unimaginable.

~ Pray to understand that "humanitarian" is not a dirty word meaning "wimp", "atheist" or "subversive" or worse, but is defined as a "person devoted to promoting the welfare of humanity, especially the elimination of pain and suffering."

~ Pray to live by the words of an American general-statesman-editor-humanitarian, Carl Schurz, who said, "Our country, right or wrong. When right is to be kept right' when wrong to be made right."

Such daily supplications in the school might lead future generations to "works" without which faith is dead.

Meanwhile, denominational praying will continue to thrive where it has long languished, in the churches, synagogues, tents, mosques, homes and hearts of the family. Nowhere in the Old or New Testament or the Constitution of the United States are public school children instructed to perform some homogenized mockery of religion.

Bible Reading

The atheist boy's protest against Bible reading in class and his mother's refusal to send him to school are being criticized for a wide variety of wrong reasons. Some say the protest is wicked and immoral, presumably because it violates our Judeo-Christian traditions during the cold war against a nation with a different religion; the worship of Marx and Lenin and adoration of current disciples in the Kremlin. Others say it is silly and trivial, because the refusal of one maverick to conform to majority standards is of no consequence when compared to other problems and crises, and undeserving of all the newspaper space devoted to it.

We say that the issue is significant. The basic American freedom of religion means tolerance not only of the beliefs but also the nonbeliefs of others. The important matter here is not what the boy and his mother believe or do not believe, not whether their conviction is good or bad, useful or useless, pleasing or displeasing, but whether they have the right to practice an unpopular faith that does not interfere, with the rights for safety of other citizens.

The right to be different, to stand out against the state and the majority, is the meaning of freedom that makes our country, in its diversity and unorthodoxy, the hope of the world ...

November 6, 1966

Just One Day

Editor: Dr. Alfred Gottschalk has rendered a valuable service in noting in his October 4 *Sun* article the deep universal significance of Yom Kippur, the Day of Atonement, in compelling us to "choose life" and to "confront the collective conscience of the Judeo-Christian heritage."

The trouble with the Day of Atonement – as with Christmas Day and its message of peace and good will to mankind – is that it's for one day a year.

Why are we disappointed, or surprised that these one-day-a-year efforts to rise above our human nature have failed to change it much?

It has been formed over two million years if you start counting with the appearance of *homo habilis* who began using stone tools, or over 450,000 years at least if you start with *homo sapiens* – according to the World Book Encyclopedia.

In all those eons, those hundreds of millions of days of gestation of our nature, the Jews have devoted only a few thousand Yom Kippurs and the Christians less than two thousand Christmas Days to trying to improve their human nature, while spending 364 times that many days abusing it.

Perhaps it's worth a bit more effort – like just a few moments each morning – examining our shameful behavior yesterday and vowing to do better today, not on grand abstractions but on the simple routines and details of our daily lives, the repetition of little acts at work and home that really determine our nature.

Perhaps we need to put more faith in everyday deeds of decency and kindness than in one-day wonders.

October 13, 1986

Save the Children

"I don't want any privilege for myself or my family that other people do not have. It makes me uneasy in my conscience to have opportunities that are denied to other people."

So said humanitarian Sidney Hollander, Sr., Maryland's beloved warrior for social justice, who died 20 years ago. His memory was honored again recently at Har Sinai Congregation, when the Maryland Chapter of the American Jewish Congress presented its annual Sidney Hollander Award of Distinction to Ruth Wolff Rehfeld, who has served many Baltimore area community service organizations as volunteer and staff person.

If Sidney Hollander, Sr. is looking down on the society he devoted his life to improving, he might wonder if much has improved. He would see:

Three out of four low-income Maryland families are at constant risk of running out of food, usually toward the end of each month, when food stamps have been exhausted. Over 60,000 children are hungry in the land of pleasant living.

Hungry children suffer two to three times as many health problems as better-fed kids, and they fall behind in school or drop out.

U.S. infant mortality statistics resemble those of impoverished Third-World countries.

Seeing all this, when other Americans are splurging $50,000 on a car and hundreds of thousands of dollars on a yacht, Sidney might wonder if many today feel any twinges of conscience at having privileges and opportunities denied to the less fortunate.

He might recall his 1939 testimony, as president of the National Jewish Community Relations Advisory Committee, before the joint Senate/House Committee on Immigration, pleading to save Jewish children from the impending Holocaust. (He was advocating adoption of the German Refugee Bill, which got nowhere.)

Reporting on a fact-finding trip to Europe, he stood before the people's representatives, whom he later referred to as the "stony-faced inquisitors." They listened to the eye-witness accounts of cruelties "without change of expression."

Sidney said of the children's parents, who were facing extermination: "Such a fate they were prepared to meet, almost with resignation, for themselves; their agony was for their children. Toward these they felt as you and I would were our own left without home, without protection and at the mercy of a merciless state. The same question met me everywhere: Will America do nothing for them? Do the people there not understand?

".... Is there no chance? Will not America open its doors? I reminded her how tens of thousands have been kept alive through our help. America has always been kind to children, and America is still America."

Was it then? Is it now? Are we again abandoning our children?

Sidney Hollander died before the Reagan-Bush cultivation of self-indulgence, irresponsibility, suspicion and even hostility toward the poor.

In Sidney's time, we rejected "a flood of alien hordes." Today, we reject our own children. We have other priorities. Again we turn our backs on what we don't want to see: children in pain, denied refuge, food, shelter, nurture and life itself. We don't set them adrift on rafts; we just set them adrift on the streets and ignore them until they rob or murder us for a drug fix.

Then we pay attention and pay to support them, not in homes but in jails.

Is this the kinder, gentler America? Can we, who are so generous in responding to the plight of one child victim publicized on TV, do little or nothing to rescue millions of kids in distress, whose stories are so common that they are not news?

In the endless debates of the current election campaign, which candidate is addressing the questions being asked by poor parents speaking for thousands and millions of poor children:

Why must we be hungry and homeless in this bountiful land?

Where do we eat and sleep tonight?

We're illiterate; how can we go to school or get job training?

We're in rags; where do we get decent clothes?

We're sick; how can we afford to see a doctor?

Will anybody take care of us while our mother is out working for minimum wages, or looking for work that does not exist?

Will any candidate talk to us who are too young to vote, or too un-middle-class?

Many Americans are listening and responding. Many are hard-working but frustrated volunteers in social service organizations whose budgets have been drastically cut or eliminated as needs multiply.

But too many of us again turn away. We say, "We've got our own troubles," without considering that one of our biggest is our forgotten children.

June 15, 1992

In the Jews, God Findeth a Cheerful Giver

In the midst of recession affecting everybody, The Associated, the Jewish community federation of Baltimore, has just completed another successful campaign of fund-raising. That's good news for non-Jewish as well as Jewish charities.

Half or more of all giving by Jewish individuals now goes to support charitable organizations serving the general community, according to a recent report on Jewish philanthropy. It has been estimated that American Jews, who compose only 2.4 percent of the population, provide about 5 percent of all philanthropy to secular causes in the United States. This means that Jewish support of non-Jewish charities is about twice the national norm.

In proportion to population, Jews are 23 times as likely to establish a charitable foundation as Catholics, and about 12 times as likely as Protestants. (However, only one Jewish foundation is among the nation's 100 largest, Baltimore's Weinberg Foundation.)

About 10 years ago, Gwinn Owens, then editor of the Op-Ed page of The Evening Sun, pointed out that Jewish philanthropy to the arts in Maryland was far disproportionate to the Jewish percentage of population. He scolded wealthy non-Jews for failure to give higher priority to support of the arts and urged them to emulate the Jewish example.

The reasons for Jewish generosity include above-average income resulting from above-average education and motivation. More important is the Jewish attitude toward the poor and disenfranchised, a direct consequence of both recent and ancient Jewish history.

The present Jewish generation consists of immigrants, their children and grandchildren, who knew poverty not from the media or hearsay but from personal, often searing, experience. The immediate Jewish reaction to the poor is not avoidance, revulsion or outright hostility, but more like there-but–for-the-grace-of-God-go-I.

Even Jewish yuppies are not as far removed as most

Americans from discrimination and deprivation. Their forebears escaped to a hard life as immigrants from an even harder life in the shtetls, the bleak villages of Eastern Europe. Struggling to put food on the table, they nevertheless covered its bare surface with a white cloth and kindled Sabbath lights. Barely eking out a living, they had yet encouraged their children to pursue learning, to take voice lessons, to practice playing the violin. Their descendants are inclined to value the quality of life and to support the arts.

But Jewish charity goes further back in time. Its roots reach deep into the Old Testament.

Some of the biblical laws (mitzvot) are in effect a kind of tax upon citizens for the benefit of the poor. In addition to tithing, the sabbatical year was instituted so "that the poor of the people may eat," and so that debts could be canceled.

Jews are not conditioned to follow the David Dukes, Pat Buchanans and others who exploit resentment of and hostility toward the poor, who want to put them out of sign and mind, and to be rid of them by imprisonment and worse.

The words that most Jews live by are the words taught in Deuteronomy: "If there be among you a needy man ... thou shalt not harden thy heart nor shut thy hand unto him and shall surely lend him sufficient for his need ... [If] thine eye be evil against thy needy brother and thou give him naught ... it be sin in thee."

The Hebrew word for charity is the same as that for justice and righteousness. Since the ancient prophets Isaiah and Ezekiel, Jews have been taught that charity is an indispensable requirement for a life of piety. Ezekiel preached that Sodom was destroyed due to its lack of charity.

The virtues of charity and its heavenly reward have been studied by Jews in the books of Job and Esther and throughout millennia in the Talmud and rabbinic literature. Jewish scholars like Rabbi Assi have argued that charity is as important as all the other commandments put together, that it atones for sins and ensures that the giver will have wise, wealthy and learned sons.

Countless generations of rabbis have instructed that

everybody, without exception, is obliged to give charity. Even one who is himself dependent on charity is obliged to give to those less fortunate. Judges have compelled the non-giver to donate according to the court's assessment of his means, and if he refused, to be flogged and to have a sufficient amount of his property confiscated to meet the court's assessment. Rabbis have ruled that one must not give away more than a fifth of his wealth lest he become impoverished himself.

No wonder Jews are good at giving. It is a sacred vow they've been preaching and practicing for a long time. It is the "pushka" that was a cherished institution in every Jewish home, the little tin charity box which many generations fondly remember as their first sense of Jewish identity.

February 29, 1992

Chapter 4

"Of Cabbages and Kings"
Elayne Fedder

This chapter includes an eclectic collection of writings by Jack Levin, profiling Baltimore, Maryland and national figures, some well-known, to others less so, but who have contributed importantly to society. They include Lee L. Dopkin, the pioneer of Maryland's old age pension law which became a model for the national Social Security legislation, along with a comparison of Maryland Senator Paul S. Sarbanes and Maryland Governor Theodore R. McKeldin, two politicians so different in style but alike in substance.

Other comparisons include that of H. L. Mencken, "the Sage of Hollins Street," the quintessential cynic who had contempt for most people, a "northern racist," with Gerald W. Johnson, a "Southern liberal," consistently fair and tolerant.

A favorite son of Baltimore, the first black member of the U.S. Supreme Court, Justice Thurgood Marshall most celebrated for his victory in the landmark Brown vs. Topeka Board of Education decision is also profiled. Others featured in the chapter include Rabbi Samuel Rosenblatt, champion of civil rights; Sidney Hollander, Sr., an unconventional philanthropist and social activist; and William Donald Schaefer, former Baltimore mayor and Maryland governor.

These and other writings reflect the turbulent times, the fight for civil rights, civil liberties, and peace all represent Mr. Levin's unflagging insight and commitment to social justice.

Sidney Hollander, Sr.
A boat-rocker all his life

A quarter century after his death, one realizes how sorely missed and badly needed today are the unique leadership qualities of the Baltimore social activist, industrialist and philanthropist, Sidney Hollander, Sr.

He had the ability to inspire and arouse people to become participants instead of spectators in the struggle for social justice. He once stated as a guiding principle, "I don't want any privilege for myself or my family that other people do not have."

Today, Sidney Hollander would cry out that we are preoccupied with material goods and political inanities, while ignoring and denying the sufferings, despair and rage of millions of children and adolescents suffering hunger, sickness and homelessness. He would be making every effort, locally and nationally, to rouse the public from its slumber.

He did that so well that in 1940, a leader of the Junior League of America who had heard him scold other organizations, invited him to rouse the league out of its torpor by addressing its national convention in Seattle.

Sidney readily accepted. He told his hostesses that their public image was that of odd creatures from the social register photographed at dog shows and on Florida beaches; silly debutantes playing make-believe with things they did not understand; alternating between teas and cocktail parties. How, he asked, could he talk to such a bunch about democracy and social work?

He went on as follows: "Never was there a time in the history of our country when it was so possible to provide people with the things they need. Our supplies of food, steel, glass, lumber, and cement are so huge that none should have to go without. Industry has produced countless gadgets to ease the burden of toil for many of us. Yet, in the midst of all this bounty, millions lack food, clothing, shelter and all things that should contribute to security and the satisfaction of life."

That excoriating speech has been called the start of the transformation of the Junior League into a social constructive organization. Its projects in Baltimore include public advocacy, library projects, Children's House at Johns Hopkins Hospital, family centers that offer prevention-oriented programs for adults and children, a thrift shop, New Start Furnishings for homeless families and other good works.

Denied a diploma

Sidney Hollander was a boat-rocker all his life. When he graduated from Baltimore City College in 1916, he was denied his diploma because he had written an editorial in the school newspaper upbraiding the administration for its shortcomings. Fifty years later, City College finally awarded its distinguished graduate his high school diploma.

Sidney and his brother Walter started a pharmaceutical manufacturing firm. One of their products was the cough suppressant, REM. The firm was later sold to a larger company for a sum that provided the basis for Sidney's many philanthropies.

His success as a businessman and philanthropist won acceptance, credibility and respectability for Sidney's advocacy of racial integration and equality – ideas that might otherwise have been spurned by some of his peers.

Sidney grew up in an exciting time when America was feeling its oats. As a young man, he was caught up in the national euphoria ignited by Theodore Roosevelt's big-stick policies asserting America's new strength, but Sidney was also sensitive to America's shortcomings. He was a patriot, but also a constructive critic. He made some enemies, but never lost their respect.

In his honor, the Maryland Chapter of the American Jewish Congress in 1965 established the Sidney Hollander Award of Distinction to a person seen as trying to follow in his footsteps. I was honored the first year. Recipients include Jacob J. Edelman, labor lawyer; Rabbi Samuel Rosenblatt; Sen. Joseph D. Tydings; Rabbi Israel M. Goldman, a leader in the civil rights movement; Esther Lazarus, a pioneer in social service; Dr. Hyman S.

Rubenstein, psychiatrist and president of the Maryland Chapter; Sen. Charles McC. Mathias; City Councilman Alexander Stark; Dr. Harry Bard, founder of the community college movement in Baltimore; Sen. Paul Sarbanes; the Rev. Joseph M. Connolly; Judge Robert B. Watts and the Rev. Frederick Hanna, jointly, as champions of civil liberties and rights; and Ruth Wolf Rehfeld, social activist and community leader. This year's honoree is John Ferron, former director of the Baltimore Human Rights Commission.

Sidney Hollander set the pace for social action for years to come. Events of the past quarter-century have weakened our faith in government and our power to influence it. Sidney Hollander's life reminds us that we have the power if we have the will. He made it more fun to do good than to do nothing.

February 21, 1997

Sidney Hollander's 80th Birthday Party

Attending a recent affair at the newly restored Belvedere, and recalling glittering occasions there during the thirties, forties, fifties and sixties, it occurred to me that the most unusual, joyous, witty, meaningful and memorable of all was the Sidney Hollander, Sr. 80th birthday party.

It was a sort-of-but-not-quite testimonial tribute to the unconventional philanthropist and social activist, held in the Charles Room on Thursday evening, January 11, 1962.

About 150 of Sidney's friends arranged and attended the salute to the beloved warrior who had contributed so much to Baltimore's progress and elimination of racial discrimination.

They were a motley mixture: great merchants, Albert Hutzler, Sr. and the Albert Berneys of Hamburger's; Windsor Hills friends, the Shackman Katzes, a labor leader; Angela Bambace; newspaper people, the Carl Murphys and Louis Azraels; lawyers, Eugene Feinblatt (the toastmaster), Francis Murnaghan and Bill Engleman; political leaders Governor McKeldin, Councilman Jacob Edelman and congressional candidate Warren Buckler; Judges Reuben Oppenheimer, Albert Blum, Robert B. Watts and Thomas J. S. Waxter; psychiatrists Manfred Guttmacher and Jerome Frank; a surgeon Mark Gann; doctors Frank Furstenberg, Ludwig Edelstein and Edgar Freedenwald; educators Martin Jenkins, Henry Waskow and Una Corbett; a clergyman Don Frank Fenn; manufacturers and businessmen Ben Katzner, Joseph Davidson, Sandy Frank, Leon Ginsberg and Lester Levy; a stockbroker Stanley Brager; civic leaders and activists William Boucher, Caroline Ramsay and Joseph Rauh; insurance actuaries Ralph and Norma Edwards; social justice professionals Harry Greenstein, Furman Templeton, Leon Sachs and Ruth Fegley; and professors, Ernest Feise, Raymond Hawes and Broadus Mitchell, who made one of the memorable cracks of the evening.

It came after the remarks by Albert Hutzler, Sr. Mr. Hutzler and Mr. Hollander and their families had been close friends through three generations. They had taken trips together. Practically every Sunday and every Christmas Eve for more than half a century they had met, talked and watched their children grow up. They had hardly ever agreed on anything – the progressive Sidney and the conservative Albert – but they had disagreed most agreeably, with deep respect and affection for each other.

On this occasion, Albert, commenting on the fact that the controversial Sidney was scheduled for surgery for a minor throat ailment, said: "It's a shame Sidney had to spend money to have his throat cut, when so many people would have been glad to do it for nothing."

Then Broadus Mitchell, the Hopkins professor of economics, said "This is the first time in memory that a member of the Johns Hopkins Board of Trustees (Albert Hutzler) was ever funny on purpose." Incidentally, Dr. Mitchell, also a confirmed dissenter, who taught at Hopkins from 1919 to 1939, then at Occidental, NYU, Rutgers and Hofstra, is said to be living happily in Greenwich Village and to have nearly total recall of his years in Baltimore and other events in his long life. He was a close friend of the Hollanders and named his son after Sidney.

Friendship and love spiced with wit and humor, pervaded that occasion. There were toasts by Howard Murphy, Leon Sacks and Judge Waxter. It was recalled that, 10 years earlier, at Sidney's 70th birthday party given him by friends in Chicago, Sidney had responded to the lavish tributes with these words: "I've listened carefully to all that has been said this evening and I find nothing with which I can possibly disagree. At no point have the descriptions of my character, abilities, or achievements been exaggerated. If anything, they have erred by understatements; and such omissions, I trust, will be corrected before the evening is over."

Aided by fine wines and champagne and abetted by gourmet treats, the good-humored repartee accelerated to prepared and impromptu songs to Sidney, like one I recall to the tune of Abdul Abul Amir: "There are men in this town who have won great renown/ at medicine, banking and law/ but that champion, Sid, with the heard of a kid/ is the one whom we all hold in awe."

We held him in greater awe when the feast arrived. For, although the Belvedere banquet was characteristically regal and sumptuous, the committee had decided that, on Sidney's birthday, he should have his favorite dishes. So he was served oysters on the half shell, roast duck, two bowls of onion soup and two strawberry ice cream sundaes – and put it all away with gusto.

Although this was more than two years before passage of the civil rights law of 1964, and integrated parties were uncommon, many black persons were present. Practically all the guests had at one time or another visited the Hollander home, where the warmth of the welcome was related not to race but to merit and social contribution. Sidney once told an interviewer: "I don't want any privilege for myself or my family that other people do not have. It makes me uneasy in my conscience to have opportunities that are denied to other people."

Sidney's love of people, shared by all in attendance, filled the Charles Room like a warm glow on that cold winter night in 1962. When it came time for the 80th birthday boy to respond to all that had been said by all the speakers, including myself, Sidney said: "I want to invite all of you now to come back here to the Belvedere for my 90th birthday party – that is, those of you who happen to be alive at that time."

Sidney just made it to his 90th, although many of the guests did not. His battle for social justice continued for another 10 full years, in behalf of the poor, the black, the aged, the young and the sick.

Sidney Hollander, Sr.

Editor: Recent racial incidents recall the 15th anniversary this month of the passing of Baltimore's beloved battler for human and civil rights, Sidney Hollander, Sr.

No citizen of this state– except perhaps Thomas Kennedy, whose "Jew Bill" in 1826 finally conceded full citizenship to Maryland Jews –ever worked harder or longer to break down racial discrimination, segregation and social injustice. Sidney's simple explanation of his commitment to black progress was that he did not want any opportunities for himself or his family that were denied to others.

The latest racial outbreaks in New York and Massachusetts as well as North Carolina and Georgia are only the tip of the iceberg. Racism is still alive in both North and South.

The reports of its death are grossly exaggerated by those who choose to see only the undeniable racial progress in our laws and life since Sidney Hollander and others went to war against bigotry.

The sad fact is that there is not now, never has been, and probably never will be absolute color blindness in race relations. That is the pretense fostered by the present administration and by those who believe that 200 years of oppressing minorities can be undone quickly and painlessly, without inconvenience to the majority.

Government indifference and hostility to civil rights must give way to leadership. Our entire nation – not just its underclass – suffers tremendous loss of human potential in our inner cities, where poverty, unemployment, ignorance, drugs and crime are ignored at our own peril.

We can honor the memory of Sidney Hollander, Sr. and his fellow fighters by supporting passage of the Civil Rights Restoration Act and rededicating ourselves to the yet unresolved struggle for racial justice.

Rabbi Samuel Rosenblatt

Dear Sir: As a long-time colleague of Rabbi Samuel Rosenblatt in many endeavors, I was privileged to present to him, at the Gold Jubilee dinner of the Maryland Chapter of the American Jewish Congress, its highest honor, The Sidney Hollander Award of Distinction. The time was October 21, 1968, the place the Beth Tfiloh Auditorium, crowded to capacity. I think that the tribute paid then is relevant now as a memorial to the beloved rabbi of Beth Tfiloh, distinguished scholar, author, founder and past president of the Maryland Chapter of the American Jewish Congress.

I appreciate this opportunity to share with your readers a chrestomathy of his leadership as a citizen, his contributions of wisdom, guidance, enrichment and inspiration to our city, state and nation, and his tireless work for *l'tokayn olam* – improving the world into the kingdom of the Almighty,

Rabbi Rosenblatt perceived long ago that the fight against anti-Semitism was part of a bigger battle; the fight for social justice for all Americans in a free society; that equality and justice are inseparable and indivisible; that discrimination in jobs, housing, education and public accommodations, and indifference to the sufferings of the disadvantaged, are intolerable.

As Congress president and as rabbi, he declared Judaism to be the conscience of our country and its servant through social action. Through his newspaper columns and lectures, Rabbi Rosenblatt constantly conveyed to the total community the views that he expressed in the synagogue.

Here are a few examples of these words of wisdom that reached hundreds of thousands of Marylanders regularly.

In discussing the injustice of Negro anti-Semitism, Rabbi Rosenblatt nevertheless pointed out – at the time of the civil disturbances; "To assert that the race-riots reflect the sentiments of the entire Negro community is to brand all its constituents as lawbreakers. This is an undeserved slur.

"The overwhelming majority of Afro-Americans are

peaceful, law-abiding citizens, like most other Americans. The arsonists, riots and looters comprised only a small minority.

"The lot of our Negroes most certainly stands in need of improvement. Although it is impossible to solve all their problems overnight, the implementation of the plans for their solution, which is long overdue, must by all means be accelerated."

In warning that immature African nations can easily fall prey to demagogues, he said:

"An oft-quoted axiom of democracy is the declaration that 'all men are created free and equal.' Nothing could be further from the truth. Freedom is an achievement, not a gift bestowed at birth."

"Equality is a right conferred by law, not a condition inherent in nature."

In the fighting of drug addiction, Rabbi Rosenblatt proposed a characteristically Jewish solution. He said:

"For at least three thousand years we Jews have managed to escape an affliction that still plagues a large portion of the human race today, exacting a heavy toll of human life, health and happiness."

"Our group has been relative free of alcoholism. How did we do it?"

"Not by being teetotalers. In fact, it is mandatory in our religion to usher in the weekly Sabbath as well as the major festivals by pronouncing a blessing over wine."

"Yet it has rarely happened that one of our number should have filled himself up with liquor to the point of intoxication. Why? On account of the social disapproval of such conduct. A sure way to stamp out drug addiction would be to put it on the social blacklist. The moment such practices cease to be fashionable, they shrivel up of their own accord."

On intergroup relations, Rabbi Rosenblatt said: "The salvation of the world will not be affected by orgies of bloodshed and mutual destruction. It will come about when men will turn their swords into ploughshares and their spears into pruning hooks, when nation will no longer lift up sword against nation nor practice anymore for war."

"Instead of planning each other's annihilation, the nations of the earth should strive for the improvement of the human lot as a whole and for the combating of disease and poverty and ignorance and crime."

Rabbi Rosenblatt believed that the United Nations must be reformed, but must be preserved. He said:

"Whenever the interests of a larger power were involved, it has proven virtually impotent in stopping aggression or in prevailing upon the feuding parties to reconcile their differences. Yet, whether it be for better or for worse, the United Nations is the only instrument at the disposal of the human race for heading off a third global conflict, which every forward-looking statesman admits would spell the end of civilization, if not the total annihilation of humanity itself."

Of Israel, and its right to survive, Rabbi Rosenblatt told the total public:

"It would most certainly be asking too much to expect the little state, composed mostly of survivors of death camps, crematories and gas chambers, surrounded by people committed to its destruction, to exercise virtual suicide by demanding that it give up, before peace is assured, the advantageous strategic position it has achieved thanks to the ongoing belligerency and avowed evil designs of its enemies. Israel retreated once and was betrayed. Such a mistake will not be knowingly repeated by her."

On the war in Vietnam, Rabbi Rosenblatt asked, before it was popular to oppose the war:

"Are the sacrifices in human life and material worth what we hope in the end to gain? If the Vietnamese themselves have no stomach to fight for their interests, why should we put ourselves out for them? Although we are the most affluent and powerful nation on earth, do we have either the manpower or the resources to serve as the world's policeman indefinitely?"

These are but a few of the many vital issues on which Rabbi Rosenblatt constantly spoke out.

We can truly say of our gentle friend that the words of his

mouth and the meditations of his heart were most acceptable in our sight. They, and he, will be sorely missed.

Theodore R. McKeldin

Theodore R. McKeldin was born 98 years ago tomorrow into a working-class family in South Baltimore. In his long life of public service, he became Maryland's most successful politician, serving two terms each as mayor of Baltimore and governor of Maryland.

He would have found incredible the widespread use today of polling by candidates, who put a finger to the wind to see what position they should take.

Parade leader

McKeldin did not follow the parade he led it by persuasion, conviction and shoe leather politicking. He moved people from where they were to where he believed they should be, persuading the majority to change their mind. He was guided only by principles that he sincerely believed in.

Many in the Maryland GOP disagreed with him on key issues, but he controlled the party because he was a recognized winner, having been elected governor in 1950 and 1954. He was elected mayor of Baltimore in 1942 and 1962.

He did not wait for opposition to social injustice, religious, ethnic and gender discrimination to become politically correct before vigorously attacking those prevalent attitudes. When he knew that something was wrong, he blasted it.

I first heard him speak in the 1950s before an all-white, Protestant crowd in a Northeast Baltimore car dealership.

In off-the-cuff remarks, he described a recent trip to Israel, where he had visited biblical sites and had stood and where the miracle of the ingathering of exiles was taking place.

He spoke with increasing emotion, pausing to wipe tears from his eyes. I could not believe what I was seeing and hearing. Certainly his political astuteness made him aware that this audience could have cared less about what he felt, but he nevertheless told them what he thought they should hear.

Later, when he couldn't swallow the beliefs of Republican presidential candidate Barry Goldwater, McKeldin vented his strong opposition in a speech that I wrote for him endorsing the

Democratic candidacy of Lyndon B. Johnson.

He was a trailblazer in Maryland's move away from radical discrimination and toward equality.

Through persuasion and, in some cases, voluntary acts of good human relations, McKeldin opened many new positions to African Americans. He appointed the first black policy magistrate, John L. Berry. He created what would become the state's first human relations commission.

He named the first black members to state boards overseeing health, welfare and education. He called for admission of black students to the "A" course at Polytechnic Institute.

He enthusiastically supported the repeal of all Jim Crow laws, even when speaking on Maryland's Eastern Shore, then a hot-bed of segregation.

He worked intensely on desegregation of the state's parks, beaches and buses. He opposed the Vietnam War and capital punishment. He expressed shame that he had yielded to public pressure in allowing the execution of four people.

Another of McKeldin's special qualities was civility. I recall being in his campaign headquarters with some of his aides after midnight, waiting for McKeldin to return from a campaign speech at the Frederick fair. When he returned around 1 a.m., fresh and invigorated, his sleepy campaign manager told him that Democratic Mayor Tommy D'Alesandro Jr. had roasted him mercilessly on television that evening in supporting his opponent, University of Maryland President H.C. Byrd. The manager urged him to respond in the strongest way to the attack. McKeldin answered, "Oh no. Tommy is my friend. He was just talking politics."

The secret of McKeldin's success in Maryland politics was that he was more democratic than the Democrats.

November 19, 1998

Sarbanes and McKeldin Compared

Editor: A little socioanalysis may be more useful than the psychoanalysis of Senator Paul Sarbanes attempted recently by Drs. Peter Jay and Ray Jenkins.

The phenomenon of Mr. Sarbanes compares in some respects to former Mayor Theodore R. McKeldin. The comparison may stretch belief. No two politicians ever so differed in style – Republican McKeldin oratorial, emotional, exuberantly extraverted; Democrat Sarbanes soft-spoken, logical and reserved; one a produce of Dale Carnegie, the pulpit and platform, the other of Princeton, Harvard and TV. But they were alike in substance, in pursuit of justice and a decent life for the disadvantage, in striving to improve their world.

They were similar also in their readiness to risk hostility and defeat in defense of their principles, and in their capacity for leadership through example and persuasion – a talent sorely missing in this day of the Great Communicator.

Communication is not leadership. Communication can be simply finding out what people want to hear and then telling and retelling it. It can be appeals to prejudice, ignorance, bigotry, jingoism and greed while calling them common sense, wisdom, patriotism and enlightened self-interest. It can be expressing the most insane, homicidal and suicidal ideas in dulcet tones that make them sound rational, caring and, above all, non-threatening.

That was not the way of Mr. McKeldin. He not only told racists what they did not want to hear, but he made many of them accept the inevitability if not the morality of social justice which they bitterly resented and resisted. He did what was supposed to be politically impossible; got himself elected twice governor of Maryland and twice mayor of Baltimore by sticking out his neck, by daring to appeal to the best in voters, by bringing them up to his level instead of descending to theirs.

So does Paul Sarbanes. He is not "brooding". He is still energetically breeding respect for the basic values in American tradition and law that a so-called conservative administration is trying its damndest to subvert.

Bucking the government-inspired vogue of trashing liberties, he is breeding confidence that we can return to our senses.

He is breeding hope that Americans will recognize again the one great superiority of the American system over those we are spending billions of dollars to defend against – the uniquely American Bill of Rights.

Senator Sarbanes is telling us what some of us don't want to hear; that patriotism does not mean Christianity, conformity, majority rule in the schoolroom and bedroom, and our country right or wrong. He reminds us what "God Bless America" and the Stars and Stripes really stand for; separation and petitioning for redress of grievances; peoples' right to be secure in their persons and houses against unreasonable search and snooping, to get due process of law and to enjoy equal protection of the law – and a lot of other stuff we don't want to be made to think about in our present smugness.

By the 1988 senatorial election, negative developments and positive leadership will have returned enough voters to reality to re-elect Paul Sarbanes by an even greater majority than in 1982.

Considering the cyclical, volatile nature of our politics, the absence of such lucky breaks as constantly falling oil prices to offset blunders, and the workings of the law of gravity on a deficit-weighted economy, that is not an unreasonable prediction. The "patient" will very likely survive his "doctors".

March 25, 1985

Lessons for Us All from McKeldin

Sir: Before the memories of Theodore R. McKeldin are congealed into monuments, it is important that practicing politicians learn the lessons that emerge from the life of Maryland's most successful politician.

Lesson: You do not have to dodge every controversial issue, abandon belief in human decency, dignity, fairness and honor, sacrifice every moral, principle and cynically appeal to the worst in the voter in order to get yourself elected.

Lesson: Even though – like McKeldin – you crave victory so badly you can taste it and will compromise, concede, equivocate, rationalize, and negotiate almost without limit to win, there must remain always a boundary, a line beyond which you will never retreat, even if defending it means defeat and political death.

Lesson: The voters cannot like and respect you when you no longer like or respect yourself.

Lesson: Eventually, they seek a man who leads and does not follow them, who appeals to their better and not their baser instincts, because they know they are composed of both and want to become better persons than they are.

Lesson: Although honesty and integrity do not always pay they pay more often than deceit and cynicism in the long haul. The fight for civil rights for all Americans was the line beyond which McKeldin never retreated.

It should be remembered that McKeldin as candidate led that struggle long before the Supreme Court decision, when members of minority groups in Baltimore could not buy food in most restaurants, use a public washroom in an emergency, get a job in city or state departments, even the fire department, work on a hospital staff or attend state and city colleges.

McKeldin could have played it safe by appealing to the prevailing majority racism, or, at least, by evading, avoiding or obfuscating the issue, but he never did.

He dared to open the Polytechnic "A" course to black

students before the law required it, to end racial desegregation on state employment applications, to appoint the first black magistrates and deputy sheriffs, to employ minority members in the public domain, to name the first members of the state Commission on Inter-Racial Problems and Relations, to support repeal of Jim Crow laws, to abolish segregation in the Maryland National Guard, and to condemn at every opportunity – in public and private life – the practice of racial and religious discrimination that he abhorred.

His opponents, like Dr. H.C. Byrd in the election of 1954, tried hard to develop and exploit majority resentment against McKeldin, but they failed.

In the end, the good citizens voted for McKeldin, the good man who could be counted on to diligently practice what he eloquently preached.

August 27, 1974

Thurgood Marshall: Favorite Son left behind rich legacy

Today makes the anniversary of a major event in the long struggle for civil rights and civil liberties for all Americans.

Exactly 31 years ago, Baltimore's Thurgood Marshall was sworn in as the first black member of the U.S. Supreme Court. The event capped Marshall's long career as chief legal counsel to the National Association for the Advancement of Colored People. He had been nominated to the high court by President Lyndon B. Johnson and confirmed by the Senate after extended, difficult hearings.

On the honor roll of great Baltimoreans whose accomplishments have saved, improved or enriched millions of lives – such men as the Baltimore merchant Johns Hopkins, who founded one of the world's great hospitals; Enoch Pratt, creator of Baltimore's libraries; Dr. Abel Wolman, a pioneer in water purification; Edgar Allan Poe and H.L. Mencken in literature – no name shines brighter than Thurgood Marshall for making legal history.

Baltimore's history of racial discrimination is well-known. As late as 1947, black students could not enroll at the University of Maryland; it was then that the first black police sergeant was appointed.

In 1948, an interracial tennis march was staged in Druid Hill Park in defiance of Park Board policy and 34 people were arrested.

It was not until 1949 that a black man was permitted to become a licensed plumber.

A Roosevelt Ally

Early on, Marshall had strong allies, including Eleanor Roosevelt, who said later that it was a time when "the country as a whole was making more progress toward ridding itself of discrimination based on race than in any comparable period since Reconstruction.

"It was a time that saw the end of the legal doctrine of 'separate but equal' which had ruled for more than 50 years –

when the barrier of segregation – legal and extra legal – began to crumble – a time that produced the first civil rights laws in half a century." All of that was mainly the achievement of Thurgood Marshall.

<u>Stellar record</u>

Before being named to the court, Marshall had won 29 of 32 cases that he had argued before the Supreme Court for the NAACP. They included such milestones as: Morgan vs. Virginia, 1946, prohibiting segregation on interstate transportation; Patrick vs. Mississippi, 1947, nullifying verdicts obtained from juries in which African-Americans had been barred on the basis of race; Shelley vs. Kraemer, 1948, preventing state courts from enforcing racially restrictive covenants.

Now, despite Marshall's efforts to equalize opportunity for blacks, affirmative action laws are being overturned in some states.

Despite his legal victories in quelling racist violence against black citizens, such incidents still occur.

Despite his victory in the landmark Brown vs. Topeka Board of Education, which outlawed discrimination in public education, segregation in colleges and universities continues in practice, if not by law.

Despite his opening the door for the middle class for African Americans, they are still excluded from too many corporate boardrooms.

As U.S. solicitor general under Johnson and as a member of the Supreme Court, he was a contrarian who never wavered in his fight to achieve social justice even when threatened with -----

Like W.E.B. DuBois, his recommendation for dealing with racists was a faceful of knuckles.

When old and ailing, Marshall was asked if he planned to retire. He replied, "Hell, no. This is a lifetime appointment, and I intend to serve it. They'll have to carry me out on a stretcher."

Eventually Marshall retired in 1991, having served for 24 years on the nation's highest court. He died in January 1993 at 84.

Gerald White Johnson: A less arrogant Baltimore 'sage'

The most frequently heard defense of H.L. Mencken following publication of his obnoxious diary, is that "he was a product of his time."

Another *Baltimore Sun* writer, Gerald White Johnson, also internationally renowned, and also a product of his time, spoke for the best of his time instead of the worst. Mencken and Johnson were Sun colleagues from 1926 to 1943, when Johnson retired.

Mencken, "the sage of Hollins Street," kept silent about Hitler, but howled his fury at Roosevelt. Johnson, "the sage of Bolton Street," denounced Hitler and praised FDR for saving the capitalist system with his New Deal reforms.

Mencken's heroes were Nietzche, the apostle of the superman whose superior powers gave him the right to despise, bully and push around the "booboisie", and Schopenhauer, the pessimistic philosopher of the force of individual will over the common herd. Johnson's heroes were such optimists as Andrew Jackson, Woodrow Wilson, FDR and, later, Adlai Stevenson, for whom Johnson wrote speeches and who called Johnson "the conscience of our time."

Mencken was the quintessential cynic. Johnson believed, if not in the perfectability, then the improvability of humanity.

The arrogant Mencken had contempt for most people; Johnson, compassion.

Mencken was a brilliant, self-educated high school graduate driven always to demonstrate how much smarter he was than the degreed academics he scorned. Johnson was a contributing editor of the New Republic, a retired professor of journalism at the University of North Carolina, relaxed and confident as educator, scholar, journalist, historian and author of more than 30 books, although he never considered himself an intellectual.

Mencken was a Northern racist, Johnson, a Southern liberal who all his life fought for civil rights, against discrimination and for progress in race relations.

Mencken was almost always critical of this country while Johnson was an unabashed patriot who believed in our two wars for democracy and yet was one of the earliest opponents of the Vietnam war. He had been a sergeant in World War I, so he knew something about war.

The main difference between the Sun sages was that Mencken showed mostly disdain, hatred and despair for most of humanity, while Johnson conveyed respect, affection and hope.

If Mencken loomed larger as a celebrity, it was because those who appeal to the mean and negative in us seem to achieve greater popularity than those who strive to bring out the kind and positive.

One of Mencken's shining moments was when, attracted by the clarity and strength of Johnson's writing in North Carolina, he offered him the job in Baltimore as editorialist for The Sun and writer of weekly articles in The Evening Sun. They rarely agreed much after that – although they did on the validity of the theory of evolution and disgust for stuffed shirts and phonies. They had a "friendly" relationship, or as close as Mencken could come to it. In his diary he attacked Johnson (as he did most of his Sunpapers "friends") as a of "conventional mind" and "notably stupid." In Mencken's view, there was only one star among the newspapers' luminaries: Mencken.

A far different view of Johnson was expressed by the Richmond Times-Dispatch in 1943: "No writer of Southern birth has been more devastating in his assaults on Dixie demagogues and dervishes than Gerald Johnson. None has deflated windbags with more consummate deftness and none has unveiled more charlatans to the public gaze ... The South salutes him as a doughty warrior in the cause of social justice."

What Johnson said of Adlai Stevenson also applied to the sage of Bolton Street: "The source of his strength was not intellect alone but also faith. He had faith in human improvement; he had the faith and the kindness and humor, to like people even when they showed no improvement."

Another difference between Mencken and Johnson was suggested when Johnson, discussing in an interview his own fallibility, recalled the remark made by the elder Oliver Wendell Holmes: "The greatest single item that ever came my way was the realization that I'm not God."

Unlike Mencken, Johnson was consistently balanced and fair, and his liberal spirit never soured into cynicism and intolerance.

Gerald W. Johnson has been called a dean of American letters and a journalist-savant, but he never took himself very seriously. Asked in 1973, when he was 82, if had any intention of writing his autobiography, he replied: "Oh, my gracious, no!" – adding that he considered the only successful one to be Benjamin Franklin's. "Writing my memoirs would be indecent exposure." When reminded that many people would be disappointed if he didn't, he said "Not half so many as would be if I did."

If only his fellow "sage" at the newspaper had shown the same wisdom about his diary!

March 22, 1990

Lee L. Dopkin:
A Modest Baltimorean helped to put it across

Baltimore and Maryland have special cause to celebrate their key roles in the 50th anniversary of the Social Security Act.

One of the earliest and most dynamic advocates of social security, and the pioneer of Maryland's old age pension law which became a model for the national legislation, was a Baltimore humanitarian, Lee L. Dopkin. His life was devoted to activism for social causes. Even his death was related; it occurred on August 16, 1988, just 33 years after Senate confirmation of the first social security board members.

After more than a quarter century in the administration of welfare in Maryland, Dopkin was appointed by Governor-elect Harry W. Nice in January 1935 to head a commission to draft mandatory old-age pension laws for the coming session of the General Assembly.

Dopkin was ready. He had been stumping all over the country to support Frank D. Roosevelt's Social Security proposals; he had his draft of legislation neatly prepared. His bill became Maryland law on April 5, 1935. It served in some respects as prototype for the national Social Security legislation passed by Congress and signed by Roosevelt four months later, on August 14, 1935.

Following passage of Maryland's Old Age Pension Law, Lee was offered the job of its first commissioner. He declined. Although never wealthy, he had resolved not to capitalize in any way on his labors in behalf of those who had faith in his leadership. Later, when invited to serve as paid administrator of the State Unemployment Compensation Board, another project he had pioneered, he again refused the paying position.

Nobody ever worked harder for social security legislation than Lee Dopkin. He wrote hundreds of letters and telegrams. He prepared and delivered speeches to anyone who would listen – from small parlor meetings to legislative bodies and national conventions. He used radio talks to create broad public support.

Self-educated after the age of 13, when family circumstances required him to go to work, he nevertheless made himself an expert on the problems of the aged, the disadvantaged, the handicapped and the poor.

His biblical zeal earned him the enmity of a few right-wingers who called him a tool of the communists and of left-wingers with contempt for reformers, but it also won the admiration and loyalty of the many who made him a prophet with honor in his own country.

Chairman in 1954 of the combined Associated Jewish Charities and United Appeal. He served the Levindale nursing home as its president in the 1930s and was honored by a number of Jewish organizations, notably the Independent Order of Brith Shalom, which named him 1950 Man of the Year.

Today, over 21.6 million workers and 10.9 million dependents and survivors – 32.5 million Americans on Social Security – are benefitting indirectly from the vision, drive and compassion of an East Baltimore boy who grew up believing that he was indeed his brother's keeper and who loved his fellow men.

His philosophy, undergirding the Social Security system, was expressed in his article published by *The Evening Sun* on March 13, 1935 –"Pension or Poorhouse".

Here are a few excerpts from his passionate protest against the anguish and humiliation which honorable old men and women experience by being relegated to poorhouses.

"Within the past century the average length of life in the United States has increased from 39 to 60 years. (In 1981, it was 71.1 years for white males, 78.5 years for white females.) This means that our population now has a much larger proportion of aged persons than it used to. In 1980 only 24 out of every 1,000 were over 65. In 1930, 54 out of every 1000 were over 65; the proportion of people over 65 continues to increase. (In 1963, it was over 120 out of every thousand; 27.4 million out of a population of 226.5 million.)

"While the natural span of life has been thus lengthened, man's economic life had been progressively shortened. Most large industries now set a deadline of 40 or 45 years for the hiring of employees, and older workers are steadily being eliminated from economic life.

"On top of this, it become increasingly difficult for the wage earner to provide for the declining years of life ....

"The traditional method of providing for old age was to rear a large family of children. But today families are smaller, children tend to scatter more, and family ties are weaker. There is no place for an old father or mother in a small apartment, nor can the young generation with its own burden of growing children contribute much to maintain the old people.

"As a result of these powerful forces, we are confronted with an urgent problem of old-age dependency .... A study made two years ago in Connecticut shows that one-third of those over 65 years old were without any income whatever, and that more than half had resources of less than $300 per year.

"The answer to this problem is clearly a mandatory old-age pension law to provide small pensions so that the aged destitute may live their few remaining years in some semblance of decency and self-respect.

"About 2,500 persons in Maryland live in poorhouses that are unworthy of a civilized community. The report submitted in 1933 by Governor (Albert C.) Ritchie's almshouse commission revealed deplorable conditions. It revealed that our present almshouse buildings are fire-traps almost without exemption; that sanitation in them is at primitive levels, that many of them are dirty and infested with vermin; that beds and bedding are inadequate; that heating systems are in many instances both dangerous and inadequate.

"Some change in our system of caring for the destitute aged is clearly imperative. Yet one still hears the question: Can we afford a pension system? The answer is that we can ...."

He then showed why "it is clear Maryland cannot well afford to procrastinate," and proposed his then-radical reform.

Dopkin carved out of solid rock the support of Social Security that has become a cornerstone of the American system.

William Donald Schaefer
As Baltimore Baron II Takes Over Maryland

Now that William Donald Schaefer, the second Baron of Baltimore, is titled governor-elect of Maryland, we note that, 239 years ago, the first Baron of Baltimore, George Calvert's claim to Maryland was affirmed by King Charles on November 30, 1647.

On about the same date A.D. 1986, the Maryland State Board of Election Canvassers formally declared Baron Schaefer's mandate official.

It was George, not Donald, who was called a "good politician" by Theodore R. McKeldin (himself no political slouch since he, a Republican in a Democratic city and state, had been elected twice governor and twice mayor.)

In an address 33 years ago, at the annual Maryland Day Celebration in St. Mary's City, McKeldin was speaking of George Calvert but his remarks could have applied as well to Don Schaefer today:

"Maryland (read Baltimore) owes its existence in its present form to the fact that George Calvert (read Donald Schaefer) was a good politician.

"Some of you may suspect that I am saying that only because I have been in politics myself, but history bears me out. I do not deny that I find it pleasant to point out how a man was enabled to do a great thing by his political skill and experience; and I think no fair-minded man should grudge me that pleasure in view of the way politicians are subjected to constant abuse for what they do, for what they fail to do and – most frequently and most bitterly of all – for what it is imagined that they are trying to do. So when we find an instance in which it is plain that everyone profited by the fact that a leader was a superb politician, I think it deserves emphasis ....

"A man who understood the trend of events and could meet emergencies wisely was highly valuable; and to understand events and act wisely is the very essence of a good politician."

McKeldin could have been talking about Schaefer's

services to him as mayor when Schaefer was a member and later president of the City Council, in saying:

"George Calvert had proved himself by a long career before he turned his attention seriously to (Maryland). He held many offices, but he was not merely an office-holder; he was what we could call in our modern slang, the King's trouble-shooter. King Charles relied much – as the event proved, far too much – on the power of .... the sword; but occasionally problems arose that could not be solved ... by power, and at such times the cry arose for Calvert and he was usually sent to disturbed zone. I doubt that this was the origin of the cant phrase, 'Let George do it', – but it might have been ....

"His skill, tact and shrewd understanding of men and events served well."

McKeldin could have been speaking of the second, instead of the first, Baron of Baltimore and of much-later black-white confrontation in Schaefer's (and McKeldin's) day, instead of Catholics against Protestants in the 1600s, when he said of George Calvert:

"He understood perfectly that passions were mounting dangerously high and he knew that no good could come of the hatreds that were being engendered on both sides.

"Many others understand that much, but much of the participants on both sides could see only one cause of the trouble, namely the obstinate wrong-headedness of the other side. It is the distinction of the first Baron of Baltimore that he grasped the truth that the poison in the situation was neither Catholicism nor Protestantism, but the hatred of Christian for Christian. The true remedy would not be the elimination of either sect, but reduction of the passion that blinded them both; and to that task he addressed himself.

It is my belief," said McKeldin of Schaefer's political ancestor, "that he was greatly assisted in gaining this clear view by his long experience in dealing with political affairs. It is the popular fashion to scoff at the politician for what is called his lack of conviction, and it cannot be denied that we do have in public life a certain number of the demagogues completely void of principle, as unsteady as weathervanes, whirled about by the slightest puff of air. But nobody can say that this man lacked conviction. Yet, like every man who has been long in public life, he had learned that no controversy can be truly described in terms of jet black and snow white. He had learned that no heresy can be as damaging to the state as the blind fury that strives to regular conscience by force."

The simple art of politics practiced by Calvert on a royal court of perhaps a few hundred differed greatly, of course, from the sophisticated wizardry used by McKeldin and Schaefer to influence an electorate of hundreds of thousands and a population of millions.

But they shared one political principle: Calvert, McKeldin and Schaefer, each in his own time, preferred moderation to confrontation because it worked better.

McKeldin was fond of Schaefer, advised him on occasion and valued his support in the City Council. McKeldin had the vision of the Inner Harbor that Schaefer made a reality, and laid the sound foundation on which Schaefer built Baltimore's renaissance.

But Maryland's master politician had no idea that his praise of Calvert's political skills of the 17th century might one day describe accurately those of his protégé, the 20th century Baron of Baltimore whose realm is now Maryland.

November 25, 1986

Chapter 5
Jewish Museum of Maryland
Elayne Fedder

Originally established in 1960 and known as the Jewish Historical Society of Maryland, the organization has evolved and changed significantly over the years, becoming the Jewish Heritage Center in 1986 and finally the Jewish Museum of Maryland.

In 1978, the then Society and the B'nai B'rith Nathan Hackerman Lodge inaugurated the first Maryland Jewish Hall of Fame as a lasting honor for Maryland Jews who contributed to social progress and advanced the cause of humanitarian service. It sought to memorialize, for future generations, the accomplishments of Jews who played a major role in promoting Jewish and American ideals and who distinguished themselves in religious, literary, medical, legal, artistic, educational and cultural sphere.

The project, which involved the Jewish community, came to fruition in 1978. Among the Jewish honorees over the years have been Henrietta Szold, Harry Greenstein, Joseph Meyerhoff, Dr. Abel Wolman, Shoshana Cardin, Judge Reuben Oppenheimer and Rabbi Morris Lieberman. A non-Jew, Thomas Kennedy, author of the bill known as the "Jew Bill" that granted rights of citizenship to Maryland Jews in 1825, was the significant exception.

Jack Levin was a key player in the concept, development and promotion of the Hall of Fame while President of the Jewish Historical Society in 1971. The Society has subsequently expanded its goals and community outreach to become a major Maryland institution.

Indicating Kennedy's Faith in the Jews

The Jewish Historical Society of Maryland will open its Jewish Heritage Center – a museum-library-cultural focus – tomorrow with a tour for large donors. The first annual meeting, open to the public, is next week in the new structure between the restored Lloyd Street and B'nai Israel synagogues, both of which are listed on the National Historic Registry.

The occasion will highlight the 160th years since Delegate Thomas Kennedy finally – on February 26, 1826 – rammed his "Jew Bill" through the Maryland legislature. For eight long years it had grimly resisted his efforts to entitle Jewish citizens to hold public office in the Free State. The legislature's surrender made possible many of the contributions to Maryland's progress that are recognized in the Jewish Heritage Center.

Kennedy's amazing triumph climaxed the Jews' struggle for full citizenship; it had begun in 1979 with their unsuccessful petition to the Maryland Assembly for the equal rights guaranteed by the U.S. Constitution. Several subsequent petitions had also failed. Maryland Jews were so disheartened that, for 14 years, nothing more had been heard about their enfranchisement.

Then along came Kennedy, the non-Jewish delegate from Hagerstown, to take up the fight. His motivation remains a mystery. He had no Jewish constituency. None of his friends, neighbors or even acquaintances were known to be Jewish. He had never even met a Jew. Only his stubborn passion for justice seemed to drive him. Defeated for re-election, he rang again, won, and resumed his incredible one-man battle against bitter opposition, to defeat discrimination against Jews in the "Christian" state of Maryland; he was vilified as an "enemy of Christianity" and as a "Judas Iscariot."

His bill enabled a Jew at last to be appointed to public office in Maryland without having to make "the declaration now required by the Constitution and form of government of the State." For the first time, a Jew did not have to lie, swear falsely and deny his identity in order to serve.

Wherever Thomas Kennedy may be now, he must regard with pride and satisfaction the results of his singular achievement. The few rotten apples recently removed from the barrel of Jewish public service have not spoiled the fruits of Kennedy's victory. Looking down from his Judeo-Christian heaven at Maryland Jewish contributions in war and peace, he could be saying to his celestial cronies, "I told you so."

But how could he have told them? All he had sought for his Jewish fellow citizens was fair play. How could anyone in 1826 have foreseen that Maryland's Jewish population of 150 would grow into a community of many thousands? Or that descendants of the peddler and laborers would become giants in business, education, the professions, arts and sciences? Or that, more than half a century after the "Jew Bill", immigrants seeking freedom and equal opportunity would surge through the door Kennedy had helped to open?

Thirty-four years after passage of the "Jew Bill", Henrietta Szold was born on Lombard Street. The found of Hadassah, the world's largest Zionist women's organization, she pioneered a new educational movement in America when she opened a night school for immigrants above an East Baltimore grocery.

One of the most eminent Maryland Jewish vindicators of Thomas Kennedy's faith was Harry Greenstein. Executive director of The Association Jewish Charities and Welfare Fund for almost 40 years, he also devoted a lifetime of public service to welfare and relief through the Depression, disaster in Europe and the Middle East, and the crises of reparations and displaced persons in postwar Europe.

Harry Greenstein was known in the United States, Europe and the Middle East as one of the outstanding social-welfare workers of our time. He founded and directed Maryland's state relief program. He helped to create and direct the United National Rehabilitation and Relief Agency. He met his greatest challenge as adviser on Jewish affairs in postwar Germany, working closely with General Lucius D. Clay and High Commissioner John J.

McCloy. Thanks to Kennedy, nothing blocked Greenstein's great humanitarian services.

The roster of distinguished Maryland Jewish scientists in government positions includes Dr. Abel Wolman. At age 94, he still walks to his Johns Hopkins University office from his Charles Street home. Dr. Wolman, Hopkins professor emeritus of sanitary engineering, has made enormous international contributions in public heath, water supply, relief and rehabilitation, mass transportation, atomic safety, marine resources, environmental and sanitary engineering. He and Joseph Meyerhoff were the first two electees to the Maryland Jewish Hall of Fame, now housed in the Lloyd Street Synagogue.

Mr. Meyerhoff's achievements in philanthropy, civic and cultural service, business, education and the arts must confound the ghosts of Kennedy's foes and leave all of us wondering where Baltimore would have been without him.

Accompanying Kennedy, Szold, Wolman and Meyerhoff in Maryland's Jewish Hall of Fame are:

> Lee L. Dopkin, a leader in the fight for passage of Maryland's mandatory old-age pension law, which eliminated the poor-house system and set the pattern for passage of national Social Security legislation. The young, aged, chronically ill, poor and unemployed benefitted from his lifelong service on may Maryland boards and commissions ....
>
> Rabbi Morris Lieberman of the Baltimore Hebrew Congregation, staunch champion of civil rights, civil liberties and the struggle to eliminate racial and religious discrimination ...
>
> Shoshana Cardin, now president of the National Council of Jewish Federations, and former leader of many Baltimore civic, educational, social and cultural institutions ....
>
> Judge Reuben Oppenheimer, retired associate judge of the Supreme Bench of Baltimore City and of the Maryland Court of Appeals, and officer of numerous professional

and community service organizations. He was president of the city and state bar associations.

Nearly 100 more Maryland Jews, living and dead have been nominated to the Hall of Fame for public services Thomas Kennedy enabled them to render their fellow citizens. Ironically, in order to win approval of his bill, Kennedy had to substitute a broader religious test for the narrower Christian one. A Jew seeking public service would thenceforth have to declare only "his belief in a future state of rewards and punishments." Secularists, agnostics and atheists need not apply. Thus, the bill that enfranchised Maryland Jews had to perpetuate the misconception of the Jews as a religious or racial group, instead of the reality: a pluralistic people with a common tradition and history.

Judaic Roots of the American Revolution

In this Bicentennial of American independence, with the United States standing apart from the many nations which disguise their anti-Semitism as anti-Zionism, and standing by Israel in its isolation, it should be noted that our nation from its very beginning has befriended Jews and adopted Judaic principles.

Alignment with Judaism is not a recent developed in U.S. policy. It did not originate with the American Jewish community of interests in freedom, democracy, civil rights and liberties, and the dignity of the individual in an increasingly totalitarian world.

It began with the Bible. The Puritans who fathered the American revolutionaries lived by the Old Testament; it was their household book and story book. They were as close to it as the modern family is to its TV set. The code they practiced and preached was the Ten Commandments. Their history was the Pentateuch. When they began to see George III as a tyrant, they began to call him "Pharaoh."

They gave their sons such Jewish Biblical names as Abraham, Adam, Enoch, Isaac, Jacob, Noah, Abel, Joshua, Moses, Samuel, Aaron, Isaiah, Jeremiah, Ezekiel, Hosea, Amos, Obadiah, Jonah, Solomon, Daniel, Zachariah, Caleb, David and Ezra; and their daughters such names as Rebecca, Sarah, Ruth, Esther, Leah, Miriam, Naomi, Deborah, Hannah, Abigail, Rachel, Hephzibah and Jezebel.

As Israel now depends upon the U.S. for material support in it struggle for national liberation, the American Revolution depended upon the Hebrew Scriptures for moral and intellectual support. The historian James Truslow Adams said of the Puritans that "in spirit they may be considered as Jews and not Christians. Their God was the God of the Old Testament, their laws were the laws of the Old Testament, their guides to conduct were the characters of the Old Testament.

The Jewish Exodus from Egypt inspired the American rebels, the patriots we honor this year, to seek liberation. The defiance of royal authority by the ten tribes of Israel in establishing their own government inspired the thirteen colonies to do likewise. The denouncing of kings and potentates by the Hebrew prophets inspired the American protestors. The Bible became the handbook of revolution.

The fires of American revolutionary sentiment were fed by Judaic precepts in the press and pulpits of the colonies. The very call to arms engraved on the Liberty Bell, "Proclaim liberty throughout the land unto all the inhabitants thereof," came from Leviticus (25:10) – *ukratem dror be'aretz l'chol yoshveha*. Jefferson, Adams and Franklin proposed for the first seal of the United States a picture of the Israelites crossing the Red Sea, surrounded by the inscription, "Rebellion to tyrants is obedience to God." Our revolutionary thunder came from the tempestuous pages of the Old Testament, not the New, which the patriots found too mild, resigned and submissive for the occasion. They wanted no part of such Tory concepts as "Render to Caesar the things that are Caesar's and to God the things that are God's." They did not believe that the meek would inherit the earth, or that the other cheek should be turned.

The fiery Boston minister, Jonathan Mayhew, quoted the prophet Samuel in warning against royalty. Harvard's president, Samuel Langdon, cited the ancient Jewish government as "a perfect republic." William Edward Lecky, the great historian, declared later that "the Hebraic mortar cemented the foundations of American democracy."

200 years before the American people and government spoke up for Israel in the UN, the Founding Fathers had spoken highly of the Jews. George Washington said, in his letter to the Savannah, Georgia synagogue that had honored him: "May the same wonderworking Deity, who long since delivering the Hebrew from their Egyptian oppressors planted them in the Promised Land – whose providential agency has lately been conspicuous in establishing these United States as an independent nation – still continue to water them with the dews of Heaven and to make ye inhabitants of every denomination participate in the temporal and spiritual blessings of that people whose God is Jehovah."

In another letter to the Hebrew Congregation of Newport, R.I., Washington made his oft-quoted comment: ".... happily, the Government of the United States, which gives to bigotry no sanction, to persecution no assistance, requires only that they who live under its protection should demean themselves as good citizens in giving it on all occasions their effectual support."

John Adams wrote to his friend, F.A. Vanderkamp: "I will insist that the Hebrews have done more to civilize men than any other nation. If I were an atheist, and believed in blind eternal fate, I should still believe that fate had ordained the Jews to be the most essential instrument for civilizing the nations. If I were an atheist of the other sect, who believe or pretend to believe that chance had ordered the Jews to preserve and propagate to all mankind the doctrine of a supreme, intelligent, wise, almighty sovereign of the universe, which I believe to be the great essential principle of all morality, and consequently of all civilization."

John Adams said further, in a letter to Manuel Josephson, regarding the consecration of a synagogue: "I wish your nation may be admitted to all privileges of citizens in every country of the world. This country has done much. I wish it may do more; and annul every narrow idea in religion, government and commerce.

.... It has pleased Providence .... that Abraham should give religion, not only to Hebrews, but to Christians and Mahometans, the greatest part of the modern civilized world."

When Benjamin Franklin wanted to praise the military genius of Washington, he compared him to Joshua, who "commanded the sun and the moon to stand still, and they obeyed him." James Madison credited Haym Salomon with a large role in the success of the American Revolution. "When any member of the revolutionary Congress was in need, all that was necessary was to call on Salomon." Madison believed in freedom of religion as "the best human provision for bringing all either into the same way of thinking, or into that mutual charity which is the only proper substitute."

With the exceptions of Maryland, North Carolina and New Hampshire, all the original states, at the urging of Jefferson and Madison, adopted constitutions granting full freedom and equality of citizenship to Jewish citizen. (It was not until 1825 that Maryland extended to Jews all rights of citizenship with passage of Thomas Kennedy's "Jew Bill".)

Yale College, which celebrated its own bicentennial seventy-five years before the nation's, has on its corporate seal, representing an open book, the Hebrew inscription, *Urim v' Tummim*, symbolic words of divination regarding light and perfection, from the breastplates of the ancient Hebrew high priests.

The influence of the Old Testament on the thought and policy of New England is evidenced by a New Haven enactment dated 1644, 136 years before the War of Independence: "In the beginning of the foundation of this plantation and jurisdiction, upon a free debate with due and serious consideration, it was agreed, concluded and settled as a fundamental law, not to be disputed or questioned hereafter, that the judicial laws of God, as they were delivered by Moses and expounded in other parts of Scripture, so far as they are a fence to the moral law, being neither typical nor ceremonial, nor having a reference to Canaan, shall be accepted as of moral equity, and as God shall help, shall be a constant direction for all proceedings here and a general rule for all courts in this jurisdiction, how to judge between party and party and how to punish offenders, till the same be branched out into particulars hereafter."

This testimony to the primacy of Old Testament doctrine helped to shape the laws of the colony and the character of Yale University. There, the study of Hebrew was not only encouraged but for a time was made compulsory, under Yale's remarkable president Ezra Stiles, who began at the age of forty to study Hebrew. He considered the learning and teaching of Hebrew a vehicle of salvation – in Cotton Mather's words, "the fiery chariot to carry one heavenwards."

Ezra Stiles wrote in his diary that no man's education could be complete without knowledge of the sacred tongue, and whoever pretended to scholarship had to be a "good Hebraician."

Women Hebraists of his day are also noted in his diary. His second wife and daughter, as well as his sons, were Hebrew students. He wrote in his diary, July 21, 1793: "My wife died 1775. She read thro' the Bible, five times the last four years of her life, once in about 9 or 10 months. Kezia [his daughter, born in September 1760] died 1785, she read it thro' five times the last five years of her life.

"Besides, reading in course privately in my study, I read thro' the Bible in my Family at family Morning Prayers from 1760 to 1791, eight times, or once in four years. My family have had full opportunity of being acquainted with the sacred Contents of the Bible."

George Alexander Kohut, a biographer of Dr. Stiles, wrote of the "patriotism and spirit of self sacrifice which the Jews showed in the Revolutionary War." He cited, among others, the Sheftalls, Salvadors, Aaron Isaacs, Salomon Rophe and Aaron Lopez, owner of thirty vessels in the European and West Indian trade and whale fisheries, who lost "nearly all he had for his fealty to the colonies." Mr. Kohut concludes: "The Moseses, Joshuas and Aarons did more than pray; they fought for the land of their adoption with the sword as well as the spirit."

In addition to their lives and honor, those who had fortunes (not many, because most were poor) put them also at the service of the Revolution. Joseph Simon, the Lancaster Indian trader, supplied rifles and ammunition to the Continental Army. Jacob Hart of Baltimore loaned money to Lafayette; Isaac Moses of New York subscribed three thousand pounds to the army for buying provisions. Bernard and Michael Gratz advanced large sums of money to patriot leaders, including "four thousand eight hundred and thirty-seven Continental dollars" to James Madison and one thousand four hundred dollars to George Rogers Clark for his Western campaign.

The entire Jewish population of all the colonies at the time of the Revolution has been estimated at no more than 2,500. Perhaps never before in history had so few contributed so much to the destiny of so many.

October 1976

Harry Greenstein
To Him, They All Had Dignity and Rights

One hundred years after his birth, and 35 years after his long tenure as director of The Associated Jewish Community Federation of Baltimore, Harry Greenstein continues to inspire "leadership that will affect Baltimoreans' quality of life into the next century." With those words, 'The Associated' awarded five Harry Greenstein fellowships last month.

But who was Harry Greenstein?

His services extended well beyond the Jewish community, and well beyond Baltimore as a whole. He made huge contributions as well to the nation and a large population of Eastern Europe through relief and rehabilitation services which were made available gratis by The Associated.

In the foreword to a biography of Greenstein, Herbert H. Lehman, former senator and governor of New York, reminds us that 60 years ago "throughout the United States there was no public social-welfare work, only private charity which was without resources to meet the challenge of the great public blight of depression." So when emergency struck, government resources were mobilized by private sector men like Harry Greenstein.

His talents were first made available in 1933 when Gov. Albert C. Ritchie appointed him state relief administrator for Maryland. Three years later he was recruited by national voluntary agencies do an organizational survey which ultimately became the United Hebrew Aid Service (HIAS).

"No area was in greater need of Harry's genius for organization and his boundless energies and fervent dedication," Lehman wrote. "Hundreds of thousands of lives were saved ... in no small measure by Harry Greenstein's brilliant work. ... To Harry, they were not faceless names or masses of alien people. They were all individuals with God-given dignity and the inalienable rights of human beings, uprooted and crushed by forces beyond their knowledge and control."

Lehman himself was the instigator of the third emergency grant of Greenstein by The Associated. He requested Harry's services as director of the Welfare Division of the United Nations

Relief and Rehabilitation Administration, serving the distressed people of Greece, Albania and Yugoslavia.

Then in 1949 Harry's prodigious talents were tapped again in the turbulent aftermath of World War II. The Associated lent him to organize relief and rehabilitation of refugees and displaced persons.

Harry Greenstein was a unique personality. Although never rich, he was a great philanthropist in the true sense – a lover of humankind. Although not strictly religiously observant, he was completely committed to the commandments of prophetic Judaism concerning relations of man to man. Although immersed in human welfare, he was devoted to the well-being of his mother and sisters.

And although occupied with grim problems of destitution and despair, he retained a keen sense of humor. Theater-goers knew his distinctive, braying guffaw. Harry's burst of booming laughter was a release from the tragedies he dealt with most of his lifetime.

He exemplified what seems lacking today: the unselfish sense of responsibility for others. Harry empathized with those mired in poverty because he and his sisters as children had carried collection boxes from door to door. His devout father's charitable activities had instilled in Harry a precocious interest in community efforts to help the poor.

During the Depression, one out of every five breadwinners was unemployed, and five out of five feared unemployment. Therefore, most Americans saw themselves as actual or potential beneficiaries of government. They did not, as today, think of themselves as benefactors of the underserving poor. There was no resentment toward the poor, only identification with them.

Harry's personal life was almost spartanly simple. His Associated salary was all that he ever felt he needed. His home, which he shared with his mother after his sisters married, was a rowhouse on West North Avenue near Monroe Street. An occasional theater tickets was one of his few personal indulgences. He remained always modest and unassuming.

He practiced the ancient Judaic principle of leaving gleanings on the field for the poor to pick up during the night so that giver and receiver would not know each other and there would be no stigma or loss of dignity. Harry had learned early the lesson he followed all his life: that there is only Justice, not Charity. In fact the two words are the same in Hebrew: *tzedakah*.

Throughout the years of Harry's services to Maryland, the United and overseas, The Associated paid his full salary. Its leaders might reasonably have rejected the outside requests for Harry's services; after all, in times of emergency communal responsibility came first. But they readily acceded, for perhaps three reasons: they knew he was the best man for the job; they honored Harry's sense of responsibility; they all were compelled by their collective historical obligation to those in distress.

In the annals of human relief and rehabilitation, the name of Harry Greenstein is written large and reflects honor upon The Associated and all the compassionate people of Baltimore.

July 10, 1995

Dr. Abel Wolman
Water

Governor Glendening has declared a statewide drought emergency – the first in Maryland history. Mandatory water conversation measures are in effect. He pointed out that Liberty Reservoir's water level is down from its normal 43 billion gallons to less than half that amount.

He has ordered Marylanders not to wash their cars or water their lawns, not to fill swimming pools, not to use water for fountains, to use washing machines and dish washers only with full loads, to repair leaks and take shorter showers.

The drought is the state's worst in 70 years with rainfall about 40 percent below normal.

All of this is new for Marylanders who have one of the world's best water supply systems. This is largely due to the achievements of Dr. Abel Wolman.

He received his Bachelor of Science in Engineering from Johns Hopkins University in 1915. During his long career he became one of the world's leading authorities on water purification and supply and developed Maryland's water system.

In the 1920s, Dr. Wolman was Assistant Engineer to Division Engineers, Maryland State Department of Health; Editor-in-Chief, Journal of the American Water Works Association; Associate Editor, American Journal of Public Health; Chairman, Public Health Engineering Section, America Public Health Association; Lecturer in Sanitary Engineering, Princeton University; Chairman, Potomac River Flood Control Committee, Cumberland, Maryland and Consulting Engineer, Baltimore County, Metropolitan District; Chief Engineer, Maryland State Department of Health; Professor and Chairman, Department of Sanitary Engineering, The Johns Hopkins University School of Engineering and School of Hygiene and Public Health.

Among his other distinctions were: Chairman, Advisory Committee on Sanitary Engineering and Environment, Division of Medical Sciences, National Research Council; Consultant to Surgeon General, U.S. Army; Chairman, Task Force on Population Migration, City of Baltimore; Consultant on the

International Drinking Water Supply and Sanitation Decade, The World Health Organization, Geneva, Switzerland and Consultant to New York City Department of Environmental Protection. He applied his skills until his death, February 22, 1989.

Dr. Wolman felt that in order to have clean, safe water to drink, we must have first of all – true governmental desire and intention – second public understanding and behavior.

Most countries pay lip service to sanitary objectives, but that's where they stop – at lip service.

Dr. Wolman believed that Moses was the first great Sanitary Engineer who demanded of his military followers that they bury their defecation. Moses' principles of sanitation were valid and still are according to Dr. Wolman.

He believed that first of all, government has to show real desire and readiness to have clean water, and that second, the public must understand and behave properly. Lip service, he pointed out, was not sufficient.

Our present strictures are temporary, but in many parts of the world, they are permanent prohibitions.

In less developed cities in Asia, Africa and South America, water conditions are primitive. There is little or no infrastructure for water supply.

In cities with ancient cultures like Alexandria, Egypt, sewage stagnates in pools just outside the buildings. In such old, but physically attractive cities, the water that used to be clear, clean and beautiful is now foul and malodorous and causes diseases to many who bathe in it.

Dwellings are supplied with water, but no sewage line. As a result, a car driving through puddles sets up a lethal spray. Walkways across these pools provide access to residences and shops. But children at play are in danger. Infant mortality is very high in such communities and water borne diseases are rampant.

By next year, it is estimated that the number of people living in cities will comprise about 50 percent of the total population in Asia, 40 percent in Africa and 85 percent in Latin America. It is expected that there will be five times as many cities as now with a population of more than one-million inhabitants each.

Such sprawling growth in the less developed countries is usually not accompanied by a comparable increase in provision of essential water and sewerage facilities.

Due to this rapid increase in urban population, the supply of water in some cities has become inadequate. Research in China and other less developed nations has shown that the reclamation of waste water is the most practical source of additional supplies. However, in many such cities without adequate sewerage, only a small portion of waste water receives treatment.

In Baltimore, with bountiful reservoirs, we have had more than an ample supply of water.

In some other cities, water laws are in conflict because of diverse demands and in less developed countries, laws and regulations are inadequate.

Serious problems in water management have to be addressed. Water resources may be renewable, but, they are nevertheless being depleted, especially by floods and droughts. Although rain water flowing into rivers, lakes and aquifers is free, it costs as much as eliminating pollution to make water available for agricultural, residential and industrial areas, and these costs must be covered.

With all of our present restrictions and inconveniences, we can thank our reservoirs and Dr. Abel Wolman's foresight and genius for the opportunity to enjoy one of the world's greatest treasures.

Baltimore Jews and Baltimore Horses

In historical accounts and memoirs of the early days of the Jewish community in Baltimore, the portraits of the Jewish doctor, the Jewish peddler, the Jewish clothing manufacturer, and the Jewish shopkeeper have been well delineated. But, there were also a great many Jews whose daily bread depended on horses, just as today many Jews are involved in the various phases of the automobile and allied businesses.

As far as I know, historians have neglected the Jewish horse dealer, the Jewish livery stable owner, the Jewish harness and saddlery dealer – even the Jewish breeder and driver of the finest stable of trotting horses that this sports-minded city boasted. This affinity between Baltimore Jews and Baltimore horses lasted from the early days of German-Jewish immigration through the first decade of the Twentieth Century.

All this was brought to mind, when I noticed a display in the lobby of Baltimore Hebrew College entitled "The Horse and Buggy Days of Jewish Education." The term "Horse and Buggy" was used, of course, as the equivalent of "ancient," and I suddenly realized that, since I had lived in "horse and buggy" times for the first 15 years of my life, I was now an "historical character," and that, since no one else had done it, I might as well try my hand on "Baltimore Jews and Baltimore horses."

The brief account lays no claim to being a scholarly paper. It has no footnotes – not even hoof-prints – and cites no documentary research, because there is none to be had, short of going through the files of over a hundred years of Baltimore newspapers, and scanning the ads of horse auctions and the racing news on the sports pages. Instead, my "source materials" are personal memories, remembrance of tales that I heard, and recollection of something which I had read "somewhere." Not very scientific, true, but after all "genuine" historians rely fondly on personal letters which, by the very nature of things, are biased by the writer's viewpoint, and are full of distorted facts, gossip and omissions.

My credentials: Up until I was at least twelve years old, horse drawn vehicles were the rule automobiles, the exception. In addition to the delivery wagons, hansom cabs, drays and fire engines, the proverbial horse-and-buggy nourished what little traffic there was on cobble-stoned McCulloh Street on which I lived. Even the doctor called in a horse-and-buggy. (As a matter of fact, as late as World War II, Dr. Ellis, the last of his breed, still made his rounds by horse and buggy; he kept his two horses at Hechter's Riding Academy at the McCulloh Street entrance to Druid Hill Park.)

In the first decade of the 1900's, when Baltimore tap water was unsafe to drink without boiling, Samuel Strouse, one of my grandmother's brothers, used to call at our house a couple of times a week to take our demijohns to be filled at the Druid Hill Park springs. Often I rode with him and, occasionally, I was permitted to drive. Carriages still out-numbered automobiles on relatively smoothly paved Eutaw Place (Belgian blocks) and Henry Sonneborn's well-matched team was a familiar sight. Another of my great-uncles lived "far out" in West Arlington, and when we came to call, he met us at the Western Maryland station with either a buggy or a wagon, depending on the size of the group.

But, the point of the matter is that many members of the Baltimore Jewish community were involved with horses <u>as a business</u>. Some of the very first Jews who came to Baltimore had been horse or cattle dealers in the "old country" and they found ample opportunity to carry on their occupation here. They brought horses and mules from the farms of Maryland, Virginia, West Virginia and Kentucky and brought them to Baltimore for sale – at first, one or two at a time, hitched behind their wagons; then, when the railroad came, in carload lots. Depending on the type of horse or mule, they were used for farm work, draft, pleasure or sport.

In those earlier days, except by boat, there were only two ways of getting from one place to another; either by horseback or horse and carriage or by "Shank's mare." Even the first B&O railway coaches were pulled by horses (Relay was so-named because that's where they changed horses) and the earliest public transit in Baltimore were horse cars. On the farms, horses, mules and even oxen pulled the plows and other farm equipment. Even when mechanized harvesters, reapers, binders, etc. were developed, they moved, literally, by horsepower.

As Baltimore city and its agricultural surroundings grew, there developed a very large market for horses and mules, and a number of Baltimore Jews were involved in the business on a major scale. Probably, Baltimore's largest dealers in horses and mules were M. Fox and Sons, and their weekly auctions of horses and mules were widely advertised and attracted large crowds of buyers from all over the state. An auction is an exciting event, and a good auctioneer must be a dramatic figure; Robert Fox, Sr. was a star in that field. Incidently, his sons adapted to the automobile age very successfully!

My most intimate memory of horse dealers was that of Joseph Kaufman, whose stables were on North Paca Street. He was the grandfather of one of my closest boyhood friends, and we used to walk from our homes on the 1500 block of McCulloh Street to see the horses. Mr. Kaufman had a contract with the Baltimore Fire Department, and we were often on hand to "inspect" a newly-arrived shipment from Kentucky. They were beautiful animals, a cross of Percherons and Morgans, usually grey in color and, when they arrived, very highly spirited, not to say rambunctious. After being properly broken and trained, they became veritable "firemen". They learned to rush from their stalls at the sound of the alarm bell, and would stand in their places, waiting to be harnessed to the vehicle – three abreast to a "steamer"; two for a horse cart. The motorization of Baltimore's fire department had to wait on the paving program – no automobile could make speed over the rugged cobblestones.

The livery stable business also engaged Jewish enterprise. If you didn't have your own stables and carriage house – as Dr. Jonas Friedenwald did – you kept your horses and rigs in a livery stable. They were scattered all over the city and you could locate the nearest one by "following your nose." You could also hire a horse and rig, a la Hertz or Avis. One of the largest livery stable's was Rice's on the corner of Madison Avenue and North Avenue (at that time the northern boundary of the city). When automobiles out-numbered horses, converting the livery stable into a garage became a natural, and Rice's Garage was probably the largest in Northwest Baltimore. The early automobile owners, for the most part, could not or did not drive themselves. To keep a $5000 automobile standing in the street was unthinkable; so, lacking a converted carriage house, the car was housed in a garage from which the chauffeur drove it to pick up the family.

By the time of World War I, Fords and Overlands outnumbered Wintons and Pierce Arrows; inexpensive sheet steel garages were erected in backyards; and Rice's like other ex-livery stables, bowed out to the service station.

However, the involvement of the Rice family with horses spanned several generations, and spread from the commercial to the sporting – including the breeding, racing and driving of trotters and pacers at the numerous "harness tracks" in Baltimore – Prospect Park, Gentlemen's Driving Park, Electric Park and others. Ned Rice, who drove a fine stable of trotting horses was one of the leading Baltimore race drivers of his day.

If the period between World Wars I and II may still be considered history, it was at this time that a number of young Jewish men appeared on the racing scene as owners of thoroughbreds. Among them was Manny Summerfield (who trained his horses as well), Henry Hecht, Irvin Grinsfelder, Harry Isaacs, and Henry Horkheimer, who, with his cousins, the Louchheims from Philadelphia, owned the "Three Cousin's Farm" which produced some fine horses, including Pompoon, one of the "greats" of the Maryland racing. This list is not by any means all-inclusive; I am sure here were others whom I have forgotten or never knew.

If horse-owning is a sport or a hobby, riding race horses is strictly a business. During this same period, one of the leading jockeys in Maryland was Manny Berg, who was known as "the king of the half-mile tracks," being the leading rider year after year. He also rode with some success on the mile tracks. Age and weight limit the length of a jockey's career; when I last saw Manny, he was a salesman for a Chevrolet dealer.

The phase of ownership of major Maryland race tracks by Jewish enterprise is too recent to be considered historic, except to point out that the Cohens of Pimlico and the Schapiros of Laurel were only following the precedent set 150 years ago when Jacob I. Cohen became the first treasurer of the Maryland Jockey Club.

After "strictly business" were the activities of a number of Jewish bookmakers who operated in that thriving business during a more tolerant era, when the police and courts winked at violation of the gambling laws as they did of the Volstead Act. As a matter of fact, for a very short time, at the outbreak of World War II, when the city was hard-pressed for sources of revenue, bookmaking was legalized and taxed. The City Council reversed itself about a week later.

It should be understood that bookmakers do not gamble; their objective is to maintain a "balanced book: – that is one where the betting is proportionally the same as that at the racetrack. Then, it matters not which horse wins; the "pay-off" is always about 10% to 12% less than the amount taken in, as this is the amount retained by the racetrack when figuring the pari-mutual prices. While the law of averages tends to equalize the bookmaking betting with that at the track in the long run, an individual bookmaker might have a distorted proportion of bets on any one race. In such cases, the bookmaker "lays-off" the excess bets with another bookmaker, or even, through an agent, at the racetrack. It takes accurate mathematics, quick thinking and lightning decisions to accomplish this. To be a success, the Jewish bookmaker had to have, not only mental agility, but an unblemished reputation for integrity and ethics, because from every angle his word was as good as his bond.

One more sidelight on the Jewish bookmakers: when the demands of the United Jewish Appeal and, later, the Jewish Welfare Fund, forced the fund raisers to seek out hitherto unexplored sources of contribution, an informal group solicited the bookmakers of their acquaintance. They responded generously – in cash, not pledges!

No story concerning Baltimore Jews and horses would be complete without mentioning "Little Joe" Wiesenfeld, whose business, for at least two generations was the leading supplier of "what the well-dressed horse would wear" – harness, saddles, bridles, blankets, and equipment of all kinds of carriage horses, riding horses, racing horses and show horses. A familiar sight at all horse shows was the Napoleonic figure of "Little Joe", himself, impeccably attired and mounted on the largest, handsomest horse to be seen.

Horses wear shoes, too, and the counterpart of Hess, Wyman and Hahn, was George Palmbaum whose customers wore four shoes instead of two and wore them out faster! Mr. Palmbaum knew enough about racing to understand that the difference in weight carried often made the difference between winning and losing. He developed and patented the aluminum horseshoe. When tested, it was a phenomenal success, and today, practically every race horse wears the products of the Victory Racing Plate Company.

I have referred to the "affinity" of many Baltimore Jews with horses; I could almost say the "affection." In fact, the horse business in any of its phases tends to become a love-affair. I can imagine the peddler who feared and dreaded the "back country"' I can imagine clothing salesmen who resented slow trains and shabby hotels; I can imagine (and have known) merchants who detested the retail business; but I can't imagine any of those old-time horse traders or horse handlers who did not have a touch of romantic feeling about their "stock in trade." The horse-and-buggy days are gone but not forgotten.

In the Jews, God Findeth a Cheerful Giver

In the midst of recession affecting everybody, The Associated: Jewish Community Federation of Baltimore, has just completed another successful campaign of fund raising. That's good news for non-Jews as well as Jewish charities.

Half or more of all giving by Jewish individuals now goes to support charitable organizations serving the general community, according to a recent report on Jewish philanthropy. It has been estimated that American Jews, who composed only 2.4 percent of the population, provide about 5 percent of all philanthropy to secular causes in the United States. This means that Jewish support of non-Jewish charities is about twice the national norm.

In proportion to the population, Jews are 23 times as likely to establish a charitable foundation as Catholics, and about 12 times as likely as Protestants. (However, only one Jewish foundation is among the nation's 100 largest, Baltimore Weinberg's Foundation.)

About 10 years ago, Gwinn Owens, then editor of the op-ed page of *The Evening Sun*, pointed out that Jewish philanthropy to the arts in Maryland was far disproportionate in the Jewish percentage of population. He scolded wealthy non-Jews for failure to give higher priority to support of the arts and urged them to emulate the Jewish example.

The reasons for Jewish generosity include above-average income resulting from above-average education and motivation. More important is the Jewish attitude toward the poor and disenfranchised, a direct consequence of both recent and ancient Jewish history.

The present Jewish generation consists of immigrants, their children and grandchildren, who knew poverty not from the media or hearsay but from personal, often searing experience. The The immediate Jewish reaction to the poor is not avoidance, revulsion or outright hostility, but more like there-but-for-the-grace-of-God-go-I.

Even Jewish yuppies are not as far removed as most

Americans from discrimination and deprivation. Their forebearers escaped a hard life as immigrants from an even harder life in the shtetls, the bleak villages of Eastern Europe. Struggling to put food on the table, they nevertheless covered its bare surface with a white cloth and kindled Sabbath lights. Barely eking out a living, they had yet encouraged their children to pursue learning, to take voice lessons, to practice playing the violin. Their descendants are inclined to value the quality of life and to support the arts.

But Jewish charity goes further back in time. Its roots reach deep into the Old Testament. Some of the biblical law (mitzvot) as in effect a kind of tax upon citizens for the benefit of the poor. In addition to tithing, the sabbatical year was instituted so "that the poor of the people may eat," and that debts could be canceled.

Jews are not conditioned to follow the David Dukes, Pat Buchanans and others who exploit resentment of and hostility toward the poor, who want to put them out of sight and to be rid of them by imprisonment and worse.

The words that most Jews live by are the words taught in Deuteronomy: "If there be among you a needy man ... thou shalt not harden thy heart nor shut thy hand unto him and shall surely lend him sufficient for his need ... [If] thine eye be evil against thy needy brother and thou give him nought ... it be sin in thee."

The Hebrew word for charity is the same as that for justice and righteousness. Since the ancient prophets Isaiah and Ezekiel, Jews have been taught that charity is an indispensable requirement for a life of piety. Ezekiel preached that Sodom was destroyed due to its lack of charity.

The virtues of charity and its heavenly reward have been studied by Jews in the books of Job and Esther and throughout millennia in the Talmud and rabbinic literature, Jewish scholars have argued that charity is as important as all the other commandments put together, that it atones for sins and ensures that the giver will have wise, wealthy and learned sons.

Countless generations of rabbis have instructed that

everybody without exception, is obliged to give charity. Even one who is himself dependent on charity is obliged to give to those less fortunate. Judges have compelled the non-giver to donate according to the court's assessment of his means, and if he refused, to be flogged and to have a sufficient amount of his property confiscated to meet the court's assessment. Rabbis have ruled that one must not give away more than a fifth of his wealth lest he become impoverished himself.

No wonders Jews are good at giving. It is a sacred vow they've been preaching and practicing for a long time. It is the "pushka" that was a cherished institution in every Jewish home, the little tin charity box which many generations fondly remember as their first sense of Jewish identity.

Hebrew Charity - Tzedakah

The Hebrew word for "justice" and "charity" is the same – tzedakah. Judaism is concerned about the world we live in, how we live, what we do, how we treat our fellow humans here and now. It does not depend upon God to provide food for the hungry but holds that we are God's co-workers, that we ourselves, each of us, can and must improve conditions to the best of our ability, and we cannot pass that buck.

Judaism's fundamental precept is also America's own, enshrined in our constitution, that all people are endowed with equal and inalienable rights, <u>all</u> regardless of differences of race, wealth, ability, intelligence, gender, education or social status. All are conceived by Judaism as fellow beings entitled to unqualified recognition of their dignity and equal humanity.

The heart and soul of Judaism is tzedakah, social justice. The same thought, expressed in various ways appears in Genesis, Isaiah, and Psalms. In Proverbs, we are told: "If even thine enemy be hungry, give others." The Bible speaks of the poor man, not as one of "them" but as "brother," deserving of loving treatment, sympathy and encouragement. The Jewish concept of tzedakah is that all wealth belongs to God. He is sole owner. We are just trustees of His bounty. Our duty is to dispense His wealth with tact and discretion, so as not to embarrass the recipients to give secretly, so that the receiver will not see his benefactor.

Part II

Jack Levin on International Affairs

Chapter 6
Jack Levin on Israel and the Arab-Israeli Conflict
Robert O. Freedman

Of all the causes in which he was involved, in none was Jack Levin more passionately involved than in defending Israel, as the following articles will demonstrate. Starting as a supporter of the Irgun, and, in his later years, becoming a major backer of Peace Now, Jack's love for Israel was demonstrated in every article that he wrote. Indeed, Jack was even willing to take on close colleagues in the Civil Rights movement such as Sidney Hollander and Chester Wickwire when they criticized Israel.

For its part, Israel was in need of defenders in the United States as, after its victory in the 1967 war, it had to fight a war of attrition against Soviet-supported Egypt in 1969-70; the Yom Kippur war against Egypt and Syria in 1973; and a continuous war against Palestinian terrorism which culminated in the Israeli invasion of Lebanon in 1982. Along the way Jack fought against the U.S. sale of F-15 aircraft to Saudi Arabia, and Arab efforts to delegitimize Israel, while all the time championing Israel as the only true democracy in the Middle East and the only state in the region that the United States could trust.

THE WORLD - America's Special Relationship with Israel
The current assessment of the special relationship of the American Jews and the U.S. government with Israel, by Noam Chomsky and other intellectuals, is that it is based upon "geopolitical, economic and strategic considerations."

True, indeed, these considerations should have been noted during the recent debate over the U.S.-Saudi-Egyptian planes deal, when the opposition was labeled the "Jewish-Israeli lobby" instead of an American lobby convinced that committing our most sophisticated weapons to states still at war with Israel did not serve American interests.

But these high-sounding considerations are not the whole truth or even a major part of the complex America-Israeli symbiosis. The cerebral and erudite professors are inclined to deal with what they may regard as a new insight (though it is not) and disdain restating the old truths about the special quality of our relationship with Israel. To them, and regrettably to most in the media, the "moral" dimension is not news. But it is necessary that the fundamental facts be remembered, since to forget or ignore them is to squander in the daily news the wisdom acquired from history and to misinterpret what makes our relationship special.

Israel is perceived by most Americans as a unique nation of refugees, survivors of an unprecedented, systematic and nearly successful effort to exterminate the Jewish people in the Holocaust which most civilized nations – including the United States – allowed to happen while millions of Jews could have been saved from gas chambers and furnaces.

Israel is seen by Americans not as an imperial military monster devised by the United States and depicted by Arab oil interests and their willing slaves as the bugaboo of racist-Zionism threatening the have-nots, not as top-dogs menacing the weak and meek – but as the world's oldest and most authentic national liberation movement, the in-gathering of exiles in their ancient, historic homeland, the salvation of the most persecuted, victimized and rejected people on Earth.

Israel's achievements in the face of formidable odds, its recreation of a people, land and language, its miracles of making deserts bloom, its repeated conversions of despair into hope and defeat into victory have given to Jews dignity and pride, to Americans admiration and to the disfranchised and dispossessed everywhere an example and dream to follow.

Israel is recognized by Americans as one of the few remaining democracies in a world increasingly authoritarian, and the sole, isolated democracy in the Middle East, not only for Jews but also for Arabs – including Palestinians who enjoy greater freedom there than in any Arab state.

Israelis are respected by Americans as a new breed of

fighting frontiersmen like our own Western pioneers, no longer passive scapegoats of oppression and degradation but brave and effective fighters for independence who have demonstrated in five wars and heroic exploits like Entebbe, a startling new proposition that is penetrating even the thickest skulls; that whoever tries to destroy Jews will be destroyed.

Arab leaders demanding an independent state for the Palestinians in what is now Israel are not fooling any American with common sense and a clear memory. They are known here to have exhorted the hapless Palestinians in 1948 to flee their homes to facilitate driving the Jews into the sea; to have refused to resettle them in any of the vast, empty Arab lands (while Israel welcomed and absorbed nearly a million Jewish refugees from Arab countries) and to have declined even to pay a decent share of the cost of feeding and housing them; to have killed far more of them in inter-Arab warfare than have Israelis in self-defense; to have aided, abetted and generously funded terrorist PLO attacks on Israeli civilians in marketplaces, movies, buses, hospitals and schools; and to have denied the humanity of their brothers by manipulating them as political pawns.

As a result of this brutalizing of the Palestinians by their fellow-Arabs and of the formalizing in the PLO covenant of the goal of annihilating the State of Israel (the only nation in the world so programmed for destruction), most Americans realize that establishing the Palestinian Murder, Inc., a few miles from Jerusalem, Tel Aviv and other Israeli cities would be an invitation to disaster not only for Israelis but also for moderate Palestinians

At a time when millions of refugees in Asia and Africa are being driven out of their homes, tortured, starved and slaughtered without concern or even notice from pundits, movers and shakers, Americans understand that the relentless concentration of world attention almost exclusively upon Palestinian refugees is yet another subtle expression of worldwide anti-Semitism: demanding of Jews the self-abnegation and self-sacrifice that are not asked or expected of the rest of humankind when survival is at stake.

At a time when millions of square miles of many peoples

land – entire nations, in fact – are occupied by their conquerors with no protest and indeed with the enthusiastic endorsement and approval of the United Nations and assorted intellectuals of the left and right, Americans are unimpressed by the lamentations over Israel's occupation – preventing attacks on innocent citizens.

Americans who live in the real world instead of an academic nirvana know that conceding a West Bank Palestinian state would not mean PLO recognition of Israel's right to exist and would instead, as clearly stated in the PLO's pronouncements, be only "a step on the path" to the total "liberation of Palestinian soil."

A few other truths that Americans hold to be self-evident and that help to explain the special relationship:

*There already exists a Palestinian state. Its name is Jordan, and its king should be participating in the peace talks, since most Palestinians hold Jordanian citizenship

*The Palestinian question is not the cause Americans know, but the result of the Arab states' refusal to accept the fact of the State of Israel.

Americans recall that during all the years when Jordan occupied the West Bank there was no demand for an independent Palestinians state, and Americans wonder, why now?

Two dates in history help to clarify America's special relationship with Israel: 1948, when Israel followed the example of the United States in establishing a democratic nation with liberty and justice for all as its goal; and 1776 when our founding fathers were inspired by the patriarchs of the Old Testament and the principles of Judaism to proclaim liberty throughout the land and to all the inhabitants thereof.

These dates were as important as 1967, the year of Israel's great military victory, in shaping the attitude of Americans toward Israel.

September 10, 1978

DISAGREEMENT

Sir: As a dues-paying card-carrying member of SANE almost since its inception, and a peace advocate of long standing in such organizations as Business Executives Move for Vietnam Peace and the American Jewish Congress, I disagree strongly with the views of my friends Jerome Frank, Sidney Hollander, Jr., and Sam Schmerier in opposing arms for Israel to defend itself and in commending Congressman Parren J. Mitchell for his vote against United States aid to offset the massive Soviet arming of Israel's enemies.

I have written Congressman Mitchell to this effect ...

Middle East warfare is initiated and pursued, not by Israel, but by those who have been since 1947, and still are, trying to destroy it.

Israel's primary concern is self-defense against relentless attack, not imperialist expansionism.

No nation in the world wants peace more than Israel, taxed at 85 percent and paralyzed by mobilization...

African blacks, who have benefitted for decades from Israel's scientific, technological, cultural and social assistance and brotherhood, understand that their leaders have been bought and paid for with Arab oil money and Soviet guns made for killing other blacks.

American blacks are not ideologues and militant Africa-firsters who carry next to their hearts a photo of Idi Amin, the admirer of Hitler.

Congressman Mitchell's first responsibility is not to represent a vague Third World but a real Seventh district.

February 1, 1974

Have They Forgotten

Sir: More in sadness than anger we note the misunderstanding and distortion of the meaning of Israel by the recent self-styled "National Black Political Convention." Its resolution condemned the congressmen who supported aid to the tiny democracy defending itself against the surprise Arab-Soviet military onslaught.

The congressmen, of course, will not exactly quake at the fulminations of the tribe of Imanu Amiri Baraka, formerly LeRoi Jones, which represents the blacks of this country to about the same extent as the Ku Klux Klan represents the whites.

It does, however, concern those of us who have fought long for human rights that the world's most persecuted people, the descendants of the hunted and tormented of history, the survivors of the death camps and crematoria, are begrudged the most basic human right of all – the right to live – incredibly by blacks who brand the friends of Israel as – of all things – racist!

Have the Braaka blacks forgotten, in their preoccupation with the so-called Palestinians, that the State of Israel is a national liberation movement of refugees struggling for survival and freedom, and under constant attack by powerful enemies?

Have the new-left, third-world blacks forgotten the flood of 300,000 black Sudanese refugees forced out of their homes by the Arabs, the estimated half million blacks slaughtered by the Arabs after Sudan gained its independence, and the enslavement of blacks by Arabs for centuries, continuing to this day as incidents of chattel slavery in Saudi Arabia, Aden, Kuwait, Yemen, Muscat, Oman, Qatar and the Sudan?

Have the power-to-the-people blacks really accepted as their allies the feudal monarchs, exploiters, and oil sheiks in gold Cadillacs, and their Soviet masters, mentors, and armorers, aligned against the only true people's government in the Middle East? Politics does indeed make strange bedfellows.

March 25, 1974

Dear Sir:

Regarding the disgraceful participation by the U.S. in the U.N. consensus statement condemning Israel for establishing settlements in the administered areas, the American collaborators with the Arabs must know that Israeli use of the occupied lands has changed nothing geographically or demographically.

They must know that the resettlement of population has been mostly resettlement of Arabs; that, since the Arab powers failed in their attacks on Israel in 1967, the Arab population of the administered areas has been allowed to increase by more than 127,000, at least 30 times the number of Israeli settlers in the same period; that Israel has permitted more than 50,000 Arabs to return to the areas as permanent residents under the Family Reunion Scheme; and that there has never in all history been such a humane occupier as Israel, offering its nearly half a million Arabs their highest standard of living, equal citizenship, equal pay, equal working, voting and language rights, and hundreds of Arab educational institutions with over a hundred thousand students.

They must know that this benign treatment of Arabs has not changed the professed determination of many Arab spokesmen to destroy the state of Israel, or their capability of doing so with massive armaments supplied by both the USSR and the U.S.

They must know, and apparently do not care, that when the U.S. collaborates with the anti-democratic U.N. majority – however briefly – we hamper the prospects for peace, confirm to the Arabs and the USSR that we can be maneuvered into pressuring Israel, and seriously damage U.S. interests in the Middle East.

November 23, 1976

Russia's Occupied Territories

Sir: Soviet Foreign Minister Andrei Gromyko's regrettable illness while attacking the Camp David accords at the United Nations interrupted not only the speech but also the high comedy of his righteous wrath at Israel.

He charged that "ten years after the aggression, its consequences still have not been eliminated. While the aggression itself goes unpunished, Israel continues to hold sway over the territories it has seized." Who should know better the evils holding sway over seized territories?

With the USSR, however, when it comes to occupying and dominating other nation's lands with police forces held constantly ready to crush any movement toward unsanctioned change, it is not a matter of do as we do, but do as we say. Soviet tanks, "as is well known" are liberators, and flowers are to be strewn in their path by grateful multitudes.

Mr. Gromyko's comic-ironic monologue followed, by only a few weeks, the tenth anniversary of the USSR's brutal occupation of Czechoslovakia, an area of nearly 50,000 square mile with a population of nearly 15 million. That event was marked by neither speeches in the U.N. nor celebrations in the Soviet press, which has constantly condemned Israel's occupation of an area about one-third the size of Czechoslovakia with one-fourteenth the population. Also unsung was the distinction between the USSR's unprovoked aggression and Israel's self-defense against forces that tried several times to destroy it.

Israel has now pledged to withdraw its military forces from the Sinai at once and from the West Bank after a reasonable transitional period. Will the USSR follow suit?

When is the USSR going to withdraw its 32 Soviet divisions still stationed in four European states more than 30 years after the end of World War II?

When will Mr. Gromyko announce to the United Nations the departure of the northern group of Soviet troops garrisoned at Legnica, Poland; the souther group at Tokol, Hungary; the central group at Milovice, Czechosolvakia, and the group of Soviet forces in East Germany at Zossen-Wundsdorf near East Berlin?

When will Victor G. Kulikov, former Soviet chief of staff and marshal of the Soviet Union, currently commanding the Warsaw Treaty Organization forces, and all the Soviet commanders of WTO ground forces, navies, air forces and air defense – when will all these Russian occupiers be packing their bags and going home?

The world is waiting anxiously for the USSR to follow the example of the U.S., England, France and Israel in withdrawing its military forces from other people's lands in Europe and Africa.

We look forward to Russian practice of Russian preachment that occupying others' territory is "criminal action ... aggression ... a mockery of international law and the most elementary concepts of justice."

October 12, 1978

Khouri's Fury

Sir: Edmund Khouri, Baltimore's resident Arab propagandist, is, if nothing else, dependable. He can be counted upon to generate profound sympathy and support for Israel among reasonable people by the crudity, frenzy and transparency of his lies – the bigger, the better, he seems to believe, as did Hitler.

A few of Mr. Khouri's lies – and the truths they serve to emblazon:

The lie that Jews abandoned Israel as a homeland for 1,905 years re-emphasizes the historical truth that Jews have lived in Israel continuously since biblical times, that they have comprised a majority of the inhabitants of Jerusalem for all of the last century, have always lived there, and that the dream of return to Zion has sustained them through centuries of persecution, even finding expression in their prayers and liturgy.

The lie that Zionism is a love of Jews for Jews and hatred of everything else reinforces the revulsion of Americans, led by our President, Congress and delegates to the United Nations, when the General Assembly obscenely equated Zionism with racism, succumbing to Arab-Soviet oil pressures and branding the world organization itself as a band of fools, cowards and frauds.

The lie that Zionism is a "colonial" movement makes it all the more evident that Israel is the only democracy in the Middle East, an oasis of liberty in that vast desert of dictatorships of right and left.

We are also reminded that Israel is less "colonial" than any other nation on earth and is the only state bearing the same name, speaking the same language, holding the same faith and inhabiting the same land as 3,000 years ago. Mr. Khouri also brings to mind that there never was an Arab state in Palestine, never a Palestine Arab nation, never any separate political or social unit ruled by Palestine Arabs.

The lie that Israel discriminates reminds us that Arabs enjoy full equality of citizenship and greater freedom, health and prosperity in Israel than in any of their own explotive societies.

The lie of the "secular democratic" state as the answer for Jews and Moslems is borne out in the daily slaughter of Christians by Moslems in the secular democratic paradise of Lebanon.

But the clincher is Mr. Khouri's prediction that Zionism will never survive in the "enlightened world" – presumably that of the brutal Brezhnevs, murderous Arafats and Amins, and slave-trading sheikhs.

Enemies like Mr. Khouri make friends for Zionism.

January 3, 1976

Israel and Russia

Sir: Why do Israelis distrust Russians, now the colleagues of the U.S. in pressuring the Israelis to surrender at the "peace" table what the Arabs have failed repeatedly to win on the battlefield? What is the basis for Israeli "intransigence?" Could it be their preference for survival over the solutions that the Arabs and Soviets have shown to have in store for them?

In 1966, when Arab military forces were being marshalled for an attack on Israel, when Egypt's Nasser was excoriating the United States and Israel, when the leftist Ba'ath military clique seized power in Syria and opened a new war of terrorism, the USSR gave military and economic aid to the Syrians who had the capability of threatening Western oil interests in Iraq, King Hussein's regime in Jordan, and, of course, Israel.

The USSR gave to Nasser not only military and economic but also diplomatic aid; and tried to bring him together with the Ba'ath Syrians while Russian warships entered the Mediterranean to keep tabs on the U.S. Sixth Fleet. Soviet weapons on all Israel's frontiers backed up the Arabs' threats to "wipe Israel off the map." Israel stood alone in facing Russian arms.

When Nasser's troops entered Sharm el-Sheikh, and he ordered withdrawn the U.N. forces that were supposed to be protecting Israel against blockade, the U.N. meekly complied, yielded to Nasser's demands, and enabled the Egyptians to take over the Tiran Straits. Israel stood alone on the battlefront.

During the War of Attrition, in 1969 and 1970, it was Russian arms in massive quantities that were hurled at Israel, which stood alone against them.

Before the Yom Kippur war in 1973, when – thanks to the USSR – the Arabs were massing more tanks than attacked the Maginot Line and who knew well what was going on, kept it secret from their American partners in peace efforts. The Arabs attacked. Israel again stood alone against Russian weaponry.

Is it strange that Israel is reluctant to entrust its fate to great powers who have so often stood by while Jews were fighting to survive, or who actually aided and abetted efforts to exterminate them? Is it puzzling that Israel declines to put back into Arab and Soviets hands the daggers they have so often plunged into Israel's back?

The judgment of President Carter, in restoring the USSR to the authoritative role it has lost in the Middle East, is indeed open to question by the American people and their representatives in Congress.

October 10, 1977

Dear Sir:

Regarding the sale of F-15 jet fighters to Saudi Arabia in the name of "realism" (Sun, April 24 Page-Op article) Stanley Karnow is bending over backwards so far to be courageously objective in expressing his minority view that he seems to have suffered a blackout.

If he has not lost his senses, why does he attribute mainly to "Israel's sympathizers" the opposition to the Administration's gimmicky package deal that has aroused all citizens concerned about America's interests and image in the world? What about America's sympathizers?

How would this infamous deal help the United States?

By showing our government to be untrustworthy and false in welching on its assurance that the F-15 planes would be provided unconditionally to Israel, not its foes?

By dramatizing the unreliability of American commitments, since Israel, based on the U.S. guarantee of planes, withdrew from vast, strategic areas of the Sinai and jeopardized its security?

By demonstrating that our government repudiates solemn and formal promises to Israel priority in arms supply and rejection of pressure on Israel?

By denying America's special relationship to Israel as its only dependable democratic ally in the Middle East?

By concealing the real possibility that the USSR could get parts or data on the U.S. most advanced weaponry through lax Saudi security with Syrian, Iraqi and Palestinian workers at Saudi air bases?

By ignoring the fact that Saudi Arabia has violated past agreements with the U.S. in training Egyptian pilots on its F-5ES, and that Saudis are known to have pledged to transfer military equipment to Arab confrontation states if war comes again?

By trusting Saudi promises not to use the planes, "if it offended Israeli sensibilities" at its Tabuk base, where they would be 10 minutes from Eilat and 27 minutes from Tel Aviv or anywhere else in Saudi Arabia, where they could easily reach any target in Israel?

By tilting the precarious military balance of power toward the Arabs and their sponsor, the USSR?

By presenting as "moderates" on oil matters the Saudis who have raised prices over 500 percent since the oil embargo and who would have raised them higher if they did not need us more than we need them?

By ignoring the fact that the Saudi oil industry does not need "placating" because it relies primarily on American technicians, equipment and management – as do Saudi power plants, industries, banking, trade, education, agriculture, transport, communication and armed forces?

Mr. Karnow says he does not believe in appeasement. "In realistic terms" (his expression) that is exactly what he recommends in urging that F-15 jet bombers be put in the unsteady hands of Israel's – and America's – enemies.

April 24, 1978

Dear Sir:

Has the worldwide "Be Kind to Arafat" club acquired a new member – the Baltimore Sun, which seems to be bending over backwards to "yes-sir" Yassir?

The latest in what appears to be attempted fumigations of the PLO stench in the Sun's "Perspective" section, was the showcased "interview" of Arafat, allowing and indeed encouraging him to perfume his program of murder and assassination with incensive replies to handpicked questions.

To date, I have not found in the Sun a single line of refutation of Arafat's glorified propaganda, or a single question raised that might have embarrassed or even discomfited him, or altered the image created by that article of a most reasonable nice-guy. Apparently, the Sun believes that it should publish the Great Liberator's selected views in the interests of truth, justice and freedom of information, but should stoutly resist exposure of opposing views as efforts to manipulate the press, influence the public or belabor the obvious.

Although many letters must have reached the Sun countering the Arafat arguments, to my knowledge not one has been published, including the enclosed, which I mailed the day after publication of the Arafat selling job.

If this is an unfair accusation, I'd appreciate hearing from you.

May 22, 1980
[encl. below]

Dear Sir:

The interview of Yassir Arafat featured on the front page of "Perspective" April 27th (we await an equally prominent display of dear friend Ayatollah Khomeini's opinions of the United States) omitted many important questions.

The interviewer might also have asked:

Mr. Arafat, you refer to the Israeli settlement policy as a conspiracy against your people. Is this the same people who in this century slaughtered the Jewish settlers of Hebron, where Jews have lived since biblical times, and who are committed to subordinate or else exterminate their Jewish neighbors?

You quote how much the American taxpayer is alleged to pay in supporting the Israeli citizen, the only friend he has in the Middle East. Does your concern for the American taxpayer extend to how much he is shelling out each day for outrageously overpriced oil to your Arab brothers, and for defense against your sponsors, the Russians?

You call Begin a terrorist, presumably because he waged war against the British army of occupation that turned away from Israel the Holocaust survivors who had nowhere else to go. What do you call your brave freedom fighters who avoid any combat with soldiers and use their Russian weapons exclusively in murdering Israeli women and children in markets and nursery schools?

You say that the Palestinians are suffering, stateless, homeless refugees. Was it not the Arab leaders in 1948 who exhorted them to leave their homes so that the Jews could be driven into the sea? Was it not the Arab nations that kept them suffering, homeless and stateless during all the shameful years of refusing to contribute to their support and denying them entry into any part of their vast lands (while tiny Israel was absorbing hundreds of thousands of Jewish refugees from Arab oppression)?

Were the Palestinians not stateless and suffering during the nineteen years of Jordanian rule over the West Bank, and why were they not then demanding a state of their own? Could it be that they really consider themselves citizens of the State of Jordan and do not need a second state? And are not these constantly publicized refugees better off by far than most of the seldom-mentioned millions of refugees roaming the earth today who have no relatives in the oil business?

You say, Mr. Arafat, that "sooner or later we will achieve our goal." Does that goal remain what you keep stating to Arabs (but not to Americans) and keep affirming formally in your covenant: the destruction of the State of Israel?

A final question, Mr. Arafat. You say, "In the PLO, we have democracy." Who elected you leader?

April 28, 1980

The Meek Shall Inherit the Grave

Criticism of Israel's move against the PLO comes down to this – excuse or ignore PLO actions against Israelis, and deplore Israeli reactions against the PLO.

Ignore the PLO's murderous violence against innocent Jewish, American and Arab victims around the world; ignore the PLO's pouring of artillery fire for seven years into Israeli villages while claiming sanctuary and immunity by hiding behind the Lebanese; ignore the PLO's profligate shedding of Israeli blood, and deplore violence only when Israel thwarts the efforts of those committed to destroy it.

Ignore Israel's effort to eliminate what the Lebanese welcoming Israeli forces also want eliminated – the PLO subjugation of Lebanon; and deplore the plight of civilians in warfare as if Israel had invented the tragic consequences.

Ignore Israel's unparalleled sacrifices for peace in handing back the Sinai to Egypt; and deplore only that Israel is not peace-loving – presumably like the PLO and its Soviet and Arab backers.

Ignore that Israel – granted security from further PLO attack – will restore its occupied area of Lebanon to the Lebanese if the PLO and Syrians will do likewise, and deplore only that expansionist Israel, having cleared out its tormentors, will not vacate so that they can move back and continue their carnage.

Was this criticism reveals is that, to a small and happily shrinking minority, Jews are not supposed to defeat their enemies and survive. Historically and theologically, they are supposed to be martyrs, weak and pathetic victims of persecution instead of strong reactors against violence who can give back more than they have to take.

That minority will have to accept that there are New Jews in history who will never again go quietly when led to slaughter while the world minds its business and looks the other way; who have learned that the earth which the meek inherit is the grave, and who will not jump into it to oblige the ignorers, deplorers and double-standard bearers.

July 15, 1982

Dear Sir:

The un-Egyptian word that best describes the views of Mr. Ismail Fahmy, the anti-Camp David Egyptian Foreign Minister whose 'Precarious Peace" article you found worthy of publication (Sun, June 29th) is chutzpah.

The arrogance of such statements as "Israel obviously planned to profit from the so-called peace with Egypt is beyond understanding.

Has any nation ever signed any pact without expecting some benefits? The "profit" Israel sought, after surviving five wars in 35 years resulting from Egyptian hostility, was peace. What was Egypt's profit, after losing the wars it started or provoked?

Return of the Sinai Peninsula, most of which Israel had held for almost 15 years.

The "profit" of the Sinai oil wells, which Israel had developed and from which it received about half of its energy needs, now costing several billion dollars a year to replace.

Homes, farms and towns which cost Israel hundreds of millions of dollars in compensation to settlers.

Military facilities and airfields whose replacement cost Israel billions in addition to the U.S. one-time grant.

Advancing the Egyptian-Israel border 40 miles closer to Israel, 60 miles from Tel Aviv, 25 miles from Beersheva.

Regaining control over the entrance to the Gulf of Eilat and its vital trade.

Sparing Egypt its periodic humiliation and loss of manpower and material in warring against Israel.

Wasn't that enough of a bonanza for Egypt to stop Mr. Fahmy from prattling about profit to Israel?

If the 'so-called' peace is precarious, it is not Israel but Mr. Fahmy and the Arab rejectionists who make it shaky. They also make clear that Israel does not act but only reacts to its enemies' intransigent determination to destroy it.

Long after Mr. Fahmy's tirade has been forgotten, the judgement of the Nobel committee that awarded its peace prize to Menachem Begin and Anwar Sadat will be remembered.

Defending Wiesel and Israel

Nobody asked, or expected, the conscience of world Jewry and voice of its 6 million martyrs; Eli Wiesel, in his Nobel Prize acceptance speech, to refer to the Palestinians, but he did, surprisingly. So he is not blind to their problem, as Normon Solomon said in his December 23 *Opinion*Commentary piece. He is acutely sensitive to it.

Mr. Solomon, however, is blind in his inability to admit that the central fact of Middle East tensions is not the Palestinians but the unrelenting determination of Israel's Arab neighbors to continue their commitment to wars to exterminate Israel.

Mr. Solomon, who is lucky enough to live in the world's strongest nation surrounded by vast oceans and friendly neighbors, is blind to what happens to human beings facing threats of annihilation every hour for 40 years.

Mr. Solomon, blissfully unaware of any daily threats to his existence, is lecturing Holocaust survivors who have had to fight world apathy, hostility and five murderous Arab wars just to keep breathing. He blinds himself to the fact that the Palestinian question is the result of, not the cause of these conflicts and that it would never have existed had the Arab nations surrounding Israel not waged this constant warfare.

He is blind to the map showing how a West Bank enemy state could cut Israel in two at its narrowest point and achieve the Arab fantasy of driving the Jews into the sea.

The Palestinian people were not "made homeless by Israeli policies" but by their rejection by Arab states which could long ago have resettled them in 5 million square miles of surrounding Arab lands – as Jewish refugees from Arab lands have been welcomed in tiny Israel.

Israel is militarized not because it wants to be, but because it has to be militarized to exist. Jews do not say that Israel can do no wrong. They do say that Israel alone should not be expected to rise above the natural law of survival and bare its jugular to the cutthroat's knife, and that unattainable and inhuman standards of morality should not be demanded of Israel which are never expected of other nations, including our own.

What other nation, besieged as Israel is, would maintain a vigorous democracy, respect human and civil rights and even forgo the death penalty, except for Adolph Eichmann?

What other "victims" have enjoyed such improvements in their daily lives under "occupation" as the West Bank Palestinians? Their numbers have increased by nearly half since their 1967 war against Israel. By 1982, their percentage of hospital births more than tripled, as did the number of doctors and maternal/child centers. Classrooms doubled. Ownership of electric refrigerators, cars and trucks increased tenfold. Thousands commute daily to jobs in Israel. Not all are throwing rocks.

What they have been denied is the statehood which they never wanted under Jordanian occupation between 1948 and 1967, which they and their sympathizers now demand, and which Palestine Liberation Organization officials proclaim is a first step toward their objective of "liberating" all of Israel.

There are none so blind as those who will not see that peace – not violence or terrorism – is the only solution to the Palestinian problem; and none so deaf as those who will not hear, or heed, the PLO threats which Israelis have learned from bitter experience are not rhetoric.

"The victory march will continue until the Palestinian flag flies in Jerusalem and in all of Palestine – from the Jordan River to the Mediterranean sea from Rosh Hanikra to Eilat," said PLO Chairman Yassir Arafat in a speech at the University of Beirut December 7, 1980.

"We shall not rest until our usurped land is liberated and until the Palestinian people return with dignity and pride to their independent state, with Jerusalem its capital," said King Fahd of Saudi Arabia in Riyadh, January 21, 1981.

"We shall never allow Israel to live in peace. We shall never allow it total security. Every Israeli will feel that behind every wall there might be a guerrilla who is aiming at me ..." said

PLO political department head Farouk Kaddoumi in a 1981 interview in West Germany's *Stern*.

"The liquidation of Israel is one of the means we adopt to achieve unity and freedom in the Arab world. We know that liberation is a long-term goal, but I am about to determine that, at the end of this year, a democratic Palestinian state will be established," said Hani al-Hassan, political adviser to Yassir Arafat, in a speech at the American University, Beirut, January 9, 1982.

Elie Wiesel is not blind to the seriousness of such threats. They are clearer to the Holocaust survivor than to Mr. Solomon in faraway peaceful Portland, Oregon.

Rev. Chester L. Wickwire
8214 Bellona Avenue
Baltimore, Maryland

Dear Chester:

I consider you my friend and a friend of all people suffering discrimination and oppression. That describes the Palestinians in the second half of this century. I think you agree that it also applies to the Jews in the genocidal first half, in dozens of preceding centuries, and in Arab and Muslim states today.

As underdogs, the Jews are all-time champions. That may help to explain, though it does not excuse, the paranoia and obsession with security and survival that underlie their reaction to the Intifada. I don't think they want to be top dogs; I think they want to survive what they see as yet another savage campaign to destroy them and the sovereignty and legitimacy of their tiny state.

As a member of Baltimore Friends of Peace Now, I support those Israelis who, despite all odds and the agonies of history, believe that, with empathy and sacrifice, peace is possible; who have not surrendered to the bleak and bloody inevitability of violence breeding more violence ad infinitum; who seek to trade land for peace, to live and let live as equals within defensible borders.

But I don't think we can expect of Israel a standard of moral conduct that is not expected of any other country that has beaten off repeated wars of extermination by surrounding enemies who are still waging war against it.

It must be conceded that the Middle East is not the Middle West and that people enjoying peace and security do not behave like those under constant threat of annihilation.

It takes a leap of imagination for Americans to picture the lands of Israel's belligerent neighbors – Syria, Iran, Iraq, Saudi Arabia and the Arab Federation – superimposed on a map of western United States - sweeping halfway across our country from the Pacific almost to the Mississippi and from the Canadian border into Mexico. In this vast expanse of the United States, Israel would occupy a small area on the coast of California – at its narrowest waist about 10 miles from the Pacific in downtown Los Angeles.

It takes an even greater leap to imagine that all of the states and their population of 250 million are at war against about 4 million Californians; that they have already waged five wars to wipe out the little band of Westerners; that they are still trying to drive them into the Pacific; that they have given the Californians not a moment's peace in over 40 years; and that they nevertheless demand that the Californians must have kind and gentle feelings toward murderous enemies and oblige them by committing suicide.

With the media emphasis on Israeli soldiers reacting to Arab civilian attacks, more than imagination, indeed a prodigious feat of understanding is needed to comprehend the predicament of the most oppressed people in history, the Jews, the victims of the ages who are now seen as victimizers, the reactors to violence who are accused of perpetrating, even inventing it.

Critics of Israel's efforts to suppress the Intifada cannot feel that Israeli reaction because they have never walked a mile – or a few millennia – in Israel's shoes. Since Israel is a democratic society open to the media, the critics are constantly exposed to violent Israeli reactions, hardly ever to violent Arab actions or to Arab assaults on Arabs or to inhumane Arab exploitation of Palestinians as weapons in the ongoing Arab wars against the Jewish state.

Perceiving from day-to-day as mid-westerners instead of historically as mid-easterners, the critics see only the brave Palestinian fight for national liberation. They do not, or will not, see the world's oldest battle for national liberation, Israel's desperate and determined struggle to survive. That is not as easy to show to the TV-viewer or the tourist as today's picture of an Israeli soldier chasing a child-puppet whose masters have manipulated him to hurl a rock or gasoline bomb at the soldier.

Nor is it easy for critics who have not barely survived the rocks, bombs and furnaces to understand why the soldier is there and will stay there until assured that he can live in peace within defensible borders.

The critics would sympathize with the soldier's survivors if he had been killed like so many other Israelis in Arab invasions. But the critics will have to understand if he considers the price too high to pay for their sympathy.

All of this is an attempted clarification, not justification. As I've tried to say in the enclosed copy of an ad in this week's New Year's issue of the *Jewish Times*, peace is the only way out.

Warmest personal regards and sincere wishes for a healthy, happy Jewish New Year 5750.

Jack L. Levin

Israel's free press invites critics, while Arab mayhem is hidden

As fabulous as "Arabian Nights", the media myth about the Middle East that seems most resistant to fact is that peace-loving Arabs minding their own business have been victimized by outsiders.

The legend has been nurtured by reporters who are excluded from closed Arab and Persian societies while they can function freely in democratic Israel. The hard, bad news, therefore, seems all to come from the Israeli side. Violence against Arabs by Jews defending their lives, homes and families is front-page news, while violence against Arabs by other Arabs or Persians is often not news at all. Journalistic ignorance is Arab bliss.

For every Arab harmed by an Israeli in six Arab wars to destroy Israel, hundreds of Arabs have been tortured and slaughtered by their countrymen. But that fact is like the tree falling in the forest that makes no sound if nobody is there to hear it crash.

So let us wander briefly into the wilderness of Middle East conflicts. If we listen carefully, we can hear echoes of Arabs felling Arabs by the thousands.

In Jordan in 1970, Hussein killed 15,000 of his country's Palestinians, more in the three days of Black September 1970 than had been killed by Israelis in the three wars that Arabs had launched against Israel up to that time. More recently in the one small town of Hama, Syria, a rampaging Assad dispatched 20,000 of his suspected political opponents and their entire families.

In Beirut several months ago, Shi'ite militiamen and Palestinian fighters engaged without benefit of TV coverage in the bloodiest week since 1982 in that tormented city. The Shi'ites, in that week only, killed 350 and wounded 1,300 Palestinians (plus 60 with a car bomb in the Christian section). The Palestinians disposed of some 20 Shi'ites with poisoned tea.

One reason rarely mentioned for this media indifference to

Arab violence is that eyewitnesses and correspondents are intimidated. Horrible atrocities are unreported in the Lebanese press, says the London Times, although "thousands of people" know what is going on. Many reporters have been withdrawn "because of the risk of being kidnapped or killed ... If we print (the stories) we will get a bomb through our window."

Arab internecine wars and blood-feuding Bedouins are nothing new. Civil wars have raged between Arabs and Kurds in Iraq and blacks and Arabs in the Sudan.

In the Moroccan-Algerian war some 20 years ago in another part of the forest, the Polisario suffered staggering losses at the hands of fellow Arabs. In Ethiopia, the savage Colonel Mengistu has shown Arab unbelievers who is boss.

Still flaming after five years of carnage is the Iran-Iraq war, in which more Arabs have been killed by Persians than Americans were killed by Vietnamese in the entire war in Southeast Asia. Iraq alone has lost an estimated 75,000 dead and twice that many wounded.

From these unseen, unheard wars of Arabs against Arabs and Persians come no sounds of bombs exploding and no sights so familiar to us from the media coverage of Israel's struggle against the PLO in Lebanon. No heart-searing glimpses of the Arab mother grieving over her small child killed in an Arab air raid. No anguish of the old man wandering pathetically through the ruble in search of his little dog. With this television blackout, Arab mayhem against Arabs is out of sight, out of mind.

There is the traditional competition among Egypt, Syria, Iraq, non-Arab Iran and Libya for leadership of the Middle East. There are personal feuds between Mubarak and Khadafi, Mubarak and Assad, Assad and Hassan Bakr, and the party feuds as in the Ba'athist cliques in Syria, Iraq and Egypt.

There are the inter-Arab wars of medievalist against modernist, of conservative against radical, of religious zealot against zealot, of Arab against black (as in the Sudan), of oil-rich Saudi Arabia, Kuwait, Iraq, Libya, Algeria and some Gulf states against oil-poor (or less rich) Egypt, Jordan, Sudan, Morocco,

Lebanon and the two Yemens.

If there had never been a state of Israel, Arabs would be murdering Arabs today as throughout their history. The Middle East has long been a cockpit of squabbling tribes, sects and factions.

With the exception of Egypt, the present Arab map is a scrambled jigsaw puzzle of pieces left over from the collapse of the Ottoman, British and French empires. Many Arab countries suffer from a chronic fever of violent irredentism and nationalism. Many of their rulers are unstable, obsessive musclemen who bullied their way to power. They rule their armed forces, security apparatus and bureaucracy with ruthless, relentless control, backed in some cases by a superpower patron.

Many of the pieces are made of fractious smaller fragments stuck together as with chewing gum: Kurds in Iraq, Palestinians in Jordan; a familiar jumble in Lebanon, tribes in South Arabia, guerrillas in Dhofar supported by South Yemen against the rulers of Muscat and Oman.

Besides fighting a war against Iran, Iraq has designs on Kuwait. Assad is building his Greater Syria in Lebanon and points west. The Saudis have irredentist claims on the Union of Arab Emirates (and vice versa) particularly oil-soaked Abu Dhabbi, and they bankroll North Yemen against the radicals of South Yemen.

Besides wars and civil wars, terrorism is another favorite pursuit in Arab countries. U.S. citizens and interests are the target of about one-third of terrorist attacks, says Robert B. Oakley, director of the U.S. State Department's Office for Counter Terrorism and Emergency Planning. He testified recently before a Senate committee that the Middle East is the primary source of world terrorism, that the main terrorists are fanatical Palestinians and Shi'ites, and that their principal bases are Iran, Syria and Libya – especially Syria which is using terrorism to block Jordanian King Hussein's peace moves.

The chances of improvement are slim. Political and social reform are unlikely in the world's least-free states. The New

York-based civic group, Freedom House, just released its annual survey of freedom around the world, ranking each country on political rights and civil liberties granted its citizens.

Its conclusion about the Middle East is that Israel is the only country there that is free, and Iraq is the least free, followed closely by Syria, Saudi Arabia, Libya, Algeria and Iran among the "not free". Listed as only "partly free" were Egypt, Jordan and Morocco.

What, then, of the argument that, if only the Israelis were move flexible, if only they would give back the launching sites of past wars against them so that their enemies can try again to destroy them, if only Israel would obligingly cease to exist, then there would be peace in the Middle East?

On the contrary, it seems that, for nearly half a century, the only frazzled thread uniting Arabs is their unequivocal, unrenounced and unalterable determination to subjugate or eradicate the state of Israel.

If there is a semblance of peace in the Middle East with Arab infighting mostly unheard and unseen, it is not because Arabs are at peace with Israel, but because, being in a perpetual state of war against Israel, they are less likely to war openly against each other in their timeless tradition. If Israel goes, there goes the neighborhood for the "Arab Nation."

The Intifada in Freeze-frame

Those who focus on Israel's reaction to the Intifada present an accurately detailed but misleading picture of but a moment in a long movie of violence.

It is like a still shot of a barroom brawl. It shows a scowling black-hat blazing away with both guns at cowering white-hats who have used up their ammunition. The picture does not show the shooting of several black-hats just for entering the saloon. It does not show the white-hats clobbering the black-hats with fists, chairs, tables and bar stools. It shows only the surviving black-hat firing back at his would-be murderers.

As an example is Hal Wyner's essay (Other Voices, October 13). Wyner's frozen-frame does not, of course, show all that happened before. It does not show the wars of attempted extermination that Palestinians have supported, cheered and helped to wage against Israel. It does not show any of the terrorist acts against Israeli civilians in which Palestinians have participated: the Olympic athletes slaughtered, the women, children and elderly Jews machine-gunned in supermarkets, synagogues, air terminals, schools, shops, buses and homes.

As underdog victims of racism, brutality and tyranny the Jews are all-time champions. That may help to explain though it does not excuse, the paranoia and obsession with security and survival that underlie Israel's reaction to the Intifada. Most Israelis instinctively hate violence and do not want to be top dogs; they just want to survive what they see as yet another savagery in the endless Arab campaign to destroy them and the sovereignty and legitimacy of their tiny state. No people in history have made greater sacrifices for peace than the Jews.

As a member of Baltimore Friends of Peace Now, I support those Israelis who despite the odds, difficulties and agonies of history, believe that, with empathy, peace is possible; who have not surrendered to the bleak and bloody inevitability of violence breeding more violence ad infinitum; who seek to trade some land for some peace, to live and let live as equals within defensive borders.

But I don't think we can expect of Israel a standard of moral conduct and cheek-turning that is not expected of any other country that has suffered as Israel has at the hands of surrounding enemies who are still waging war against it.

It must be conceded that the Middle East is not the Middle West and that people enjoying peace and security do not behave like those under constant threat of annihilation. It takes a leap of imagination for Americans to picture the lands of Israel's belligerent neighbors – Syria, Iran, Iraq, Saudi Arabia and the Arab Federation – superimposed on a map of western United States, sweeping halfway across our country from the Pacific almost to the Mississippi and from the Canadian border into Mexico. In this vast expanse of the United States, Israel would occupy a small area on the coast of California – at its narrowest waist about 10 miles from the Pacific in downtown Los Angeles.

It takes an even greater leap to image that all of the states and their population of 250 million are at war against about 3-1/2 million Californians; that they have already waged five wars to wipe out the little band; that they are still trying to drive them into the Pacific; that they have given the Californians not a moment's peace in over 40 years; and that they nevertheless demand that the Californians must have kind and gentle feelings toward their murderous enemies and oblige them by committing suicide.

With the media emphasis on Israeli soldiers reacting to Arab civilian attacks, more than imagination, indeed a prodigious feat of understanding is needed to comprehend the predicament of the Jews, the victims of the ages who are now seen as victimizers, the reactors to violence who are accused of perpetrating, even inventing it in a world addicted to it.

Critics of Israel's efforts to suppress the Intifada cannot feel the Israeli reaction because they have never walked a mile – or a few millennia – in Israel's shoes. Since Israel is a democratic society open to the media, the critics are not constantly exposed to violent Arab actions or to Arab assaults on Arabs or to inhumane Arab exploitation of Palestinians as weapons in the unrelenting

Arab wars against the Jewish state.

Absorbed in TV and oblivious to history some critics see only the brave Palestinian fight for national liberation. They do not or will not see the world's oldest battle for national liberation. Israel's stubborn, desperate struggle to survive against terrible odds.

That is old stuff to journalists with what's-new tunnel vision. It is not as easy to show to TV viewers or tourists as today's picture of an Israeli soldier chasing a child-puppet whose masters have manipulated him to hurl a big rock or gasoline bomb at the soldier.

Nor is it easy for critics who have not barely survived the rocks, bombs and furnaces to understand why the soldier is there and will stay there until assured that he can live in peace within defensible borders. The critics would sympathize with the soldier's survivors if he were killed like so many other Israelis by the brawlers in the white kaffiyehs.

November 8, 1989

Considering Israel

Editor: In her otherwise irrational comparison of Israel with South Africa (*The Sun*, March 3) one comment by Doris Rausch is interesting, perceptive and revealing: that Israel, long since lost its right to any special consideration by this country or by the world at large.

When did Israel – meaning the Jewish people – ever get consideration – special or otherwise – from the world at large?

Was it when one-third of the world's Jewish population was being exterminated and the world, including this country, turned away?

Was it when a remnant to the world's oldest national liberation movement was at long last allowed to gather its tormented exiles in its tiny historic homeland after being denied refuge everywhere else?

Was it when Arab hordes outnumbering the Israelis 100 to 1 tried their damndest in five wars to overrun and annihilate the fledgling state – did the world then give Israel special consideration?

In helping Israel, the U.S. is acting pragmatically as well as morally: Israel is America's only dependable ally in the entire Middle East, the one and only democracy, a vital friendly forward base of American naval and air power. America's embattled outpost is under constant threat or attack by surrounding autocratic, tyrannical and barbaric regimes that are still at war against Israel and still committed to finish Hitler's work.

We U.S. citizens aid Israel because it is a sound investment and because Israel's enemies are our enemies. They are not the Palestinians, but the Arab states which cynically incite and use the hapless Palestinians, now and for the past half century, as weapons in the Arab wars against the Jews.

Somehow, the slaughter of Arabs by other Arabs (over 20,000 mowed down and paved over in one town alone, Hama, by Syria; at least 15,000 Palestinians in Black September, 1970; by moderate Jordan, etc. was not news. The fact that nearly one-third of all Palestinians killed last year in the West Bank and Gaza were murdered by fellow Palestinians is not news. The brutal killing of thousands of rebellious Arabs by British and French imperial powers (whose national existence was never at risk, as is Israel's) was not news. Only Arab insurrection casualties caused by Israel Defense Forces (the destruction of whose nation is still avowed by the PLO) makes horrifying front-page headlines and shocking TV features news in this violent cruel and savage world.

Now that is truly "special consideration."

April 17, 1990

May 21, 1993
President Bill Clinton
The White House
1600 Pennsylvania Avenue
Washington, DC

Dear President Clinton:

We respectfully urge you to consider reviewing the espionage conviction of Jonathan Pollard.

There can be no question of his guilt – although he was misled into an admission of guilt by false promises of leniency.

There is a grave question, however, of unjust discrimination; other spies such as the Walkers have received much lighter sentences for more serious crimes of greater threat to our national security.

We believe that Pollard has paid with years in solitary confinement for his misplaced loyalty and incredible stupidity, and that his sentence is due for review and commutation.

Thank you very much for considering this request.

                Signed by: Jack L. Levin
                                  David J. Levin
                                  Ester M. Levin
                                  Roslyn Wills

When the Eternal Victims Struck Back

At this season 50 years ago appeared a startling new development in the long history of the Jewish people. For the first time since ancient days, Jewish victims began fighting back as Jews against their oppressors.

Nothing like it had happened since the Maccabees resisted Greek efforts to force them to abandon their religion and since Shimon Bar Kochba, with his followers, fought successfully for three years against the mighty Roman legions. Through most of the millennia that followed, Jews became known as "the Martyr Race" who passively accepted persecution rather than yield to pressure to convert.

Of course, Jews had fought bravely as citizens of other nations in the American, French and Russian revolutions, the American and Spanish civil wars, and the great wars of the 19th and 20th centuries (although often as second-class participants.)

Resisting the British

But in 1946, the Israeli Irgun Zvi Leumi, the Organization of the National Army, started the battle against the British army of occupation in Palestine. Those forces had been ordered by the British foreign minister Ernest Bevin to turn back the rickety ships crowded with wretched survivors of the Holocaust.

The Irgun, under such commanders as Menachem Begun, was determined to admit these fellow Jews to the only land that would take them in. The fighters struggled to prevent the refugees compulsory return to live with those who had robbed and brutalized them and murdered their families. This effort required driving out the British army of occupation, a formidable task for the ill-equipped Irgun fighters.

The Irgun was condemned by virtually all the Jewish establishment organizations of the time. David Ben Gurion, Golda Meir and other Israeli leaders were still in London pleading with Bevin to relent and admit the hapless refugees to Palestine.

The Irgun was officially perceived as terrorists, hooligans, fascists and worse – hotheads upstaging the Haganah, the main body of the Israeli army, which was preparing for the anticipated attack of five Arab armies after the imminent declaration of Israeli statehood. The Haganah was keeping its powder dry for the decisive battle; it resented the Irgun's activities.

Many saw the Irgun as patriots doing the same job as the Minutemen of 1776 – driving out the British army. Two of us were Jews: Jimmy Swartz of Mano Swartz Furs was in charge of fund-raising. I was organizer and publicity director of the newly formed Maryland Chapter of Americans for a Free Palestine. (That organization, founded by Ben Hecht and Peter Bergson, lasted only two or three years, but they were exciting ones.)

The third man was Oliver B. J. Krastell, a West Baltimore Irish Catholic furniture retailer, whose zeal as chairman of the chapter was rooted in his low opinion of the British occupiers of Ireland and his concern for the Jewish people. He taught me that no one is more effective at raising money for a Jewish cause than a good Christian.

In 1946, we formally organized the Maryland chapter, enrolled members and raised funds and support for the Irgun's battle to save the Holocaust survivors.

After Israel declared its independence, the three of us, with a few friends, organized the first Rally for Israel and the Irgun in Baltimore's huge Fifth Regiment Armory.

The response from the Jewish community was immediate and overwhelming, despite Irgun's notoriety. The overflow crowd was estimated by police at more than 14,000 the largest assembly of Baltimore Jews before or since. The crowd packed the Armory, filled Hoffman Street and extended up Linden Avenue on a rainy night. Amplifiers had to be set up outside so that those standing in the rain could follow the proceedings.

The new hero

Behind the speakers was a huge blow-up of Arthur Szyk's drawing of an Irgun fighter, the new hero of Jewish history. It inspired the audience and the speakers.

Maj. Samuel Weiser, a former member of Field Marshal Montgomery's staff, was the principal speaker. He had organized the George Washington Legion of American War Veterans who had volunteered to fight for the Irgun in Palestine. Also featured on the program were Barney Ross, boxing champion and U.S. Marine Silver Star winner, Sen. Herbert R. O'Conor, Rep. Abraham Molter of New York and Baltimore's exuberant Mayor Thomas D'Alesandro.

Invocations were delivered by the Rev. John S. Martin of St. Vincent's Catholic Church and Rabbi Samuel H. Vitsik of Beth Hamedrash Hagodol Congregation.

Mrs. Louis Untermeyer, a former judge, delivered a message written for the occasion by her husband, the editor-author Karl Shapiro. Baltimore's Nobel prize-winning poet, contributed a poem that was read by the actor Murray Slatkin. Tevya's speech to the United Nations, an excerpt from Ben Hecht's 1946 drama on Broadway, "A Flag is Born," was presented passionately by 14 year old Alice Shecter, winner of the city-wide Hebrew school's declamation contest.

Roar of the crowd

It was not the messengers, however, but the message that kept the crowd roaring. The state of Israel was at long last a reality. All Jews, not just old people hoping to die in Israel, saw the dream of the ages come alive. Most took pride in that historic day. Many of the Jewish leaders who opposed the rally came to recognize the Irgun's contribution to the rescue of the survivors. Baltimore Jews, like Jews everywhere, were tired of identifying with Jews as victims, with Jews herded like cattle into the gas chambers and ovens, with Jews as the martyrs of history. There had been enough of Jews taking it. Now Jews were successfully giving it back.

There have been many occasions since for all freedom lovers to admire the courage, skills and success of the Israel defense forces, but none will equal the excitement of that rainy night when, in Shakespeare's words, the worm turned.
March 1, 1996

Chapter 7
Jack Levin on Soviet Jewry
Robert O. Freedman

Soviet Jews were always a special interest of Jack Levin. His concerns extended from attempts to free them while they were imprisoned in the Soviet Union – his letter to then Soviet leader Mikhail Gorbachev which concludes this group of his writings is a classic call to conscience – to their successful resettlement in Baltimore. Indeed Jack seems to have taken great satisfaction in the achievements of Soviet Jews once they had moved to Baltimore. Unlike the situation in other cities in the United States, Soviet Jews who moved to Baltimore have not only successfully assimilated economically into American life, they also have played a significant role in the Baltimore Jewish community and Jack was only too happy to make note of that fact.

The notable contributions of Soviet-Jewish immigrants to Baltimore's new vitality

Soviet-Jewish immigration has been slowed to a trickle, but the rich human talent has already released has been measurably bestowed on Baltimore as well as other communities and other countries. The fact of the immigration, however limited, gives special significance to an event to be held at Beth El Synagogue this coming Sunday. This will mark the 10th anniversary of the newest member of Baltimore's Jewish community – JURI (Jewish Union of Russian Immigrants). The celebration will remind us how much the USSR has lost and the United States has gained from Czarist and Soviet persecution of the Jews.

Baltimore's newest ethnic community, numbering over 1,600 Soviet Jewish immigrants, has already produced many successful contributors to business, the professions, arts, sciences and social services.

From earlier flights of Russian and Eastern European Jews to freedom in Maryland emerged many of the civic leaders who have helped to build Baltimore into one of the world's great centers of commerce, industry, medicine and culture.

Thomas Kennedy, author of the 1825 "Jew Bill", which he finally rammed through the Maryland legislature after several unsuccessful attempts, to give Maryland Jews the rights of citizenship, would be proud to see what the recent immigrants have been enabled to achieve.

Baltimore's recent Soviet Jewish community has provided six accomplished musicians to the Baltimore Symphony Orchestra, two teachers to the Peabody Conservatory of Music, a conductor, several talented musicians in local bands, two successful architects, a top executive of a title-search corporation, a manager of Baltimore City's planning department, a dozen or more owners of small businesses ranging from a neighborhood grocery store to a large insurance brokerage firm, and three computer scientists working for NASA.

More than 50 have become engineers, computer analysts and researchers, three of whom have obtained U.S. patents for their innovations.

Among its university professors are Drs. A. Katok and I. Mayergoys at University of Maryland, Dr. S. Fridman at Johns Hopkins and Dr. S. Bercovich at George Washington. Eight of the Baltimore newcomers are Ph.D.s in science... This could not have happened without help from the annual campaigns of the Associated Charities and Welfare Fund, HIAS, Baltimore's Hebrew Immigrant Aid Society for over a century, supported the Soviet Jews as the had earlier generations of immigrants, with aid in all details ranging from arranging passports, visas, citizenship papers and other documents, to handling luggage and publishing an English-Russian newspaper. Since 1880, the national HIAS organization has reunited families and helped the adjustment to freedom of over four million Jewish men, women and children, after rescue from war or persecution.

The Jewish Family and Children's Service took over from HIAS in helping the new citizens with the myriad problems of learning a new language and adapting to the culture, habits, customs and institutions of a new homeland. JFCS was the principal, primary settlement agency which helped the immigrants to survive and thrive in a totally new environment.

JFCS provided the security deposit for the first house or apartment and vouchers for the family's necessities – food, clothing, furniture. It assigned a social worker to help with arrangements for social security and other entitlements, and in due time for contact with the Associated Placement and Guidance Service.

The APGS than assessed the immigrants' work skills, taught them survival English and later, more advanced courses in adjustment to their new life, and helped them to find and qualify for entry-level jobs.

Now the beneficiaries are becoming benefactors. Rafael Chikvashvili and his brother David are active community leaders. Rafael served two terms on the board of the Associated Jewish

Charities and Welfare Fund and is currently a member of the United Jewish Appeal Young Leadership Council, the JFCS and the board of Beth Tfiloh Synagogue.

Other Soviet immigrants involved in Baltimore's Jewish community include two on the board of HIAS, three on the Baltimore Jewish Council, several on the boards of JFCS, Levindale, APGS, The Hebrew Free Loan Association, the Jewish Community Center and the Board of Jewish Education.

Soviet Jewish children are enrolled at Beth Tfiloh Day School, Bais Yaakov and the Talmudical Academy. Many families have joined local orthodox, reform and conservative congregations.

Ten years ago, the emigres were struck by the contrast between Baltimore's supportive community and the antagonistic establishment they had left behind. In the USSR, as soon as they applied for immigration visas, they had been deprived of employment, income and housing and cast out as pariahs and parasites reduced to living off relatives. Many who were established professionals with distinguished careers – scientists, rocket engineers, professors, physicians – had been reduced to the most menial jobs.

But they got out; they were the lucky ones.

Today, their brothers and sisters who have been denied the right to join their families in America and Israel are stuck at the bottom of the social order, if not imprisoned in mental institutions or labor camps.

But they have not given up. They survive in hope that, one day, they, too, will be allowed to escape to family and freedom. They live for tomorrow.

May 29, 1984

Returning the Favor

As the granddaddy of Baltimore's Soviet Jewry support movement, along with Fabian Kolker, I'm proud of how the Soviet Jewish community is growing.

The Russians are not only coming; they are coming of age.

With help from the Jewish community, the 2,000 Russian Jews who arrived in Baltimore in the past 15 years have become self-reliant American citizens. The help has come from HIAS, Baltimore's Hebrew Immigrant Aid Society, which has aided generations of immigrants with luggage, passports, visas, citizenship papers and other documents, reuniting families and easing adjustment to a new land and life. Supplementing HIAS, the Jewish Family Service, another agency of the Associated Jewish Charities and Welfare Fund, has also helped the newcomers to learn the language, history, customs and institutions of their new homeland, as well as providing first homes and apartments and family necessities. The Associated Placement and Guidance Service has analyzed skills and located jobs.

But serving the needs of those coming to Baltimore is not the only concern of the Baltimore Jewish community. Attention is being paid also to those Jews still denied their rights in the USSR.

On December 6th – the first anniversary of the historic rally for Soviet Jewry that drew nearly a quarter-million protesters to Washington – Baltimoreans assembled at Beth Tfiloh Congregation in behalf of Soviet Jews who are still forbidden to live religiously or leave for Israel or the U.S.

The main speaker was Baltimorean Soshana Cardin, newly named chairperson of the National Conference for Soviet Jewry and former president of the Council of Jewish Federations and Welfare Funds.

Besides observing a year of remembering those left behind, the occasion also recalled the accomplishments and contributions of those who got away to Baltimore.

The Chikvashvilis are examples – brothers from Tbilisi who have lived in Baltimore with their families since 1974. David is now redevelopment manager for the Montgomery County central business district. Rafael is a professor in computer science at George Washington University. As volunteers, both have filled many positions of responsibility, serving on such boards as the Associated Jewish Charities, Baltimore Jewish Council, Jewish Family Service and Beth Tfiloh Synagogue. The homes of both brothers often serve these days as hospitality centers for visiting Soviet friends now allowed to travel.

Like earlier waves of Russian Jewish immigrants, Baltimore's newest ethnic community has produced many success stories in business, the professions, arts, sciences and social services. They would have gladdened the heart of Thomas Kennedy who, in 1825, rammed through a resistant Maryland legislature his "Jew Bill" that finally conceded to Maryland Jews the rights of citizenship.

Among the latest arrivals are many members of the Baltimore Symphony Orchestra, Peabody Institute teachers, architects, physicians, professors, a top executive of a title-search corporation, a Baltimore city planning manager, computer scientists and over 50 engineers.

They are paying back to their community, city, state and nation rich dividends on the investment in their resettlement.

They are making us more aware of the individual freedom that is too often taken for granted. To them, it is a dream come true. Their enthusiastic patriotism is inspiring and infectious. They remind us that liberty, in the Soviet Union and in Israel, is best appreciated by those who have been denied it and have made sacrifices for it, and that the greatest strength of a nation of immigrants lies in their diversity of talents, energies and love.

December 21, 1988

General Secretary Mikhail Gorbachev
Central Committee of the Communist Party
of the Soviet Union
Staraya Place 4
Moscow, USSR

Dear Secretary Gorbachev:

We have something in common besides our desire to live in peace.

Soon your people and ours will be celebrating the births of our respective constitutions.

Our original constitution of the United States of America was adopted on September 17, 1787, so we will be observing its 200th anniversary.

Your much more recent constitution of the Union of Soviet Socialist Republics was adopted on October 7, 1977, so you will be marking only your tenth – but we hope with similar enthusiasm.

As we strive to live with our differences, it's worth noting how many ideals we share – at least on paper. Seems like a good time to examine the two great documents. They contain some amazing revelations.

For instance, I was pleasantly surprised to learn from which constitution come the following excerpts:

"Article 50 .... Citizens are guaranteed freedom of speech, of the press, and of assembly, meetings, street processions and demonstrations. Exercise of these political freedoms is ensured by putting public buildings, streets and squares at the disposal of the people and their organizations, by broad dissemination of information and by the opportunity to use the press, television and radio.

"Article 51 .... Citizens have the right to associate in public organizations that promote their political activity and initiative and satisfaction of their various interests.

"Article 52 .... Citizens are guaranteed freedom of conscience, that is the right to profess or not to profess any religion, and to conduct religious worship ....

"Article 54 .... Citizens are guaranteed inviolability of the person. No one may be arrested except by a court decision or ... warrant ....

"Article 55 .... Citizens are guaranteed inviolability of the home. No one may, without lawful grounds, enter a home against the will of those residing in it ....

"Article 56 .... The privacy of citizens and of their correspondence, telephone conversations and telegraphic communications is protected by law ....

"Article 57 .... Respect for the individual and protection of the rights and freedoms of citizens are the duty of all state bodies, public organizations and officials. Citizens have the right to protection by the courts against encroachments on their honour and reputation, life, health, and personal freedom and property.

"Article 58 .... Citizens have the right to lodge a complaint against the action of officials, state bodies and public bodies. Complaints shall be examined according to the procedure and within the time limit established by law.

> "Actions by officials that contravene the law or exceed their powers and infringe the rights of citizens, may be appealed against in a court in the manner prescribed by law.
>
> "Citizens have the right to compensation for damage resulting from unlawful actions by state organizations and public organizations or by officials in the performance of their duties."

Sound familiar? Why, of course, Secretary Gorbachev. These excerpts are not from the original or amended American constitution (although the concepts are in the Bill of Rights, the first ten constitutional amendments which were adopted in 1789).

No – these resounding declarations of freedom are lifted verbatim from your own sacred document. Does it mean what it says? Is it the Soviet idea of a big joke? If not, was it intended to be practiced or preached: a profession of lofty ideals and sentiments to which the USSR finds it expedient to pay lip-service but has no intention of implementing? Is it a commitment to the laws by which you claim to abide?

You must admit that the USSR's denial of human rights, your harsh treatment of dissidents and of Jews who ask only for permission to practice their religion or leave, and your (let's be honest) welshing on the Helsinki Accords, raise doubts as to whether you ever meant your constitution, and other solemn commitments – past, present and future – to be observed or ignored.

You have to admit, also, that – whatever our shortcomings (and we have plenty) – disregarding our constitution as you do yours is not one of them.

Despite constant efforts by many in and out of government to distort, undermine and evade its clear intent and instructions, despite the doubtful dedication of some Americans to all the lofty principles and pesky restraints in our Bill of Rights which partisans and fanatics often find damned nuisances, the U.S. constitution, after two centuries, remains our supreme law. You must have noticed that it determines our form of government, as both a republic whose head of state is elected by the people and a democracy which entrusts final authority to the people. It defines and dictates the respective powers of our national, state and local governments, and their relations to each other. It not only promises but in fact delivers the stated fundamental rights and liberties of every citizen.

Whatever else you may say of us, you must concede that our constitution:

> not only promises but indeed protects, preserves and enforces the separation of church and state and free exercise of religion;
> really defends true freedom of speech and the press, and the right of people peaceably to assemble for redress of grievances or even for defiance of the state;
> really safeguards the individual against abuse by the

military, the police and governmental agencies that snoop, harass and persecute;

really prevents pressure on the individual to incriminate or testify against himself;

really ensures that the citizen will not be deprived of life, liberty or property without due process of law, including a speedy, public trial by an impartial jury, and demands that he be informed of any accusation and allowed to confront witnesses;

really forbids any state from abridging citizens' immunities and privileges, and denying them strictly equal protection; and

really warrants the precious right of every citizen, of any religion, race, sex or color, to vote for officials, from dogcatcher to President, whose jobs are understood to serve the individual, not the other way around.

These constitutional rights and liberties, Secretary Gorbachev, are not cosmetics applied to conceal ugly reality, but the very essence and distinction of our system.

That is why, in summit and other meetings with you and Ambassador Shevardnadze, and even in the SALT talks, we must keep stressing human rights. We are not interfering in your internal affairs. On the contrary, we are simply asking you to pursue your own ideals and your own laws, as enshrined in your own constitution.

Sincerely,
Jack L. Levin

Chapter 8
Jack Levin on Peace and War
Robert O. Freedman

Jack Levin was as passionate about questions of peace and war as he was on every other subject. If he saw unjust wars, such as U.S. involvement in the Nicaraguan civil war, he would denounce them. On what he felt were questionable wars, such as the one against Iraq, he openly asked if the money could be better spent on health services and helping the poor. But in what he felt were legitimate wars such as World War II or aiding the Bosnian Moslems against the Bosnian Serbs, he urged strong U.S. involvement, and Jack also was enthusiastic about the creation of the U.S. Institute for Peace, which he felt would be a step toward a better world.

Open Letter to Daniel Ortega, President of Nicaragua

Dear President Ortega:

May we respectfully suggest a way to deal with President Reagan's insistence on those pesky democratic reforms in your Marxist/Leninist regime? You're reluctant to make them until he stops his proxy war against your country; and he's convinced you'll never qualify as a freedom-lover. Reopening the opposition newspaper *La Prenza*, naming a critical cardinal to head a peace commission and pledging other reforms at the Guatemala conference are not enough. Therefore, unless something is done, you can never prove worthy to meet with him to discuss peace.

Meanwhile, he is preparing to meet cordially with another leader of a Marxist/Leninist regime, Mikhail Gorbachev of the USSR, your patron who makes you a pariah.

You may wonder: why him and not me?

Well, clearly, you're more of a threat than your patron; because you're only 1200 miles from our southernmost border. True, yours is a flea nation of 3-1/2 million and his an elephant of over 283 million. True, he has thousands of nuclear warheads that could reach us far sooner than your trucks could slog through Honduras, Guatemala and Mexico to invade Brownsville, Texas. True, you're much easier to push around as customary.

But that's reality, and fantasy prevails in foreign policy.

As you know, glasnost and perestroika are in vogue. Openness and reform create the perception of reason and moderation, and dispel the image of Evil Empire. Try some; a little dab will do you.

You might begin with cultural exchanges. Send us a few musicians and dancers to foster your image as friend of art and culture.

Most important, however, is to persuade us that, although your history, traditions and conditions of desperation for centuries past are vastly different from ours, you are exactly like u. Show us formal declarations in support of civil liberties and human rights. They abound in the eleven-year-old Soviet Constitution to which Mr. Gorbachev can point with pride should President Reagan demand proof of loyalty to democratic ideals.

Of course, you also have a nice new constitution to exhibit. In 1979, your Sandinistas suspended the old one from 1974, due to the state of emergency – but you came right back with your Statement of Fundamental Rights. And, as if that were not enough to prove your commitment to civil rights and liberties, you signed a fine fresh constitution in January 1987, which of course must await peace for implementation. Meanwhile, during the state of emergency, you've put everything on hold, including habeas corpus. But don't let that bother you.

You can still reassure President Reagan that you're as devoted to democracy as the Marxist/Leninist he's going to receive shortly in Washington for discussion of arms reduction.

Here's how you might try to convince him. Announce that, with a cease fire, Nicaragua will immediately activate your frozen constitution.

                              Jack L. Levin
                              October 10, 1987

'Say Uncle'

Editor: Listening to President Reagan's August 12 address, the people of Nicaragua, whose government for years has been under attack by Reagan's renegades, must have heard echoes of President Botha's address after the recent South African "election."

Said Mr. Reagan, rededicating himself to the "democratic resistance" that specializes in making life impossible for the weakest and most vulnerable Nicaraguans: "We have always been willing to talk."

Said Mr. Botha, in calling for talks with selected black leaders: These negotiations will not be a struggle for domination and power; it will be an honest meeting of men of peace and goodwill."

Freely translated: "Let's talk; say Uncle."

August 24, 1987

The Wars We're Losing

Meanwhile, back home at the White House, on Wall Street and Main Street, problems that could hurt us as badly or worse than Iraq are getting short shrift.

Many of us have declared a cease fire and some are considering surrender, in important wars that we've been fighting and losing for years; the wars against poverty, hunger, homelessness, drugs, disease, illiteracy and national bankruptcy.

Who can worry about the [yawn] national debt of $4 trillion when spellbound by a killer-nation on the loose? Yet, the estimated cost of the military buildup and standoff, $1 million per hour, if used instead to pay what we owe, would have to continue for 4 million hours, 166,642 days, or 455 years to liquidate that $4 trillion debt on easy installments – not counting interest, which would take another 100 years or so.

In those other wars, too, people die.

The World Health Organization has estimated that, every minute, 30 children die of hunger or inadequate health care. That comes to 1,800 per hour, 43,200 per day, nearly 16 million children dying each year – plus millions of adults dying of starvation. Most of those lives could be saved.

In the war on drugs, the U.S. Customs Service reported that in 1986 nearly 2,000 Americans died from heroin and nearly 1,000 from cocaine (usage, not peddling, which takes a toll of thousands more dead each year).

Casualties in the war on AIDS are said to be soaring above 100,000 dead in the past decade.

According to census figures on the war on poverty, over 37 million Americans exist below the poverty level – a figure that does not include the millions of walking wounded – the "working poor". In Maryland alone, more than 700,000 fellow-citizens – mostly children and the elderly – require nutritional assistance at some time each year, according to the Maryland Food Committee.

These other wars are boring compared to the high-noon

confrontation that has us gripping the arms of our easy chairs. But while we are entranced by our fearless, firm-jawed Lawman Bush ready to whip out his six-shooter as he strides slow and steady toward the snarling, black-hatter desperado Saddam, a white-hatted gang in store-bought suits is blowing up the bank and setting the whole town ablaze.

There can be no doubt that our fixation on the Middle East, distracting our attention from issues that politicians want us distracted from, is letting a lot of scoundrels get away with murder.

Victory over Saddam Hussein may deter aggression and curtail the damage done by exorbitant fuel costs, but it will not put food in the stomachs of the hungry and starving, or a roof over the heads of a homeless family. Nor will it provide self-respect to millions of isolated, alienated fellow-Americans who have no sense of worth, morals and ethics. Nor will it teach people to read and count, or rehabilitate drug addicts or give medical care to the sick and dying who can't afford it. Nor will it narrow the growing gap between the outrageously rich and desperately poor in our nation.

Obviously, we and our allies must have the will and endure the hardships needed to win the war in the Gulf. However, we can do no less to win the wars at home – remembering that in war as in peace the burdens weigh heaviest on the poor, weak and vulnerable who are least able to bear them. Saddam Hussein is a dangerous foe, but our worst enemy remains our uncaring selves. We are still the only power on earth that can defeat and destroy us – from within.

Many brave young men declare they are ready to die for their country in chasing Saddam out of Kuwait. Are they ready also to ask – as John Kennedy advised – what they can do for their country in pursuing justice at home?

September 1, 1990

Then and now, a plea to resist a costly, unnecessary war

Recently I was dictating to my secretary a letter to the editor opposing a U.S. attack on Iraq. There are 106 strike fighter planes on several aircraft carriers, 55 fighter and jammer planes and hundreds of other planes poised to strike Iraq, at great cost to U.S. taxpayers.

I was struck by a sense of deja vu. About a third of a century ago, following the alleged attack on the American warship in the Gulf of Tonkin, my fellow civil libertarian and social activist, Henry E. Niles, then chairman of the Baltimore Life Insurance Co., and I were writing a letter to the editor opposing the Vietnam War's escalation. His wife, Mary Cushing, came to the office to meet with Henry and other Baltimore Quakers.

"What? Another letter to the editor?" she said. "Why don't you spend your time instead enlisting the support of your colleagues in a businessman's organization opposing the war?" She told us this would add respectability to the anti-war efforts of students, religious groups and other "radicals." As businessmen, she said, you know what damage this war is doing to the country, economically as well as morally. So why don't you speak up? The nation is ready to listen to you.

That was the beginning of "Business Executives Move for Vietnam Peace and New National Priorities," (BEM) at a time when anti-war protesters were generally perceived as wimps, cowards, draft dodgers and subversives of all shapes and colors.

There were a few mainstream anti-war organizations, such as the American Civil Liberties Union and Clergy and Laity Concerned and the American Friends Service Committee, but their voices were lost in the clamor.

BEM's general sentiment had been expressed by naval hero Stephen Decatur: "Our country: In her intercourse with foreign nations, may she always be right; but our country, right or wrong!" Our group started with 98 of Niles' counterparts and grew to more than 3,000 members.

They included such national business leaders as Joseph E.

McDowell, president of Servomation Corp. of New York; and such prominent Baltimoreans as George L. Bunting, junior executive vice president of Noxell Corp.; Sidney Hollander Jr. of Sidney Hollander Associates; Howard H. Murphy of the Afro-American; Philip Macht of Welsh Construction Co.; and the Rouse's Co.'s Malcolm Sherman.

Some were fellow Quakers, 90 percent of whom had supported the war against Hitler, Hirohito and Mussolini. At least 80 percent had been active members of the armed forces, and 10 percent had served in non-combat roles.

There are, of course, many dissimilarities between the Vietnam War and the proposed attack on Iraq, but there is one common element: The specter of loved ones returning home in body bags concentrates the mind on the high price of military adventures.

Perhaps it is time for new thinking about Saddam Hussein. He is a first-class scoundrel – and threat to world peace.

But is he the incarnation of all evil?

Does the history of brutal invasions of neighbors begin and end with Saddam? Will defeat or assassination change the situation?

Is there much moral difference between his ruthless extermination of those who stood in his way and our genocide and seizure of lands of Native Americans who blocked our westward expansion?

Although isolation as a policy is not only wrong but impossible in this shrinking world, so is U.S. intervention without the support of other nations.

We hope that the former student protester who declined to risk his life in an unwinnable war will keep other Americans out of harm's way, now that he is commander-in-chief.

It is clear that, like Henry Niles' business colleagues of a generation ago, the public today is opposed to costly, solitary American ventures into foreign quagmires.

Most of us would support Henry Niles' assertions that "war makes no moral, economic or legal sense" and that

"America's exclusive intervention in an undeclared war would be to the detriment of more valid and honorable social problems here at home."

Niles said that when you have a policy that doesn't work, be flexible and change it.

That would mean withdrawal of the U.S. armada from the Persian Gulf, saving billions of U.S. taxpayer dollars. It would also reassure millions of Muslims, Kurds, Iranians and Turks, who consider U.S. power as threatening as their murderous neighbor.

April 17, 1998

May 3, 1993

President Bill Clinton
The White House
1600 Pennsylvania Avenue
Washington, DC 20050

Dear President Clinton:

    Despite the peaceful promises of the Bosnian Serb leadership – which experience has shown cannot be trusted – we urge you and Secretary of State Christopher to press ahead with efforts to formalize a United Nations coalition to strike hard at Serbian attack forces. If we are civilized, we must do everything possible to stop mass-murder, rape, torture and "ethnic cleansing." We must do our part to increase military, economic and diplomatic pressure on the Serbs and humanitarian aid to their victims.

    Thank you for considering this view.

                  (Signed)   Jack L. Levin
                                    David J. Levin
                                    Ester M. Levin
                                    Roslyn Wills

cc: Senator Paul Sarbanes
         Senator Barbara Mikulski
         Representative Benjamin Cardin

How wars are won

On Baltimore's waterfront, the Fairfield section is very quiet now. You can almost hear the summer breezes blowing in from the Patapsco.

Fifty years ago, it was a round-the-clock, seven-days-a-week bedlam of riveting hammers pounding red-hot rivets into steel plates, a cacophony of mechanical hubbub, whistles, fog horns and the yelling and cursing of sweaty workers struggling with unaccustomed tasks – business and professional people developing blisters and callouses on soft, unskilled hands.

One distinctive sound in the din was the wailing ambulance siren as yet another hapless victim was rushed to the infirmary or hospital. Strange, heavy tools became deadly weapons in the clumsy clutches of eager amateurs. In the early days of the war, shipyard casualties rivaled those on the battlefields.

Out of this chaos, in the late fall of 1941, was born at last the first Liberty ship, the Patrick Henry. It was Fairfield's first response to the arrogance and belligerence of the Axis powers. We who had slogged through a gray, grinding Depression felt our hearts pounding. Until then, our only patriotic excitement had been on the Fourth of July, celebrating the victories of earlier achievers. This was *our* victory!

The first launching of the ships that would carry the war to America's enemies, and help to finish what they had started, lighted our sky as no fireworks had ever done.

For many of us, the launching was the most memorable event of our routine lives. We wildly cheered the speeches of shipyard officials. We had goose bumps as the skids were knocked out, the first champagne bottle smashed against its bow and the Patrick Henry slid majestically down the greased ways. We forgot the gripes and the pain; the rising at 4 a.m., the dashing half asleep to meet our rides, the launching in the company of rats scurrying under the hulls, the aching joints and muscles, the interminable monotony of seven-day weeks of mind-numbing labor.

But the mounting frequency if exhilarating launchings made it all worthwhile.

Production revved up to overdrive after Pearl Harbor. President Franklin D. Roosevelt, who had called the slow-moving vessels "ugly ducklings," renamed them "Liberty ships" because he pledged that they would "liberate the world." Our fighters did that job, of course, but our workers surely helped.

Great flocks of the ugly ducklings were born into the waters of the Patapsco. On September 7, 1942, nine months to the day after Pearl Harbor, came the John Brown, which is now on display as a museum ship at a pier on Clinton street. It was one of 384 Liberty ships launched at Fairfield – more than any produced at any shipyard in the nation. Altogether, the yards turned out 2,710 ships. Built and crewed by civilians, they carried two-thirds of all essential cargo to Allied forces. Nearly 200 were torpedoed by U-boats, but the Nazis could not sink them as fast as we could build them.

It took 42 days to build the John Brown, but by the end of the war Fairfield was mass-producing a ship a week. It was not only Fairfield workers and management who achieved this miracle of productivity, it was also the workers and management at all the industries which supplied the thousands of tons of materials used – from rivets, nuts, bolts and welding rods to heavy steel plates and huge ships' engines.

The only we nearly ran out of was names for the ships. John W. Brown was a little-known labor union leader; other uncelebrated civilians had to be dug out of obscurity for moments of glory. But nothing slowed the pace in the 18 yards producing Liberty ships.

At shipyards like Bethlehem's, at airplane plants like Glenn Martin and in bustling factories from coast to coast, American praised the Lord and passed the ammunition to thos fighting in the armies on two sides of the world.

Wages were adequate, not lavish. With shortages and rationing of many commodities, the standard of living was no consumer's paradise. But morale was high; no burnout, no malaise. We were confident of eventual victory. We gave it the highest priority and threw ourselves entirely into the task of waging the war as well on the home front as on the battlefront.

Today, too, as headlines and newscasts keep reminding us, we are at war – against drugs, poverty, hunger, crime, disease and pollution. These enemies lack the personified evil of Hitler, Hirohito and Mussolini, but their threats to our survival are as real. We are good at declaring these wars, but not very good at fighting them. Where are the emergency measures? The War Bonds? The planning of production? The rationing of resources? The setting of priorities in finance, labor and education to assure concentration on winning?

Counting all those, especially children, who are dying of malnutrition, drug overdoses, street violence, AIDS and gun slaughter, American losses in these wars must exceed those in the most destructive war in history.

We won that war by will, determination, steadfast commitment and readiness to pay the price of victory. Only by such unconditional, uncompromising effort can we triumph over present enemies.

In 1992 as in 1942, we can again dream of victory over formidable enemies which threaten not just "them" but also "us."

As Theodor Herzl, the founder of Zionism, said "If you will it, it is no dream."

August 26, 1992

Forgotten, but Not Gone

As a frequent participant in groups discussing current concerns, I am struck by their downgrading or elimination of the threat of nuclear annihilation as an important issue. The matter is rarely mentioned any more by editorialists, pundits and talk-show hosts exploring more titillating topics.

The collapse of the Evil Empire has taken the steam out of the issue of atomic mass suicide. We are Number One, and Number Two has crumpled like a deflated balloon, so why worry?

We know, of course, that even if all agreed-upon reduction of nuclear weapons is observed to the letter, Number Two will still have enough left to reduce Number One to a mass of contaminated ruins. And what about Numbers Three, Four, Five, Six and the rest? Fourteen countries, including four Soviet successor states disposing 45,000 weapons among them, are mentioned in the Army War College "World 2010" estimates of nuclear-weapons powers. Are they all to be expunged from our priority list of major concerns because some of them will not be ready for mass destruction until next year or five years from now?

As we counting on some new technological wizardry to save us from ourselves? Or have we abandoned hope that we can do anything about the death machine suspended over our heads? Have we concluded that what will be must be and decided to concentrate on Bosnia, Somalia and Haiti? In that case we are resigned to the same fate as the terrifying monsters of Jurassic Park who for millions of years roamed and ruled the earth as we do not, but who somehow vanished. Science tells us that dinosaurs were the masters of creation for more than a hundred million years before the first primal ancestors of man appeared only some 5 million years ago. If the dinosaurs had any capacity for thinking, they must have thought they would surely be around forever, as do we.

The difference between us and them is that they could not see extinction coming – and we can.

It is likely that, in the next few thousand years at least, we won't have to worry about comets and asteroids hurtling into our planet from outer space, or about a new glacial age brought on by the greenhouse effect, or about any of the phantasmagoric nightmares of science fiction. Moreover, we are at the top of the food chain. Other animals do not eat us, we eat them. We have no real enemies left – none, that is, but one: ourselves.

What does offer the possibility of instant extinction of our kind is the combination of nature with human nature, the invention of a way to use the most powerful forces in nature to exterminate ourselves.

Can there be any doubt that the Serbs, Croat and Muslims of the former Yugoslavia would be doing their ethnic cleansing with atomic weaponry if they had it? Or that the likes of Saddam Hussein, Muammar el Kadafi and the Iranian ayatollahs would justify a nuclear attack if they thought they could get away with it? Or that China, the upcoming superpower, is developing is nuclear technology and has joined the former USSR in peddling it to rogue regimes?

With world population figures exploding, especially in Third World countries that cannot produce enough food, jobs or resources to sustain their growing masses, is there not enormous pressure on nature and human nature to wipe out problems now that the means to do so are available?

For the soundest reason – to save hundreds of thousands of lives of American servicemen who might have been lost in an invasion of Japan to end World War II – we unleashed the first atomic monster on the world. Now, for an equally sound reason, to save perhaps a billion lives, we must kill off the monster's progeny.

We may have it still within our power to control and even to change our nature which controls the seeds of our destruction. We may yet find ways to prevent Homo sapiens from becoming as extinct as the triassic reptiles.

The first step is to restore to the national agenda an issue that is not getting enough attention.

Second, we must develop plans for getting genocidal

weapons out of the hands of unstable individuals in seats of power all over our endangered planet. Signatories to the Nuclear Non-Proliferation Treaty should recommit themselves to carrying out the treaty, and strive to involve other nations in the commitment.

Third, beginning with January's Geneva Conference on a permanent ban, we must put talks to reduce or eliminate nuclear arms back on the front burner.

Fourth, efforts must be intensified to shut down the nuclear black market that is growing, especially in former Soviet states. The black market price for plutonium is said to be $50 million a kilogram, and business is booming with Korea and Iran.

We must kill our monstrous creatures before they kill us. And if that means changing human nature, let's start to work on it. After only 5 million years – a mere moment in geologic time – it's still malleable.

November 24, 1993

Part III

At the Close of Life

Chapter 9
Jack Levin on Nostalgia, Aging and Death
William H. Engelman

This last section of Jack's writing includes select pieces of Jack's last years.

These selections are quite different in emphasis from those earlier writing that focused on issues. Remarkably, Jack did not slow down. But the subject matter changed. His writings – in his last decade – were of a personal nature. They dealt with nostalgia, aging and death.

The article **"Passages"** reflects his attitude toward "moving day" and he describes passionately his feelings towards his empty house as "... a desert where everything once bloomed."

He then follows up with "**A Mixed Review of the Golden Years**." It includes an inventory of "good" and "not so good" of the changes from life in his private home to life in a retirement community.

His irrepressible good humor shines through in his essay "**Musing at Sunset**" in which he deals with death, but insists he isn't ready to go thanks to his ".... internist, otolaryngologist, cardiologist, ophthalmologist, urologist, dentist and surgeons, and a cabinet full of medications ..."

Jack's op-ed piece in 1994, "**When We Danced Together, Not Apart**" will surely bring tears to the eyes of those of all ages. He describes small pleasures enjoyed with neighbors, family and friends. And he insightfully points out that "... the operative word in those memories is 'we' ..." as in "...We ate together and sat together in one room, not each in his own room munching fast food alone, staring at a TV screen." Jack didn't hesitate to express these sentiments, which most of us will recognize to be right on the mark.

This section concludes with his special to *The Jewish Times* on **"The Best $5.00 Wedding Ever."** It is too good to describe. Please read it and allow it to flavor your memory of Jack L. Levin.

Passages

We had known for two years the date that we would be moving. For over one year, we put it out of mind, like a visit to the dentist. Then we began some serious procrastinating. Finally, with about a month to go, we confronted the inevitable.

We had to start dismantling our lives, clearing out the treasured trivia of over 40 years in our home, the priceless, useless bric-a-brac that could not be shoehorned into our newer smaller apartment. Among the flotsam and jetsam that had to go were:

Stacks of my father's love letters courting my mother when he was in the Navy from 1906 to 1910, with all the formal and flowery sentimentalities; boxes of photographs and slides of long-gone relatives, pets and friends celebrating birthdays, anniversaries and other joyous events; an uncle's white steel air-raid warden's helmet from World War II; tons of records and games no longer played, books no longer read, Little League baseball, football and camping paraphernalia no longer used, booze no longer drunk; a workbench vise and tools, many inherited; a barbecue grill and Damariscotta, Maine, lobster can from half-forgotten cookouts and feasts.

There are the stately tulip poplars in whose shade you read and dozed away many a lazy Sunday afternoon, and the evergreen tree you planted as a tiny sapling nearly 40 years ago that now towers above the roof-top, the bushes and shrubs you nurtured , the lawn you mowed on hundreds of hot weekends with gallons of sweat and pride. You are swept up in a flood of fond memories.

It does not help much when friends call to say they've heard wonderful things about the life-care facility you'll be moving into, and how much you'll enjoy the easier life, making new friends, sharing new experiences, finding new listeners to oft-told tales. It only sharpens the sense of loss of dear old neighbors, routines, associations. You begin to feel kindly even to the cats and dogs for whom your grounds have been a favorite comfort station.

Moving day approaches. As you cram and lug boxes and

bags, as you rip up the years, mournfully deciding what to keep, to dump, to give away and to whom, you realize that moving is the only thing more painful for a woman than delivering a baby or, for a man, than passing a kidney stone. At least those sufferings are followed by immediate relief and joy; moving is followed only by the anguish of unpacking, of squeezing far too much into far too little space, of trying to find a familiar item in some unfamiliar haystack.

Like death and taxes, moving day arrives. The movers take over. They are miracles of efficiency, courtesy and professionalism, gliding from room to room, packing the unpackable, lifting the immovable, creating cardboard crates by magic, making everything disappear into the massive maw of the moving van.

After hours that seem like days, the house is empty, a desert where everything once bloomed. Desolation deepens as you drive down your street for probably the last time, following the van and waving a final goodbyes to lost neighbors.

At the new apartment, in the chaos of unpacking, you have a recurring fantasy that you'll wake up soon and find yourself home. But you are home – for the first time in an apartment, sharing a common roof that is not your own, on grounds you don't tend, eating food you did not prepare. In this partly collective life-care community, you will be pampered with amenities, attentions and gourmet dining. You will be free of all the problems and chores of home ownership and home cooking that you complained about and already miss.

You will also miss driving the old route to and from the office, turning into the old streets and shortcuts, seeing the old faces at stores, bank and service stations. You will have to register to vote in the county election and will miss the local candidates you've supported in the city where you were born. One bleak comfort is knowing that this is your very last move for which you'll have to pack and unpack.

But then, in the dining room you meet childhood friends you haven't seen for decades, friends of even longer standing than those you've just lost. You are refreshed by an excellent dinner and the recapture of youthful days of wine, roses, Easterwood Park and Ballow's Delicatessen.

For every ending, there is a beginning; there is a time to die and a time to be born. As stated in Ecclesiastes, chapter 3: "The hour of death is like the hour of birth." ... And vice versa.

May 17, 1991

A Mixed Review of the Golden Years

A year and a half ago, my wife and I moved to a retirement home, seeking R and R – rest and recreation. What we found are D and D, delight and some disappointment, due not to our splendid new home but to our frustrating old age.

I still work at my downtown office five days a week (transportation by a relative), but evenings and weekends are for discovering and developing new friendships and warming up old ones. After living privately in a detached suburban home for over 40 years, daily socializing at dinner and at many programmed events have become a gratifying experience. But the most attentive, tender and loving care cannot offset the deterioration of certain body parts, which makes it impossible to do the things we used to enjoy doing.

Playwright George S. Kaufman said that when a play gets "mixed reviews", that means it is good and rotten.

Our new life in our luxurious retirement community has been good and – not rotten – but not so good, because of advancing infirmities.

Good: The easy living. Virtually every chore is handled for us by skilled, accommodating functionaries – household repairs and replacements and all kinds of services, from housecleaning to laundering flatwork. For us, no more grass-cutting, leaf-raking, painting, snow-shoveling and running all over town to locate replacement parts for equipment long out of production.

Not so good: A pervasive feeling of uselessness and helplessness afflicts over-the-hill do-it-yourselfers with nothing to do. Never again will we pick up a hammer, saw, wrench or pliers and, after sweating and swearing, gaze on our handiwork with pride and satisfactions at having cut out costly professionals. Never again will we have the pleasure of grumbling over jobs we loved to hate.

Good: No cooking, no pots and pans and clean-up. Every night a different menu in the same posh venue. The food is wholesome and plentiful, the ambience that of a fine restaurant.

Not so good: Some residents complaining because the food is not prepared according to the recipes favored in their families for 50 years. Every dish is designed to please everyone, so it pleases most of us who are adaptable.

Good: By house rules, pets are now allowed. So we are liberated from indentured servitude in the care and feeding of troublesome creatures.

Not so good: We miss the cat rubbing against our leg and sneaking into our lap, and the dog, when we arrived home, wagging and wiggling in a frenzy of welcome for us and his dinner.

Good: Dining out every night with various members of our large extended family, to whom we feel closer than to some of our relatives.

Not so good: Losing them when we've just grown to love them. The average age is 83 – so, despite cheerful efforts at denial, the losses are continuous and inevitable. Also, avoiding repetition of old jokes and tales told before.

Good: No more care worries since failing vision required me to give up driving and to sell the remaining car. By using the house bus and lifts from generous family members and friends, we reach required destinations without the hassle of traffic, parking and repairs that had occupied so much of our lives.

Not so good: We feel that we have lost one of our basic freedoms guaranteed by the Bill of Rights, the right to jump in the car and go wherever and whenever we pleased. Dependence on cabs and the courtesy of others is a constant annoyance.

Good: No more unscheduled, unexpected visits, just before midnight, of friends returning from a night out, dropping in for snacks and chatter.

Not so good: Absence of the same in our well-regulated daily routine.

Good: Grandchildren and great-grandchildren, and being no burden on their parents.

Not so good: No outdoors play equipment to absorb their energies.

Good: Being expertly served and professionally cared for in a protected environment.

Not so good: In response to our complaints and differences of opinion with an occasional employee, being stroked as backward children by our your caretakers who are one-third our age, who flatter and patronize us into accepting their views, because they know what's best for us.

Good: A creative program of activities that can keep one constantly occupied.

Not so good: The shortage of meaning and purpose in some of them is why, with the support and full cooperation of our social director, we are promoting volunteerism among residents who are up to it – devoting time and effort to helping various local causes and programs, to help both receivers and givers of the efforts. The latter find some good reasons to get up in the morning.

Balancing the pluses of our care and minuses of our condition, we are happy in our new life, but feel ti could be better, despite the woes of aging.

In only one place, we've heard, is there no room for improvement – and we are not ready for that place.

We are not going gentle into that quiet night, but raging against the fading light.

February 9, 1993

Musing at Sunset

As she lay dying, Gertrude Stein was asked, "Is there an answer to death?" She replied, "What was the question?"

Until I passed age 80 a while ago and acquired an assortment of deteriorating parts, I had never thought of an end to a busy life as either question or answer. Oh, I had made the customary preparations. Persuaded by skilled salespersons, I had bought "life insurance" (lovely euphemism) and cemetery plots "pre-need." But I could not imagine, let alone consider, my own actual demise. Death was something that happened to other older people, not to me.

Now my wife and I have moved into a retirement home where the average age is about 84. We have made delightful new friends – and lost them almost immediately. We are surrounded by death. We have attended so many last rites in recent months that the funeral parlor has become like a second home. With each ceremony, one is more inclined to picture onself in the coffin, covered first with eulogy and then with dirt.

Now I think of the remark attributed to Satchel Paige, the old Negro League baseball player: "Ain't nobody goin' outa this world alive." To dwell on the inevitability of death is morbid, but to ignore it is foolish.

I pay attention these days to the impermanence of things I have always considered timeless: holding my wife's hand as we watch a favorite television program; birds chirping and darting past our open window; crickets; a distant police or fire sien reminding of someone else's problem; the laughter and chatter of children at play.

I become aware that what I have taken for granted can be taken away – and the value of these things increases.

In the will I had drawn and revised and the estate evaluation, how do I set a value on a loving spouse and partner who has been sharing my joys and sorrows for 60 years; on children, grandchildren, co-workers, colleagues and friends who have so enriched our lives?

Approaching the last chapter clarifies the meaning of all that has gone before. You realize that many of the crises in the earlier chapters were not as vitally important as they seemed at the time. I regret that I never told my grandparents of my gratitude to them for choosing to risk emigrating to a strange land instead of staying where I might have been born. I regret – as months and days dwindle down – some of the time squandered on livelihood and news programs – time which could better have been used for living and listening to music. I regret all the years of insensitively when I was too busy to see the wonderful world around me.

With failing eyesight, my gaze lingers on the faces of friends and family members, as if to fix them in an album of treasured memories, on familiar flower and scenes, on growing trees and children.

With slowing pace, I made an effort to keep up with striding companions. With one-third of heart function, along with the weariness comes awareness. The embers seem to burn brighter when the fire is going out. As the room grows darker, it seems briefly to get warmer. I begin to understand how the bedridden Marcel Proust could write pages about the glint of a spoon in a glass of tea.

My wife and I appreciate our good fortune to live in a continuing-care community, with friends of comparable age and condition. It's comforting to know that we will not have to face the sunset of the golden years in loneliness and isolation, as do so many less fortunate older citizens, and that we will not burden our children.

We share the hope expressed by the writer Rabindranath Tagore: "Let me not pray to be sheltered from dangers but to be fearless in facing them ... Let me not look for allies in life's battlefield, but to my own strength ... Let me not crave in anxious fear to be saving but hope for the patience to win my freedom ..." We agree with Edgar Allan Poe that "The boundaries which divide Life and Death are at best shadowy and vague. Who shall say where the one ends and where the other begins?"

My affairs are in reasonable order. But be patient, dear

heirs and assignees, I am not ready to go. With the help of my internist, otolaryngologist, cardiologist, ophthalmologist, urologist, dentist and surgeons, and a cabinet full of medications, I intend to hang on for dear life. I will not be pried loose for even a moment from a single one of the little pleasures I cherish – and I've discovered that there are happily so many of them. These are things seen more clearly in fading light.

July 1, 1994

When We Danced Together, Not Apart

A ninety-some-year old is supposed to be responsible, civil, reasonable and serene; a teenager, just the opposite. Yet, comparing this aging, obstreperous Twentieth Century with its teenage that I recall, the qualities have been reversed: conformist in its callow youth, rebellious in its golden years. How did it get so topsy-turvy?

This is not a nostalgic lament for good old days that never were. All that can be said of flies, rats, pollution, disease, discomfort and short rations is – good riddance. But how did we get from the way we were to the way we are? Technological advances are only a part of the answer.

Once upon a time, early in the century, there was no television, no video games, no radio, no talking movies, and yet the family – incredibly – had fun.

Once upon a time a family like mine – parents, grandparents, my sister and me – lived in a tiny box of a row house in East Baltimore, with no inside plumbing except for a single cold-water faucet in the kitchen, and no central heating, (just a coal stove), no electricity, no air conditioning, no fans and an ancient icebox. And yet, unbelievably, we did not feel deprived.

In summer, we kids played a wide variety of games on the sidewalk squares – hopping, skipping, jumping – cooling off with chips of ice picked off the floor of the ice wagon after the ice man had chopped off a 10-cent hunk and tonged it inside to the icebox. Or we went to the square, played on the grass and watched the big goldfish in the pond,

Or, in our tiny backyard, in the shade of the outhouse, we devised a secret bank. We removed two bricks from the path, buried an open tin can, fashioned a coin slot that just fit between the replaced bricks, and deposited our pennies. We loved the clink as they slid down the slot into the can. After a week or so of secret hoarding, we would lift the bricks, remove a few pennies, and treat ourselves to a Tootsie Roll from the store, or Eskimo Pie from a vendor with a cart like the street sweepers.

Sometimes, when the tiny parlor was not insufferably hot, we would crank up the Victrola and listen to songs by Galli-Curci and Caruso and comic Abie Kabbibble records.

On summer nights, we sat on the front steps chatting with neighbors about the newspaper headlines: would President Wilson stop the kaiser from committing all those atrocities and sinking our ships; would they find the killer of little Clara Stone? (That one murder case was town talk for weeks when a slain child was uncommon news.)

If there was no breeze and no rain was predicted, we took blankets to the park, spread them on the grass and enjoyed the band concert. Sometimes we slept through the night beside other families as safe as in our own beds.

Down-the-bay excursions to Tolchester were extra-special. Anticipation was the best part – inhaling the aromas of chicken frying, hard-boiled eggs soaking in vinegary beet juice, pickles, relishes and favorite sandwiches and snacks being prepared for the picnic baskets.

We rose with the sun, trotted with our loaded baskets to the streetcar, bantered with other families with the same destination, hurried to buy tickets, then up the gangplank. After a frantic rush to get folding chairs positioned at the rail, where you got the best views and breezes, we would converse with the group next to us about how lucky we were to get these good seats and would it rain.

At Tolchester Beach, we hurried to be among the first off the boat, to run with our baskets up the long pier to get a picnic table under a tree. We rode the rides, especially the goat carts, played on the beach and feasted. Back on the boat at sunset, we heard stories and sang songs with other families on the moonlit sail home.

Winter nights were also a time of togetherness. Warmed by the nearby coal stove, we clustered around the small dining room table, under the gaslight dome, playing cards or dominoes, hearing Dad's animated reactions to items in the newspaper while we worked the daily follow-the-dots puzzle and Mom darned socks and passed along neighborhood gossip.

The operative word in these memories is "we". We talked with each other – sometimes in strange dialects of German, Irish, Italian, Bohemian, Chinese and Yiddish, but we communicated. We listened to each other. We shared experiences with each other. We were keenly aware of each other – as family members, neighbors, friends and friendly strangers. We ate together and sat together in one room, not each in his own room munching fast food, alone, staring at a TV screen. We played with and against each other, not alone against a video game. We worked together with each other, not alone with a computer.

We argued, sometimes fought; but we did not shoot to kill. The few of us who had guns used them mostly to make noise on New Year's Eve and the Fourth of July.

We were poor but did not know it, because so were most of our neighbors. We ere not obsessed with possessions, like moderns pounded by TV and radio temptations hour after hour, day after day.

We traveled together on trolleys and buses, not alone in a 2,000 pound car taking us individually to and from work. We shared reactions to movies with friends and neighbors and sang with them, following the dot that touched each word of the lyrics on the screen.

We dealt with no supermarkets but with an often opinionated individual baker, butcher, grocer, tailor, iceman, laundry man or woman. When dancing, man and woman held each other; they did not avoid contact.

Could it be that somewhere between the teen-time and old age of this century we have lost much of our common humanity?

Without the terrible unifying force of war and other disasters, can there ever again be another "we" generation?

October 7, 1994

To Have and to Hold Forever

Among the guests at a recent celebration of our 60th wedding anniversary was a young couple planning to be married soon. Each was a college graduate from an upper middle-class family.

"Tell us the secret of your success in marriage," said the groom-to-be, half jokingly.

"Yes," added the bride-to-be, "We don't want to be one of the every two marriages that break up today."

My wife and I looked at each other, shaking our heads. "I'm afraid you couldn't possibly understand," I said.

How could we explain the 1930s to today's young people?

How to communicate to kids who have never wanted anything they didn't get almost instantly, what it meant to scrimp and save for it for years and often never get it; what a difference that made in one's perception of the value of things; what it meant to forego cherished dreams like a college education because the family breadwinner had been long unemployed; what it meant to have to adapt, to be flexible, to make do, to compromise in an uncompromising world?

How could they comprehend a world in which people walked miles to save five cents carfare, skipped meals and rent payments, wore clothing to shreds and shoes until holes appeared on the soles, and saw belongings repossessed because of an inability to keep up installments or dumped onto the street when rent was long overdue?

How could they imagine this great nation of hope and abundance in 1923, when we decided to marry? When unemployment reached 12,800,000 – more than a fourth of the civilian labor force; more than a quarter million homes were foreclosed, and financially ruined people were jumping out of windows in skyscrapers.

How could we explain the bonding that resulted from interdependence and shared sacrifice instead of just time spent together at a show or baseball game, bonding like metal that must e melted in order to meld?

Most impossible to convey to our young friends would have been our eager participation in the intellectual ferment of the early '30s.

It was not just socializing, but a hunger for social action that drew us to the Saturday night soirees at 2110 East Pratt Street. Our host/teacher/provocateur was Baltimore's and New York's renowned radical socialist, V. F. Calverton (real name George Goetz), the publishing-editor of Modern Quarterly.

It was not abstract intellectualizing but intense identification with some of the passionate prescriptions for a better life that swirled about that book-lined, smoke-filled room.

How could young people who never had any reason to want to change their comfortable world understand what Saturday night Calverton's meant to us? What hope it gave us to sit at the feet of such mighty critics of the status quo as A.J. Muste, Clarence Darrow, Sherwood Anderson, F. Scott Fitzgerald, Langston Hughes, Norman Thomas, labor leaders like Louis Budenz, black intellectuals like Alain Locke and Charles S. Johnson, and other challengers of those we blamed for the bleakness of our young lives?

How could young moderns for whom Saturday night means an expensive show, know the thrill of chipping in our quarter for the whiskey and exploring wild ideas with other spellbound locals like Louis Azrael, Harry Bard, Una Corbett, Elmer Sebastian, our hometown Trotskyite, Bessie Peretz, and Joe Buchoff who provided quips for comic relief?

To us, there was never a show more stimulating and encouraging than V.F. Calverton, student and teacher of psychology, anthropology, sexology, sociology and government.

We were seekers of the truth that would change our live, give them meaning and purpose, something more than the treadmill of eking out a meager livelihood. We sought "tikkun olam," to improve the world, and we reveled in the tempting choice served up at Calverton's.

But we never joined any of the radical groups that belabored each other, each convinced that its was the only way.

We were, however, stimulated by the explosion of ideas and visions of a better future to become members and later, leaders of such social justice groups as the Americans for Democratic Action, the American Civil Liberties Union, The American Jewish Congress, the Baltimore Jewish Council and other progressive and charitable groups.

Civil rights and civil liberties could not be taken for granted but had to be fought for. Social upheavals, revolutions and wars were not far-off affairs, but close to home, disrupting our lives, demanding adjustment, compromise and sacrifice.

My wife and I had spent almost a half century together before the onslaught of the "me generation" in which our questioners had grown up. We have learned the joy of sometimes placing other's needs before our own, and losing instead of winning an occasional argument.

"Well," said the groom-to-be, still waiting, "any words of wisdom?"

"Yes," I said, "when you promise to share, to love and cherish each other – make sure you mean it, no matter what."

August 24, 1994

En Route to the Good Night

Dylan Thomas' advice is open to questions: "Do not go gentle into that good night," he said. "Rage, rage against the dying of the light."

I've been raging like crazy, but the light keeps dying and I can't see a big bullseye target on a barn door. With all the raging, I have less than 10 percent of normal eyesight, which make me legally blind.

Here are a few of the things that keep me raging:

At the top of my list is dependence on others to drive my wife and me on social occasions with other couples. Especially in bad weather. For decades I was the designated driver. In blizzards, I was the one who tossed a shovel and broom into the car trunk and picked up and delivered my guests. Now my wife and I are the perpetual passengers, dependent on friends and cabs. We are in mourning for our beloved family car and independence.

I rage at the Big Slowdown. It takes as long now to decipher a newspaper headline or sub-head with a magnifying glass as it used to take to speed-read an entire page of newspaper stories. On a short walk, I slow my pace to avoid collision because my sight is limited to only a few steps.

I rage at having to wait for my busy wife or secretary to read to me the tiny-type message labeled large on the outside URGENT/IMPORTANT or ACTION ALERT, which almost every mailing claims to be and few are.

I rage at the movies where sound effects tell me that exciting things are happening on the screen which is only a gray blur.

I rage against losing the facial features of our two beautiful grandchildren, but I seem to be acquiring a sharper sense of "hearing" their visible expressions.

As sight deteriorates, other senses of touch, smell and taste seem to sharpen a bit from greater use and dependency. But footsteps falter without visual guidance and obstacles loom up at the last moment before collision.

I rage at the stinginess of creditors whose faded bills are so lightly printed that mount due cannot be found or deciphered under the strongest magnifying glass.

The bustling supermarket, which used to be fun to visit, has become a bedlam of avoiding cart-crashes, overshooting aisles with unseen numbers and peering at unidentifiable packages with illegible labels. I hate imposing on a good-hearted friend to read and lead us through the chaos. It's enough, Mr. Thomas, to keep anyone raging.

After a lifetime of activity in various organizations – and still participating in meetings – I cannot recognize old colleagues who greet me. I have to ask, "Who are you?"

I try to conceal my rage with a benign smile that I wear constantly on social occasions, so that the uncomprehending will not get the idea that they are being slighted.

Even so, there is enraging confusion. A couple came up to me recently and when I asked the man "Who are you?" he replied "Bill and Suzy." Then sensing my plight, Bill added their last name.

And how's this for raging against the dying of the light? At a popular restaurant buffet, I was carrying two plates of food through the crowd in the dimly lighted ambiance toward our table. Suddenly a person appeared to be standing in front of me motionless. I politely asked if I could get by. No response. I repeated the request, less politely. Still no response. Finally, Mr. Thomas, I let him have it. When the figure failed to move, I realized I was berating my own image in a narrow mirror on a column.

It is disconcerting – and a bit surprising – when I look in the mirror and no one is there. It's a habit when shaving. But, since I use an electric shaver now instead of a razor, who needs a reflection anyway?

Worse than losing one's image in the mirror is losing so much of the city one loves and grew up in. I had become somewhat accustomed to the vanishing of the Emerson and Rennert Hotels, the Hearst Tower Building in whose penthouse we had offices for many years, the old Sun Building at the center of town, the Post Office, the National Exchange Bank and the yellow McCormick Building that marked the beginning and end of happy excursion trips down the bay. I miss the buildings that are long gone, but now I'm missing those that are still there, because I can't read the signs.

These drive me to rage: invisible (to me) men's room signs, restaurant menus, traffic signals, entrance, exit and elevator signs, floor numbers, directions on bottles and jars (especially how to open them).

I hide annoyance with well-meaning friends who offer vitamins, advice, nostrums, and magnifying lenses, and who cannot understand that there is nothing deader than a dead optic nerve.

But, what I can see, more clearly than ever, is the goodness of individuals. In the readiness of relatives, co-workers and friends to offer to help immediately when they sense the need; in the caring patience of volunteers who read to me beyond weariness; in the generosity of such institutions as the Maryland School for the Blind which provide cassettes, disks and playback, I am heartened to rediscover what we are losing in public life:

The capacity to see things through the other fellow's eyes.

As Anne Frank said, "In spite of everything, I believe that people are really good."

That's enough to quiet the useless raging and to ease the passage into the good night.

February 27, 1995

Requiem for a Fun War and a Melting Pot

Seventy-nine years ago on April 6 of the fateful year 1917, the United States declared war on Germany, I became aware of it through my first grade teacher, my parents and my old playmates. Uncle Sam and I ran on parallel tracks.

When he appealed for funds to press the war effort, I responded by raiding my Tootsie Roll savings to buy 25-cent war savings stamps in school. I was stirred by the theme, "Lick a stamp and help lick the Kaiser." At the movies, when the Kaiser's scowling face appeared, I hissed and booed as loudly as any other kid.

When the four-minute speaker was introduced by the theater manager, after the piano player's thundering roll, "to bring the message from President Wilson," I whistled and stomped with the best of them. And when he finished his harangue to support the war effort by buying Liberty bonds, I cheered and clapped as lustily as my parents.

When the park bank played "Over There", the new hit song by George M. Cohan, I sang every word of the lyrics.

When Mrs. Schmick, our next-door neighbor, bought the rolls of other war songs for her player and permitted me to sit beside her and pump the pedals, which I could just about reach, I was a full participant in the war effort. I remember such tunes as: "Let the Rest of the World Go By," "When Johnny Comes Home," "Smile a While," and "Peg O' My Heart."

When my father read aloud to us a paranoiac's letter to the editor speculating on an imminent invasion of our homeland by the enemy, I grabbed my trusty sawed-off broomstick and rushed outside to join my buddies in repelling the foe. And when the armistice was declared, I felt I had helped to win the war.

Patriotic beehive.

But I felt closest to the war effort on my Saturday visits to the Henry Sonneborn clothing factory where my father, an assistant foreman in the labeling department, kept me busy cutting a few labels off a roll. He was one of 4,000 employees, mostly recent immigrants, who produced army uniforms in World War I. The firm had won the contract because it had been the world's largest clothing manufacturer, producing 3,000 suits a day at Paca and Pratt streets in Baltimore.

That massive 10-story structure, now occupied mostly by The First National Bank of Maryland, today displays a plaque identifying it as a historic site.

I accompanied my father to work and marveled at the beehive of activities. I could see on each floor from the open elevator – the cutters, sewers, pressers sweating over their hissing machines; the button-hole makers, the finishers and labelers. Looking down the long aisle in my father's department, I saw a tower of army overcoats advancing toward me and underneath them.

Saturday was the happy half-day. I looked forward all week to lunch with my father at the little restaurant with the paddle-arm chairs, where we feasted on the special of hot dogs, baked beans and lemon meringue pie.

The most remarkable thing about the Sonneborn factory was the high employee morale. From the designers to the label sewers, everyone gave all-out efforts. Many had sons and brothers on the battle front wearing the Sonneborn-made uniform. Some had already received the news of the loss of a loved one at Chateau-Thierry, the Marne or Belleau Wood, where 8,000 American troops had been reduced to 2,000. The clamor of the factory machines seemed to me always accompanied by the bombardment of artillery shells. The Sonneborn factory was my war front.

A simple world.

This was a fun war for a six-year old in a simple world. Everything was good or bad, right or wrong, with no in-between and no on-the-other hand. And at the movies, watching a western, you could always tell the heroes from the villains by the color of the hats.

Although I did not know it then, the Henry Sonneborn Company, Maryland's largest employer next to Bethlehem Steel, was also Maryland's foremost melting pot for generations of immigrants. It not only converted textiles from any nations into clothing; it melded people.

I enjoyed the babel of polyglot arguments over whether or not to join the newly formed Amalgamated Union. The immediate issues, I later learned, were management's imposition of a speed-up elimination of less-fit workers, monitoring workers' motions and using women to do skilled work that had been men's prerogative.

Many characters emerged from the Sonneborn melting pot. Jacob J. Edelman, one of the "greenhorns" who got his start in the Sonneborn cauldron as a union organizer, became a distinguished city councilman and chairman of several of its most important committees. He was the cutting edge of the union, its eloquent spokesman and business representative, and under the New Deal, a federal labor referee.

With the end of war-time uniform production, the recession of the early twenties and Sonneborn's downsizing, many notable clothing firms became Sonneborn off-shoots, with the funding and guidance from Mr. A. Frank, founder of the linings firm that bears his name. These included L. Grief and Bros., J. Schoenemann & Co. and Strouse Brothers. Most of these have disappeared. Among the survivors are A. Frank & Son, Haas Tailoring, Jos. A. Bank, Hartz and Co.

Now that immigrants are less tolerated, we might recall a time when they were more needed to provide muscle and sweat for building railroads, dams and infrastructure, and to fill the tough factory jobs to help win our wars. We benefitted from the strength of their diversity. They were not perceived as outsiders or the welfare wards of hard-working tax-payers.

In that tolerant time, Uncle Sam and I sped along on parallel tracks toward the common goal of making the world safe for democracy and the land of the free, friendly and brave. But that was when we were both very young,

I was side-tracked years later when I read the post-war novels by Ernest Hemingway and Erich Marie Remarque. They explored a new world in which wars were not fun, life was not simple and melting fell out of fashion.

July 31, 1996

Year-round Good Will

According to the Ancient Talmudic legend of the Lahmed Vovniks (the Thirty-Six), there are at any given time 36 righteous, saintly individuals in Israel and 36 in the Diaspora who try to improve the world by helping others. I think that I have used up the quota for North America. As a blind man with congestive heart failure, which making walking difficult, I am constantly receiving help from good people.

Among the "Lahmed Vovniks" to whom I am indebted are my wife, son, daughter-in-law, neighbors and Roslyn and Lem Wills – my long-suffering secretary and her husband without whose help I could not function at all – and a retired insurance executive, Samuel Weinblatt who is my dedicated volunteer reader.

For most of us the season of good will is the five-week period after Thanksgiving. After New Year's day, its back to business as usual. But for those like Sam, who volunteer to help others on a weekly basis, the happy time of giving and receiving lasts all year.

A New Friend

I did not know him when, at the suggestion of the Maryland Society for Sight, he called me offering his service. We are now good old friends.

When my phone rings at about 5:20 p.m. each Tuesday, I know who is calling.

"Hi, Sam," I answer, "How are you?"

"Fine, 8:15 o.k.?"

"Sure, I look forward to your visit as always."

"I'll be there," says Sam.

Sam has been there for me virtually every Tuesday evening for three years, excepting only a few weeks for visiting his children and grandchildren living elsewhere. Each week, he brings a folder containing articles clipped from publications of interest to me. His readings are more stimulating than tapes and recordings because they provide an opportunity for discussion.

Volunteers like Sam are brightening the lives of the blind all over the United States. Hospitals, health care and religious institutions, schools, libraries, and countless social organizations like Meals on Wheels and home care for the elderly facing severe budget cuts and growing needs, could not operate without support of thousands of volunteers.

The trend to volunteer is receiving a powerful push from corporations seeking to improve their public image.

When Robert K. Goodwin, president and chief executive official of The Points of Light Foundation of Washington, said recently, "Enlightened corporations have known for generations that their long-term viability and profitability is related to corporate citizenship, but only recently have firms been encouraging employees to become active in their communities."

When Nancy Goldberg, associate director of Boston College's Center for Corporate Community Relations (CCCR), of Massachusetts said, "Volunteerism puts a face on a company," they were preaching to the choir.

A poll of community relations executives take by CCCR shows that 79 percent of Americans passed up the TV sitcoms to volunteer for at least one cause during the year, an increase over the 43 percent recorded in a poll two years earlier. Actually, the 49 percent is a majority of those able to volunteer since the 51 percent includes not only those who do not give, but also those who cannot because they are preoccupied with their own daily survival.

Volunteerism improves morale, reduces employee turnover, attracts better employees and benefits the entire community.

I am suggesting to the Maryland Society for Sight that it send to each client a Volunteer Readers Appreciation Fund form with spaces for name, address and phone of the client and the volunteer reader and provision for committing a small weekly donation to the society. It will remind the grateful client that, although the volunteer receives no compensation, the society does need financial support.

That can be expressed by pledging a nominal sum. It will be emphasized that the services are provided without charge or obligation and that any financial expression of appreciation is purely voluntary.

There is much to be ashamed of in our nation's history; slavery, racial and religious discrimination and indifference to the poor, but so much more to be proud of, especially the achievements of our volunteers.

Their invaluable work is more than a feel-good exercise. It helps to relieve the needs of the desperately poor and sick. It is not charity or pity, but empathy and love. It brightens the world with year round goodwill.

How Wars Are Won

On Baltimore's waterfront, the Fairfield section is very quiet now. You can almost hear the summer breezes blowing in from the Patapsco.

Fifty years ago, it was a round-the-clock, seven-days-a-week bedlam of riveting hammers pounding red-hot rivets into steel plates, a cacophony of mechanical hubbub, whistles, fog horns and the cursing of sweaty workers struggling with unaccustomed tasks – business and professional people developing blisters and calluses on soft, unskilled hands.

One distinctive sound in the din was the wailing ambulance siren as yet another hapless victim was rushed to the infirmary or hospital. Strange, heavy tools became deadly weapons in the clumsy clutches of eager amateurs. In the early days of the war, shipyard casualties rivaled those on the battlefield.

Out of this chaos, in the late fall of 1941, was born at last the first Liberty ship, the Patrick Henry. It was Fairfield's first response to the arrogance and belligerence of the Axis powers. We who had slogged through a gray, grinding depression felt our hearts pounding. Until then, our only patriotic excitement had been on the Fourth of July, celebrating the victories of earlier achievers. This was *our* victory!

This first launching of the ships that would carry the war to America's enemies, and help to finish what they had started, lighted our sky as no fireworks had ever done.

For many of us, the launching was the most memorable event of our routine lives. We wildly cheered the speeches of shipyard officials. We had goose bumps as the skids were knocked out, the first champagne bottle smashed against its bow and the Patrick Henry slid majestically down the greased ways. We forgot the gripes and the pain; the rising at 4 a.m., the dashing half asleep to meet our rides, the lunching in the company of rats scurrying under the hulls, the aching joints and muscles, the interminable monotony of seven-day weeks of mind-numbing labor.

But the mounting frequency of exhilarating launchings made it all worthwhile.

Production revved up to overdrive after Pearl Harbor. President Franklin D. Roosevelt, who had called the slow-moving vessels "ugly ducklings," renamed them "Liberty Ships" because he pledged that they would "liberate the world." Our fighters did that job, of course, but our workers surely helped.

Great flocks of the ugly ducklings were born into the waters of the Patapsco. On September 7, 1942, nine months to the day after Pearl Harbor, came the John Brown, which is now on display as a museum ship at a pier on Clinton Street. It was one of 384 Liberty Ships launches at Fairfield – more than any produced at any shipyard in the nation. Altogether, the yards turned out 2,710 ships. Built and crewed by civilians, they carried two-thirds of all essential cargo to Allied forces. Nearly 200 were torpedoed by U-boats, but the Nazis could not sink them as fast as we could build them.

It took 42 days to build the John Brown, but by the end of the war Fairfield was mass-producing a ship a week. It was not only Fairfield workers and management who achieved this miracle of productivity; it was also the workers and management at all the industries which supplied the thousands of tons of materials used – from rivets, nuts, bolts, and welding rods to heavy steel plates and huge ships' engines.

The only thing we nearly ran out of was names for the ships. John W. Brown was a little-known labor union leader; other uncelebrated civilians had to be dug out of obscurity for moments of glory. But nothing slowed the pace in the 18 yards producing Liberty Ships.

At shipyards like Bethlehem's, at airplane plants like Glenn Martin and in bustling factories from coast to coast, American praised the Lord and passed the ammunition to those fighting in the armies on two side of the world.

Wages were adequate, not lavish. With shortages and rationing of many commodities, the standard of living was no consumer's paradise. But morale was high; no burnout, no malaise. We were confident of eventual victory. We gave it the highest priority and threw ourselves entirely into the task of waging the war as well on the home front as in the battlefront.

Today, too, as headlines and newscasts keep reminding us, we are at war – against drugs, poverty, hunger, crime, disease and pollution. These enemies lack the personified evil of Hitler, Hirohito and Mussolini, but their threats to our survival are as real. We are good at declaring these wars, but not very good at fighting them. Where are the emergency measures? The War

Bonds? The planning of production? The rationing of resources? The setting of priorities in finance, labor and education to assure concentration on winning?

Counting all those, especially children, who are dying of malnutrition, drug overdoses, street violence, AIDS and gun slaughter, American losses in these wars must exceed those in the most destructive war in history,

We won that war by will, determination, steadfast commitment and readiness to pay the price of victory. Only by such unconditional, uncompromising effort can we triumph over present enemies.

In 1992, as in 1942, we can again dream of victory over formidable enemies which threaten not just "them" but also "us".

As Theodor Herzl, the founder of Zionism said, "If you will it, it is no dream."

August 26, 1992

Forgotten, But Not Gone

As a frequent participant in groups discussing current concerns, I am struck by their downgrading or elimination of the threat of nuclear annihilation as an important issue. The matter is rarely mentioned any more by editorialists, pundits and talk-show hosts exploring more titillating topics.

The collapse of the Evil Empire has taken the steam out of the issue of atomic mass suicide. We are Number One, and Number Two has crumpled like a deflated balloon, so why worry?

We know, of course, that even if all the agreed-upon reduction of nuclear weapons is observed to the letter, Number Two will still have enough left to reduce Number One to a mass of contaminated ruins. An what about Numbers Three, Four, Five, Six and the rest? Fourteen countries, including four Soviet successor states disposing 45,000 weapons among them, are mentioned in the Army War College "World 2010" estimates of nuclear weapons powers. Are they all to be expunged from our priority list of major concerns because some of them will not be ready for mass destruction until next year or five years from now?

Are we counting on some new technological wizardry to save us from ourselves? Or have we abandoned hope that we can do anything about the death machine suspended over our heads? Have we concluded that what will be must be and decided to concentrate on Bosnia, Somalia and Haiti? In that case we are resigned to the same fate as the terrifying monsters of Jurassic Park who for millions of year roamed and ruled the earth as we do not, but who somehow vanished. Science tells us that dinosaurs were the masters of creation for more than a hundred million years before the first primal ancestors of man appeared only some 5 million years ago. If the dinosaurs had any capacity for thinking, they must have thought they would surely be around forever, as do we.

The difference between us and them is that they could not see extinction coming – and we can.

It is likely that, in the next few thousand years at least, we won't have to worry about comets and asteroids hurtling into our planet from outer space, or about a new glacial age brought on by the greenhouse effect, or about any of the phantasmagoric nightmares of science fiction. Moreover, we are at the top of the food chain. Other animals do not eat us, we eat them. We have no real enemies left – none, that is, but one – ourselves.

What does offer the possibility of instant extinction of our kind is the combination of nature with human nature, the invention of a way to use the most powerful forces in nature to exterminate ourselves.

Can there be any doubt that the Serbs, Croats and Muslims of the former Yugoslavia would be doing their ethnic cleansing with atomic weaponry if they had it? Or that the likes of Saddam Hussein, Muammar el Kadafi and the Iranian ayatollahs would justify a nuclear attack if they thought they could get away with it? Or that China, the upcoming superpower, is developing its nuclear technology and has joined the former USSR in peddling it to rogue regimes?

With world population figures exploding, especially in Third World countries that cannot produce enough food, jobs or resources to sustain their growing masses, is there not enormous pressure on nature and human nature to wipe out problems now that the means to do so are available?

For the soundest reason – to save hundreds of thousands of lives of American servicemen who might have been lost in an invasion of Japan to end World War II – we unleashed the first atomic monster on the world. Now, for an equally sound reason, to save perhaps a billion lives, we must kill off the monster's progeny,

We may have it still within our power to control and even to change our nature which controls the seeds of our destruction. We may yet find ways to prevent Homo Sapiens from becoming as extinct as the triassic reptiles.

The first step is to restore to the national agenda an issue that is not getting enough attention.

Second, we must develop plans for getting genocidal weapons out of the hands of unstable individuals in seats of power all over our endangered planet. Signatories to the Nuclear Non-Proliferation Treaty should recommit themselves to carrying out the treaty, and strive to involve other nations in the commitment.

Third, beginning with January's Geneva Conference on a permanent ban, we must put talks to reduce nuclear arms back on the front burner.

Fourth, efforts must be intensified to shut down the nuclear black market that is moving, especially in former Soviet states. The black-market price for plutonium is said to be $50 million a kilogram, and business is booming with Korea and Iran.

We must kill our monstrous creatures before they kill us. And if that means changing human nature, let's start to work on it. After only 5 million years – a mere moment in geologic time – it's still malleable.

November 24, 1993

real enemies left – none, that is, but one – ourselves.

What does offer the possibility of instant extinction of our kind is the combination of nature with human nature, the invention of a way to use the most powerful forces in nature to exterminate ourselves.

Can there be any doubt that the Serbs, Croats and Muslims of the former Yugoslavia would be doing their ethnic cleansing with atomic weaponry if they had it? Or that the likes of Saddam Hussein, Muammar el Kadafi and the Iranian ayatollahs would justify a nuclear attack if they thought they could get away with it? Or that China, the upcoming superpower, is developing its nuclear technology and has joined the former USSR in peddling it to rogue regimes?

With world population figures exploding, especially in Third World countries that cannot produce enough food, jobs or resources to sustain their growing masses, is there not enormous pressure on nature and human nature to wipe out problems now that the means to do so are available?

For the soundest reason – to save hundreds of thousands of lives of American servicemen who might have been lost in an invasion of Japan to end World War II – we unleashed the first atomic monster on the world. Now, for an equally sound reason, to save perhaps a billion lives, we must kill off the monster's progeny,

We may have it still within our power to control and even to change our nature which controls the seeds of our destruction. We may yet find ways to prevent Homo Sapiens from becoming as extinct as the triassic reptiles.

The first step is to restore to the national agenda an issue that is not getting enough attention.

Second, we must develop plans for getting genocidal weapons out of the hands of unstable individuals in seats of power all over our endangered planet. Signatories to the Nuclear Non-Proliferation Treaty should recommit themselves to carrying out the treaty, and strive to involve other nations in the commitment.

Third, beginning with January's Geneva Conference on a permanent ban, we must put talks to reduce nuclear arms back on the front burner.

Fourth, efforts must be intensified to shut down the nuclear black market that is moving, especially in former Soviet states. The black-market price for plutonium is said to be $50

The Best $5 Wedding Ever

The recent loss of my wife Ester after 69 years together, five courting and 64 married, stirred up many memories. My fondest is of our $5 wedding on August 31, 1934.

It happened one hot August afternoon in the depression year when Hitler was on the rise.

In that dreadful time, my wife-to-be and I lived with our respective families helping to meet mortgage payments, food and household expenses. Even a modest wedding ceremony was out of the question, so we decided to elope and inform our families later. We sought guidance from a co-worker who qualified as an expert on several counts –he had shopped around, compared the costs of rabbinical service for his marriage, and most important, he had a car.

It was not much of a car, a second-hand Model-T Ford two-seater, but it could take the three of us to Alexandria, Virginia. In Alexandria, our friend had found a low-fee rabbi we could afford. We left work early, and, with three corned beef sandwiches, squeezed into the tin lizzie and rattled off along Route 1 on the long trip.

In a picnic mood, I began serenading the bride-to-be with the old song from the Gay Nineties, "Daisy Bell," a favorite of singers and tap dancers at the Victoria Theater on East Baltimore Street. We stopped for gas in Laurel, then wormed our way through the dense D.C. traffic.

We bounced down a cobbled back street of Alexandria and stopped in front of a weather-beaten brown shingle cottage. The parlor had been converted with benches, a *bimah* and ark, into a small synagogue.

The rabbi, a small bearded man already wearing his prayer shawl and *yarmulke*, called to his wife in the kitchen, "Sara" he said in Yiddish, "they're here. Get the boys."

From the strong smell of fish cooking, we knew that the wife was preparing Sabbath dinner. She called to the boys who had been playing in the back yard. Barefoot, they came running into the synagogue, and immediately set to the task they had done before. They unrolled the *"chuppah"*. Each one took a pole. The wife, emerging from the kitchen, wiping her sweaty face and hands with her apron, took the third pole and handed the fourth to our friend. She was so pregnant that when the rabbi crowded bride and groom under the canopy, her belly was pushing me. She became aware of it and backed off. It was over quickly. The rabbi bid us to kiss, handed me the marriage certificate, and had me crush underfoot the small glass reminding of the destruction of the Temple. Everyone yelled *"mazel tov"*. I paid the $5 and we headed home.

A month later, when I had obtained a slightly better paying job and had found a tiny furnished apartment, we informed our parents. They were happy, but they wished they had attended.

At our low-budget wedding, there were no printed invitations, no fancy clothes, no caterer, no orchestra, no champagne, no ice sculptures, no shoes and rice, no bill in six figures, but it was a fine wedding.

Today, more than half of all first marriages end in divorce; 60 percent of second marriages fail. We found that airing complaints and arguing did not weaken, but actually strengthened our marriage. Usually, we worked out problems to our satisfaction. We confronted differences. Our standards were respect for each other, civility, communication and compromise.

Our marriage worked for 64 years, while today many with fancier weddings do not last 64 weeks.